SURVIVAL SCOUT

T0018087

WARNING! The following story takes place over less than twenty minutes. In the event of an actual earthquake or tsunami, do not stop to explain geology or fluid dynamics. Also, please communicate with a responsible and capable adult before approaching water, walking along roads, or hosting reptilian exchange students.

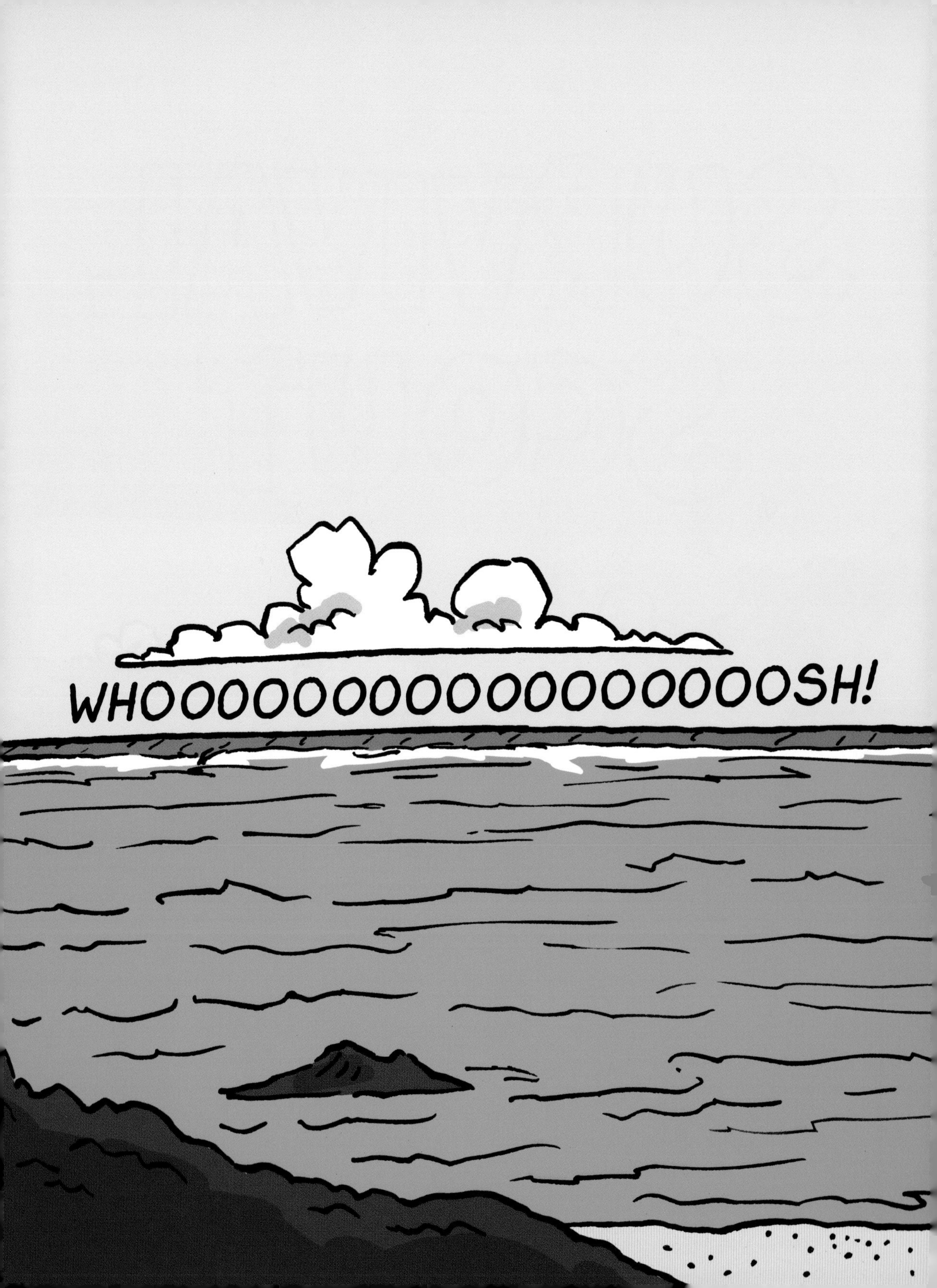
WHOOOOOOOOOOOOOOOOOOOOOOSH!

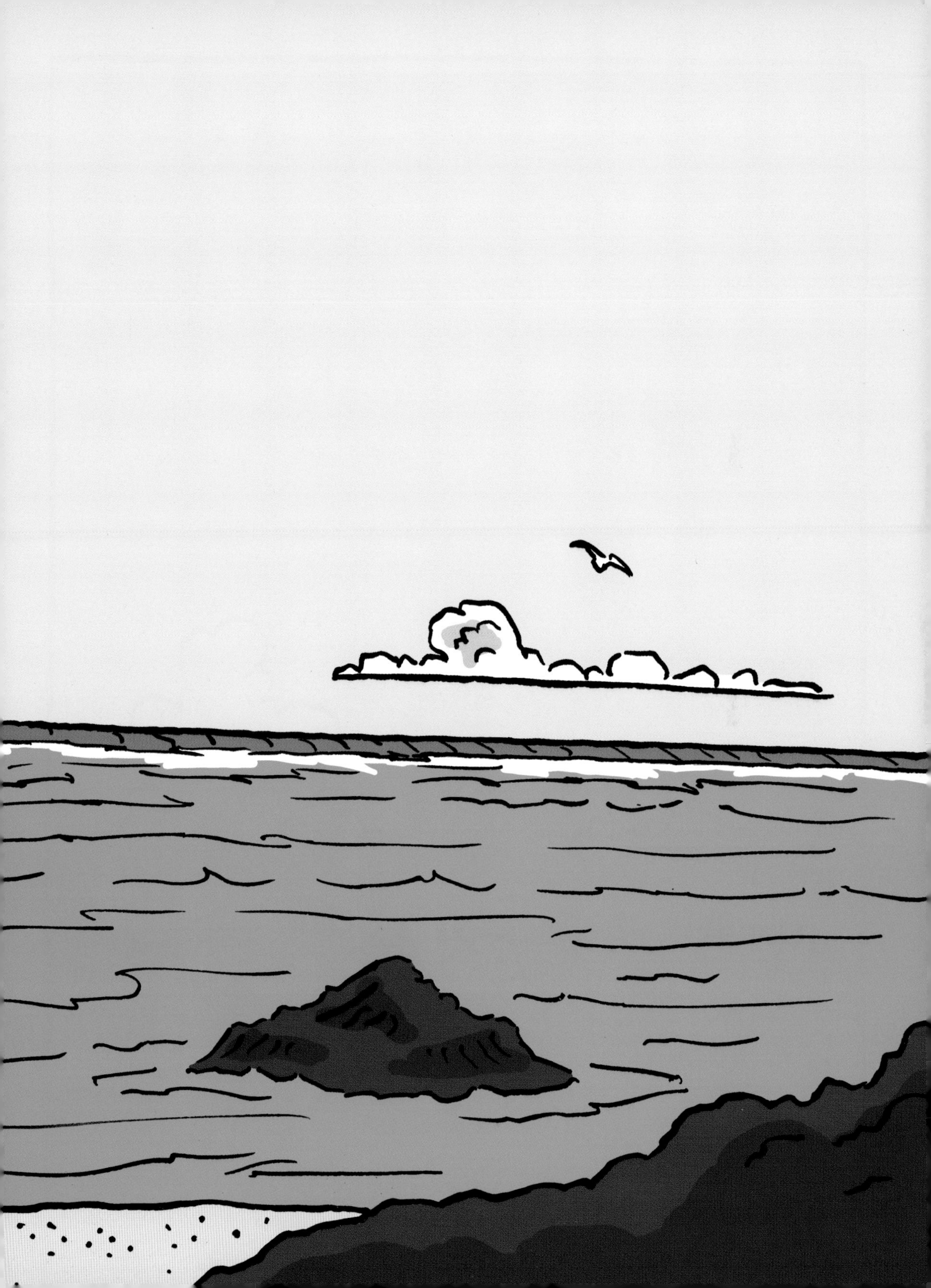

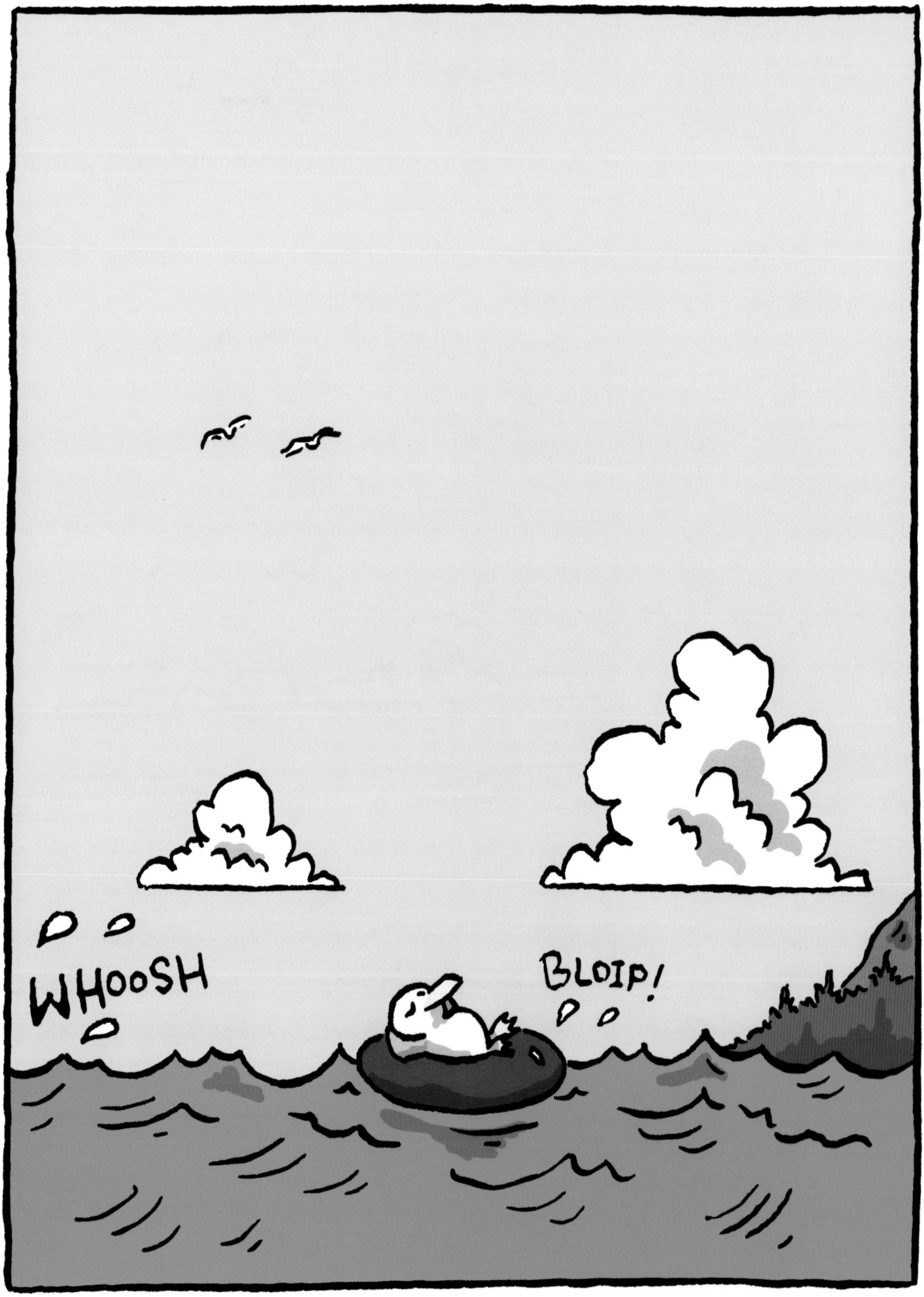
WHOOSH
BLOIP!

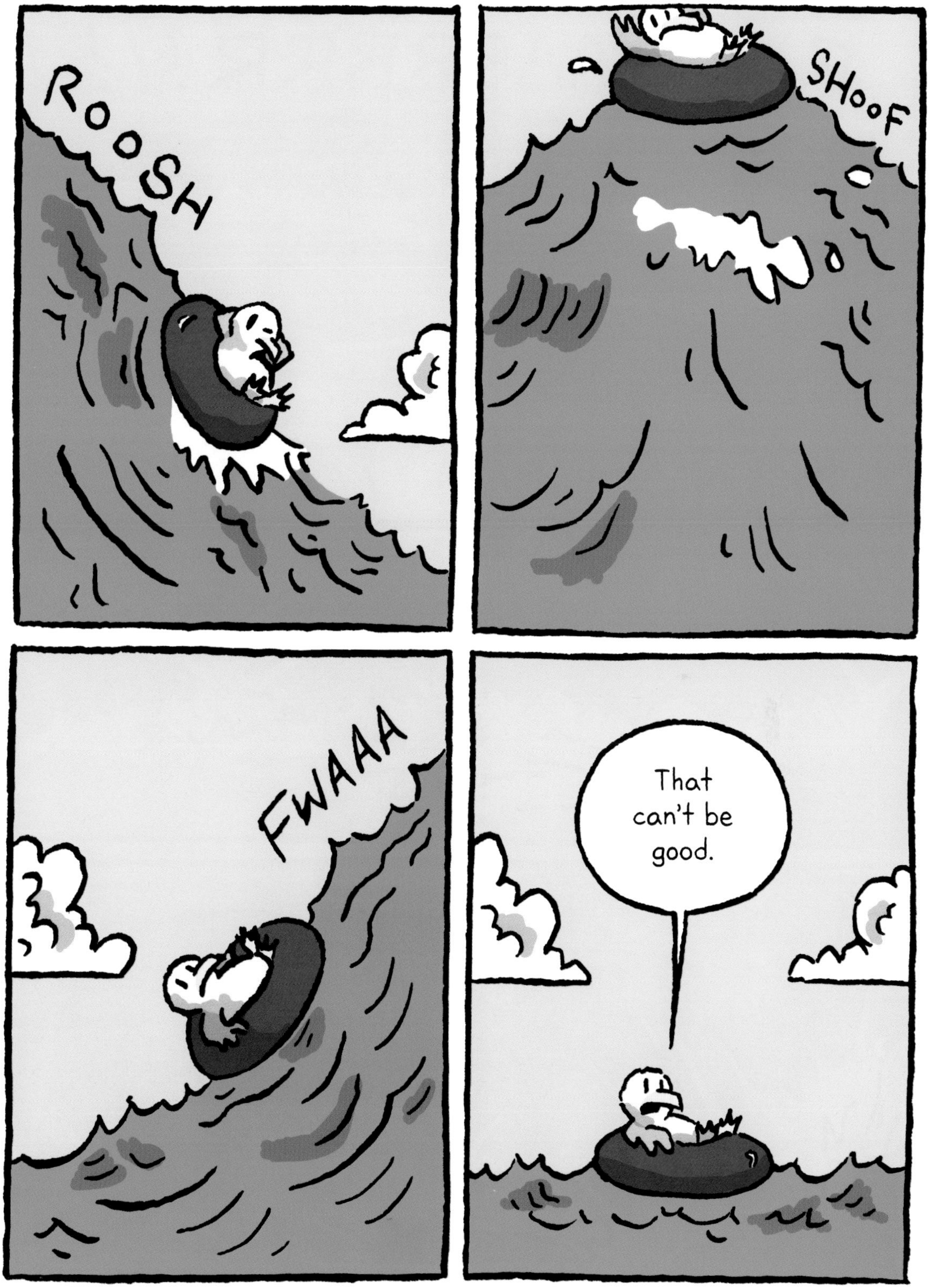
ROOSH
SHOOF
FWAAA
That can't be good.

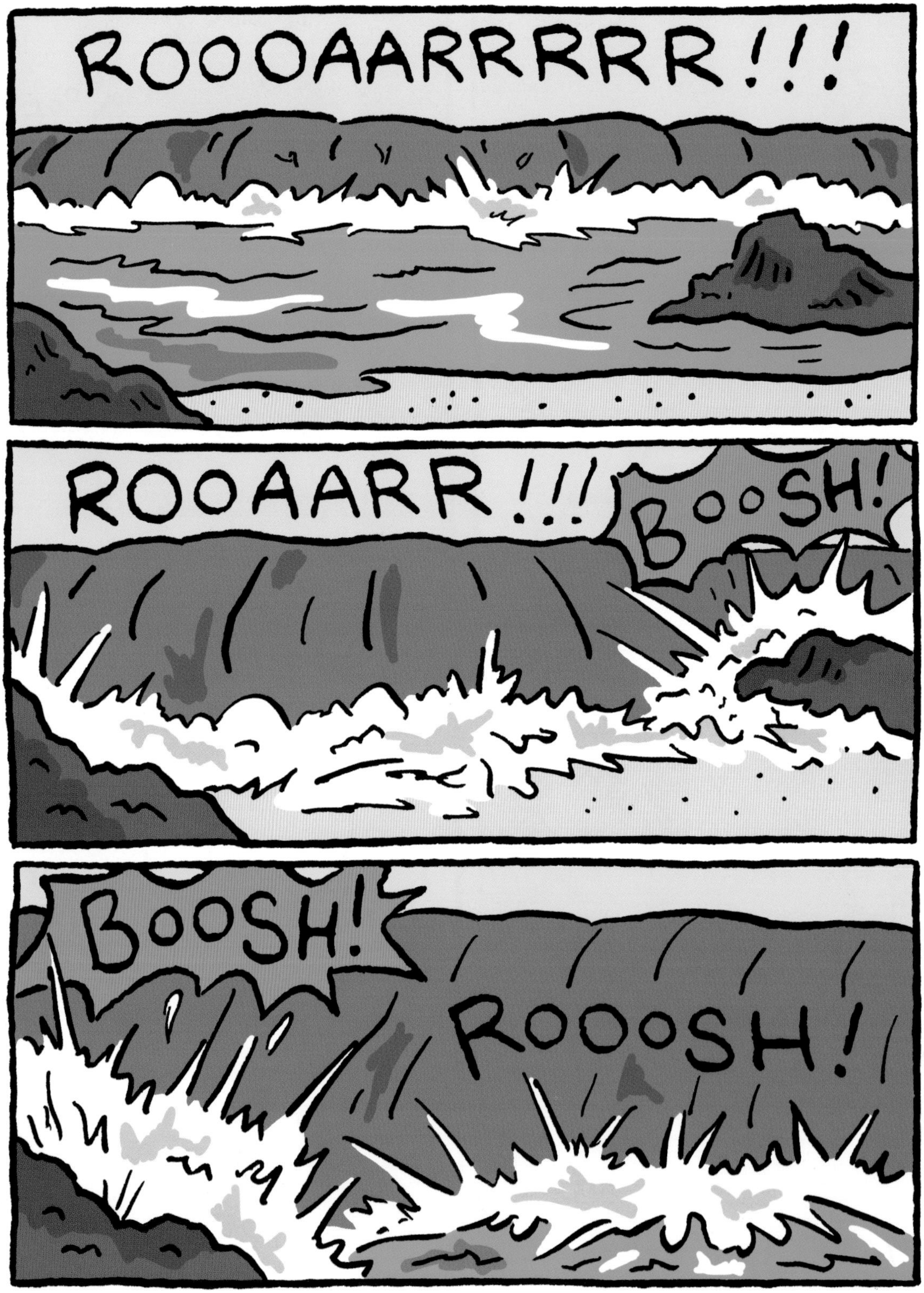
ROOOARRRRR!!!
ROOAARR!!!
BOOSH!
BOOSH!
ROOOSH!

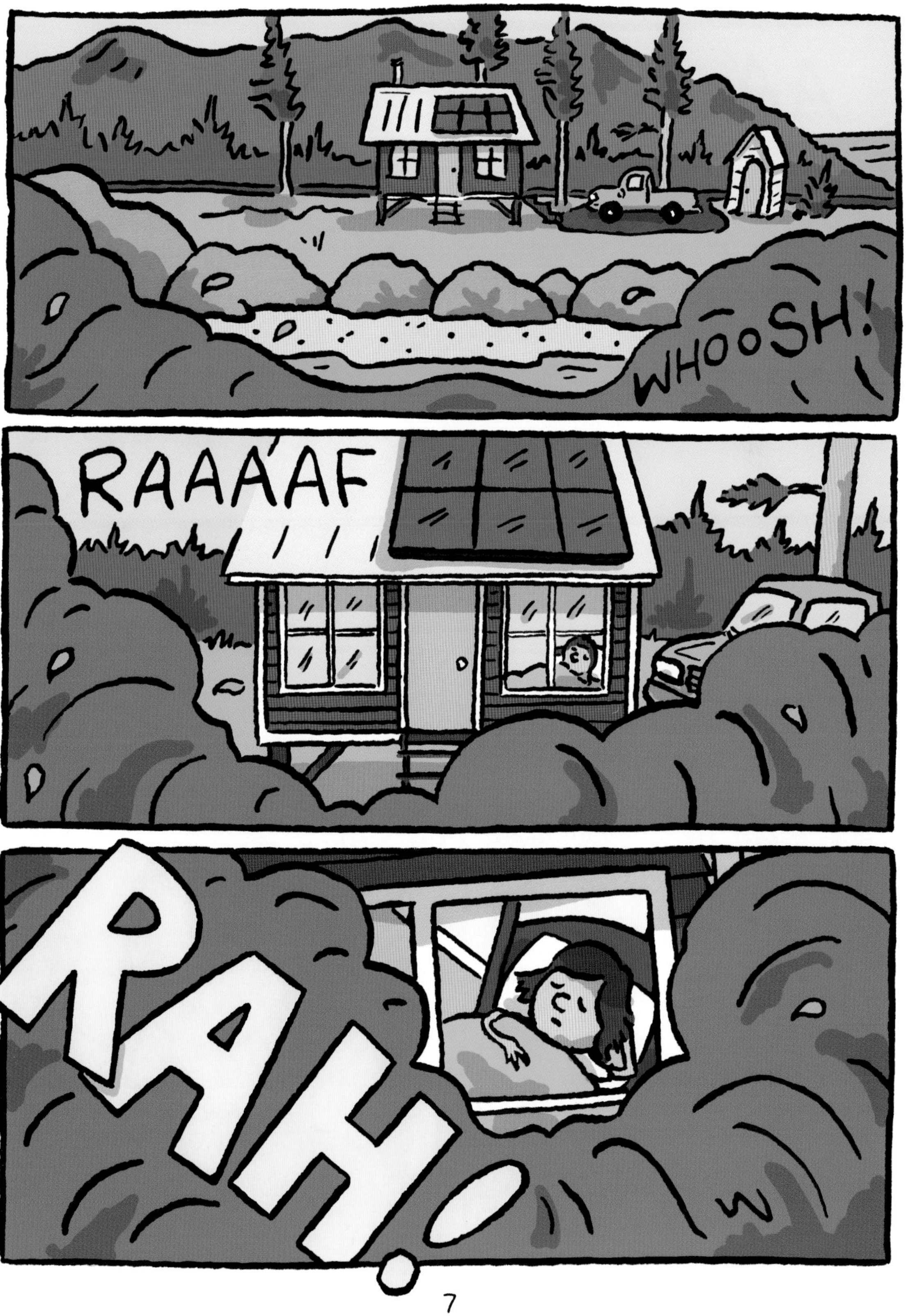
WHOOOSH!
RAAAAF
RAH!

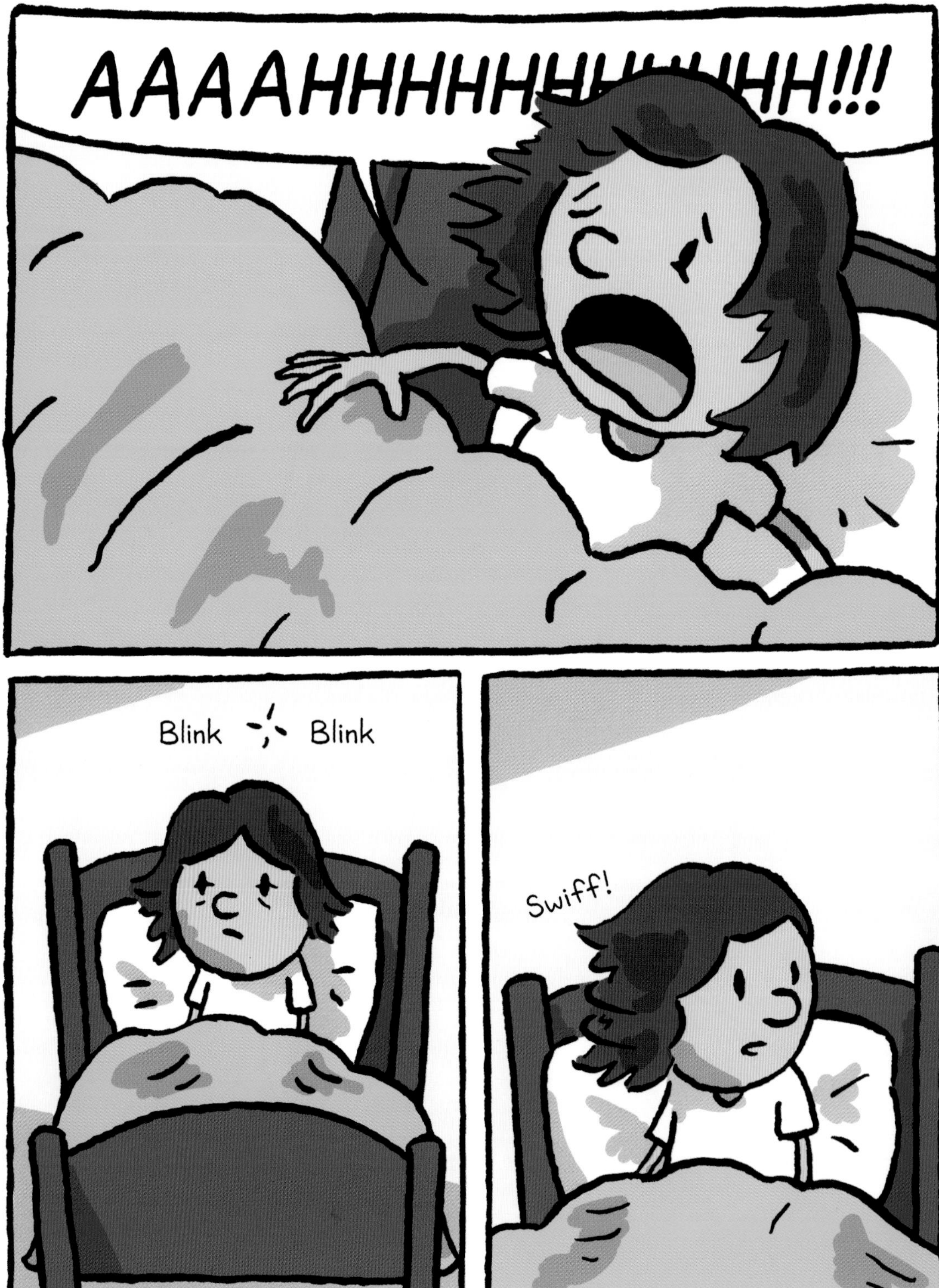
AAAAHHHHHHHHHHH!!!
Blink Blink
Swiff!

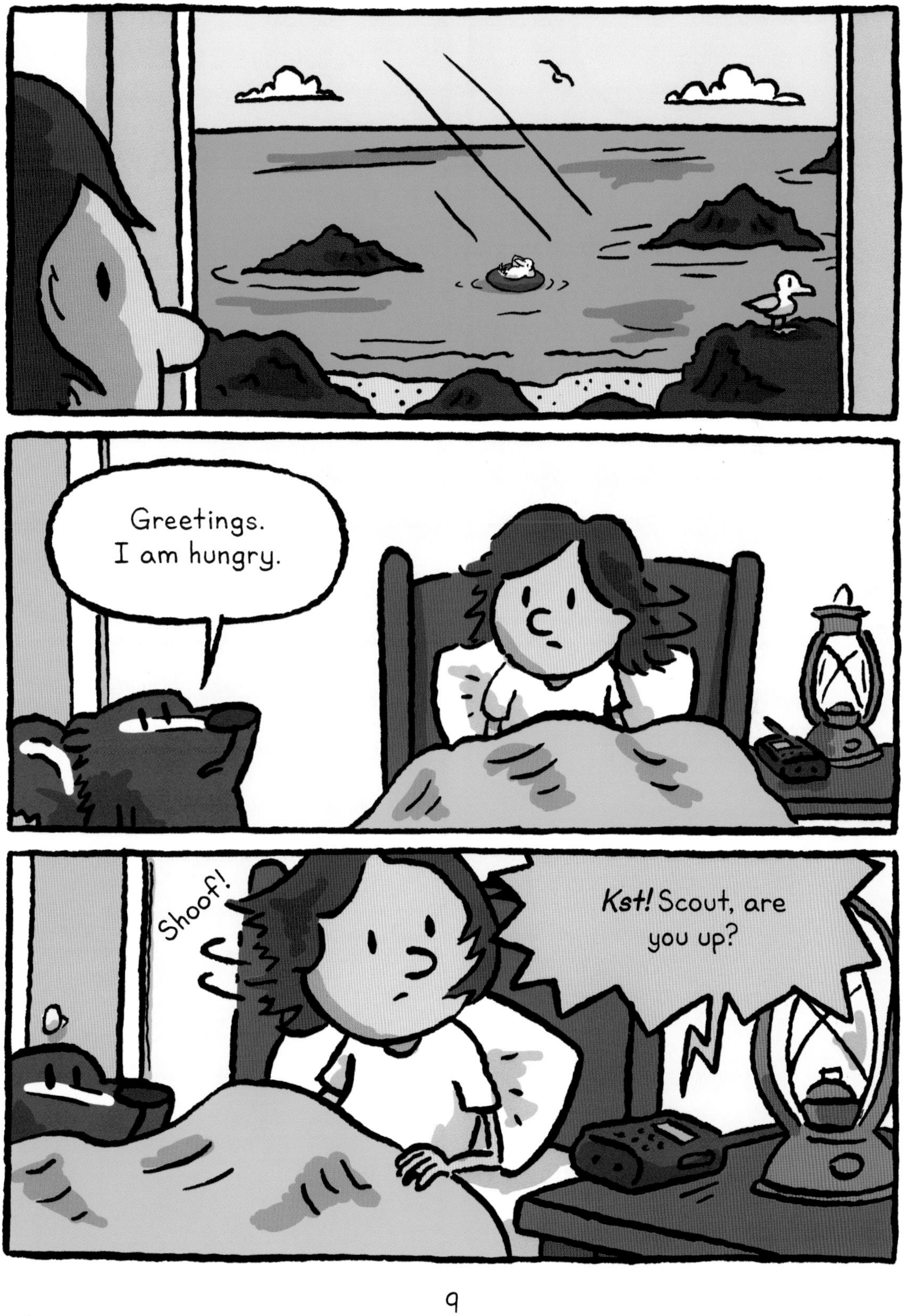
Greetings.
I am hungry.
Shoof!
Kst! Scout, are you up?

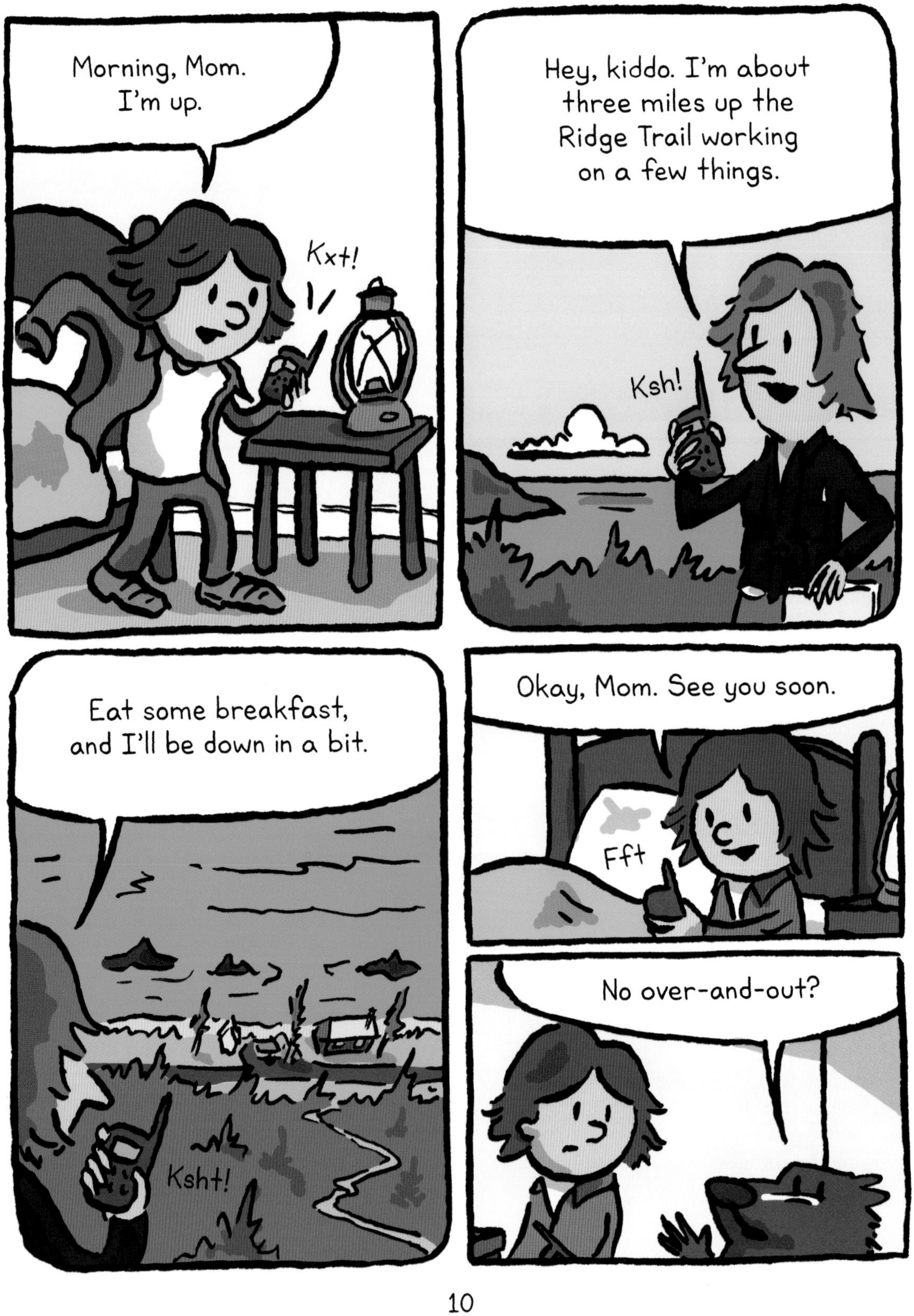
Morning, Mom.
I'm up.
Kxt!
Hey, kiddo. I'm about three miles up the Ridge Trail working on a few things.
Ksh!
Eat some breakfast, and I'll be down in a bit.
Ksht!
Okay, Mom. See you soon.
Fft
No over-and-out?

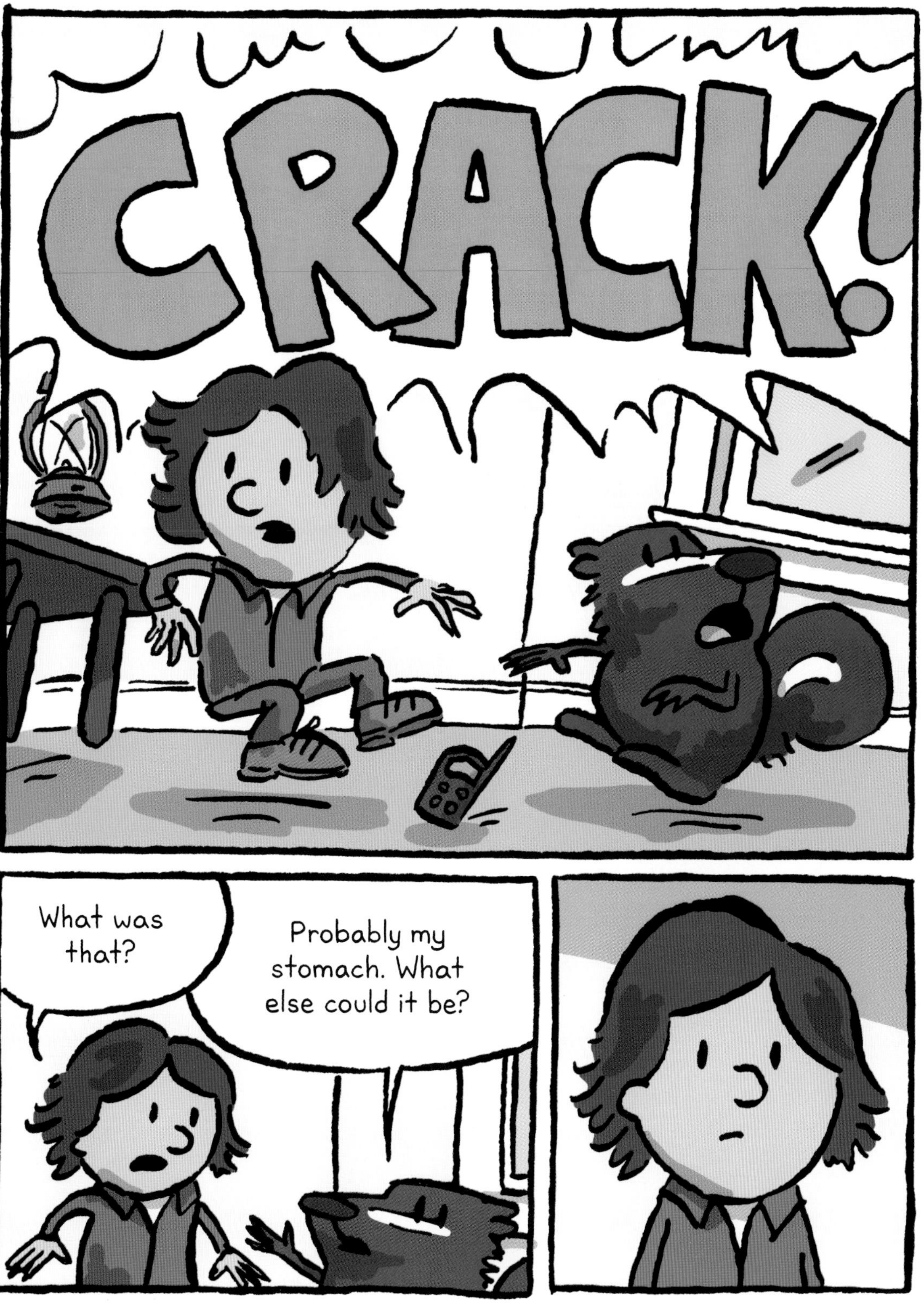
CRACK!
What was that?
Probably my stomach. What else could it be?

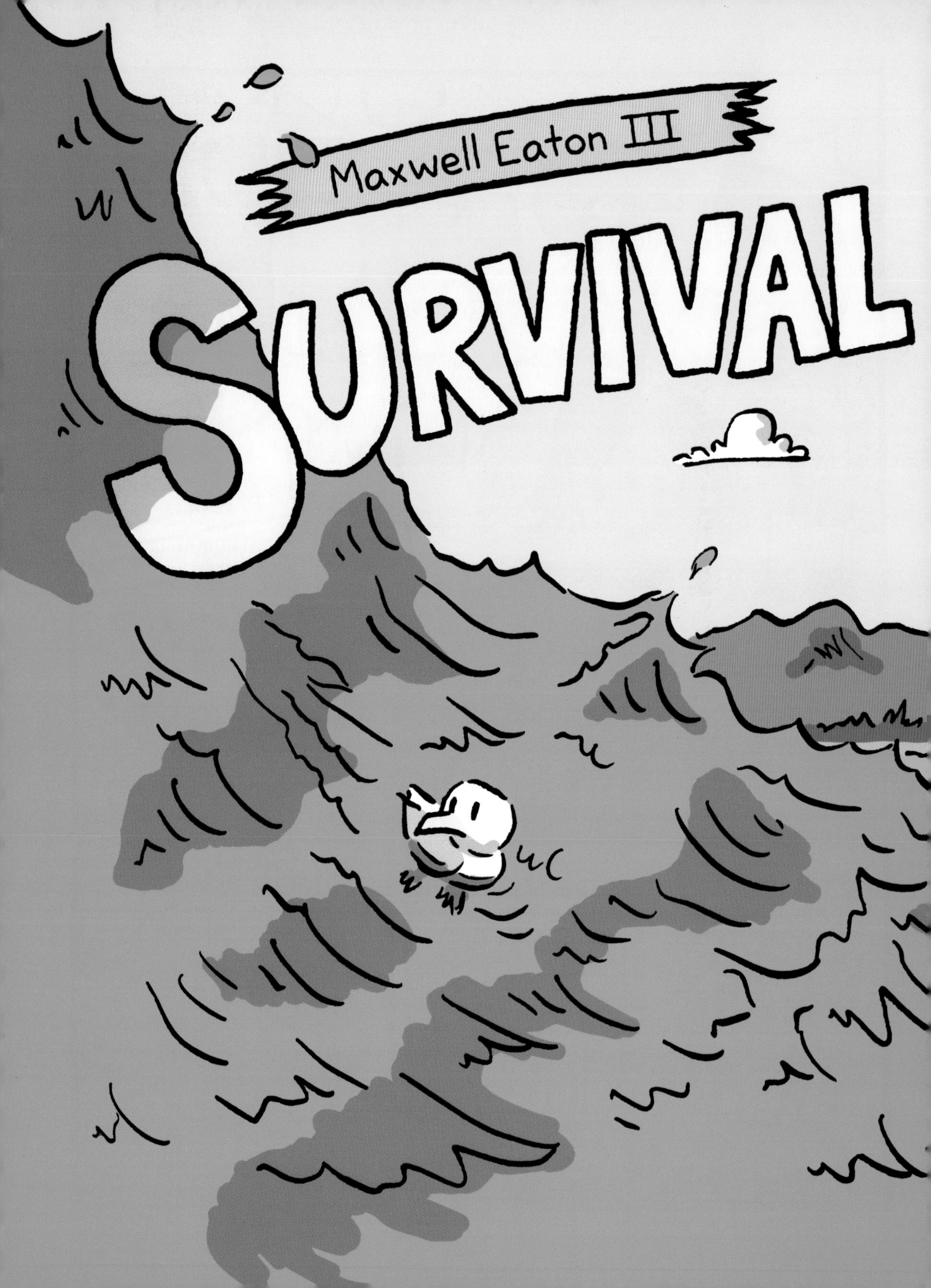
Maxwell Eaton III
SURVIVAL

SCOUT
TSUNAMI

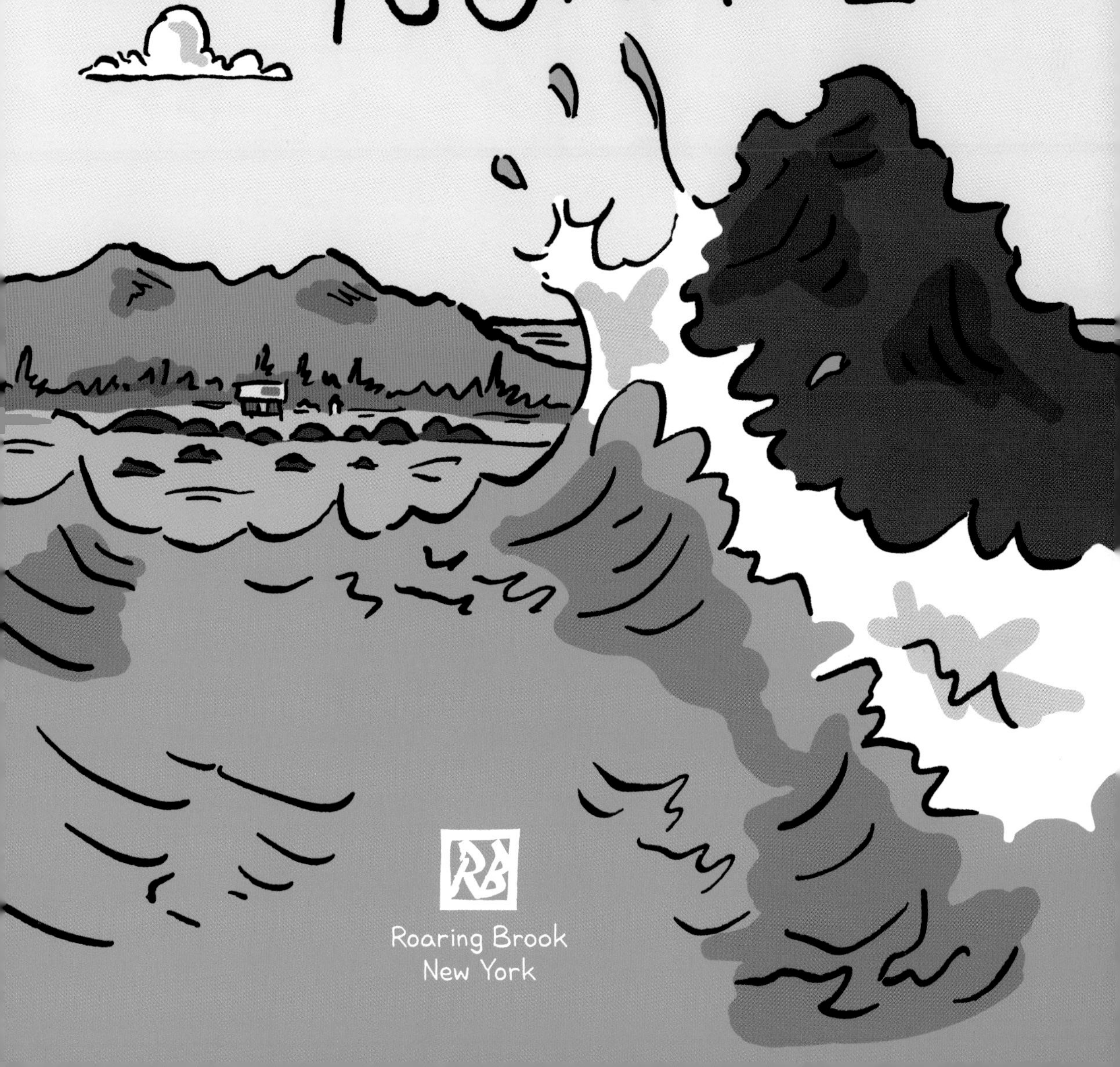

Roaring Brook
New York

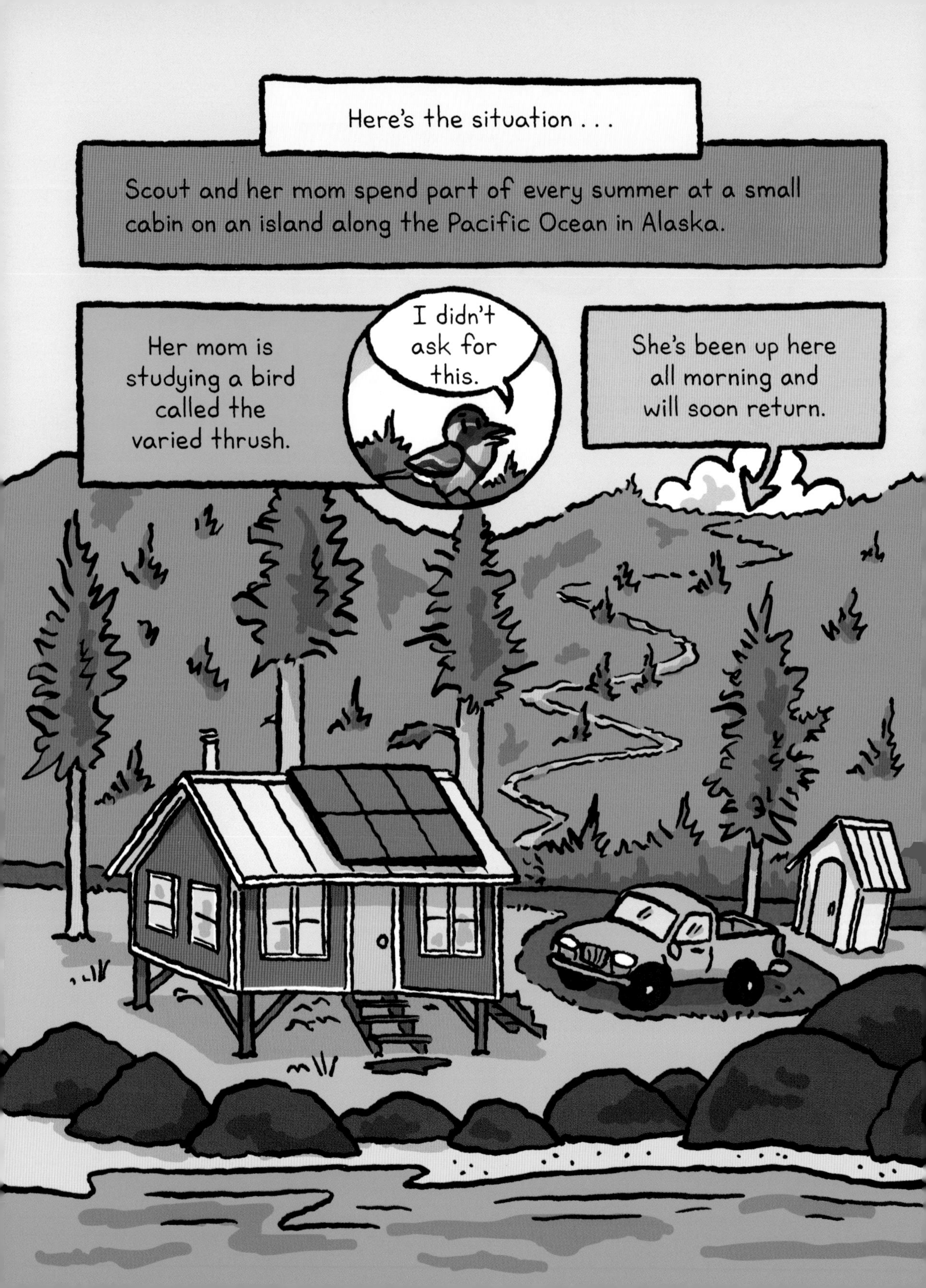
Here's the situation . . .
Scout and her mom spend part of every summer at a small cabin on an island along the Pacific Ocean in Alaska.
Her mom is studying a bird called the varied thrush.
I didn't ask for this.
She's been up here all morning and will soon return.

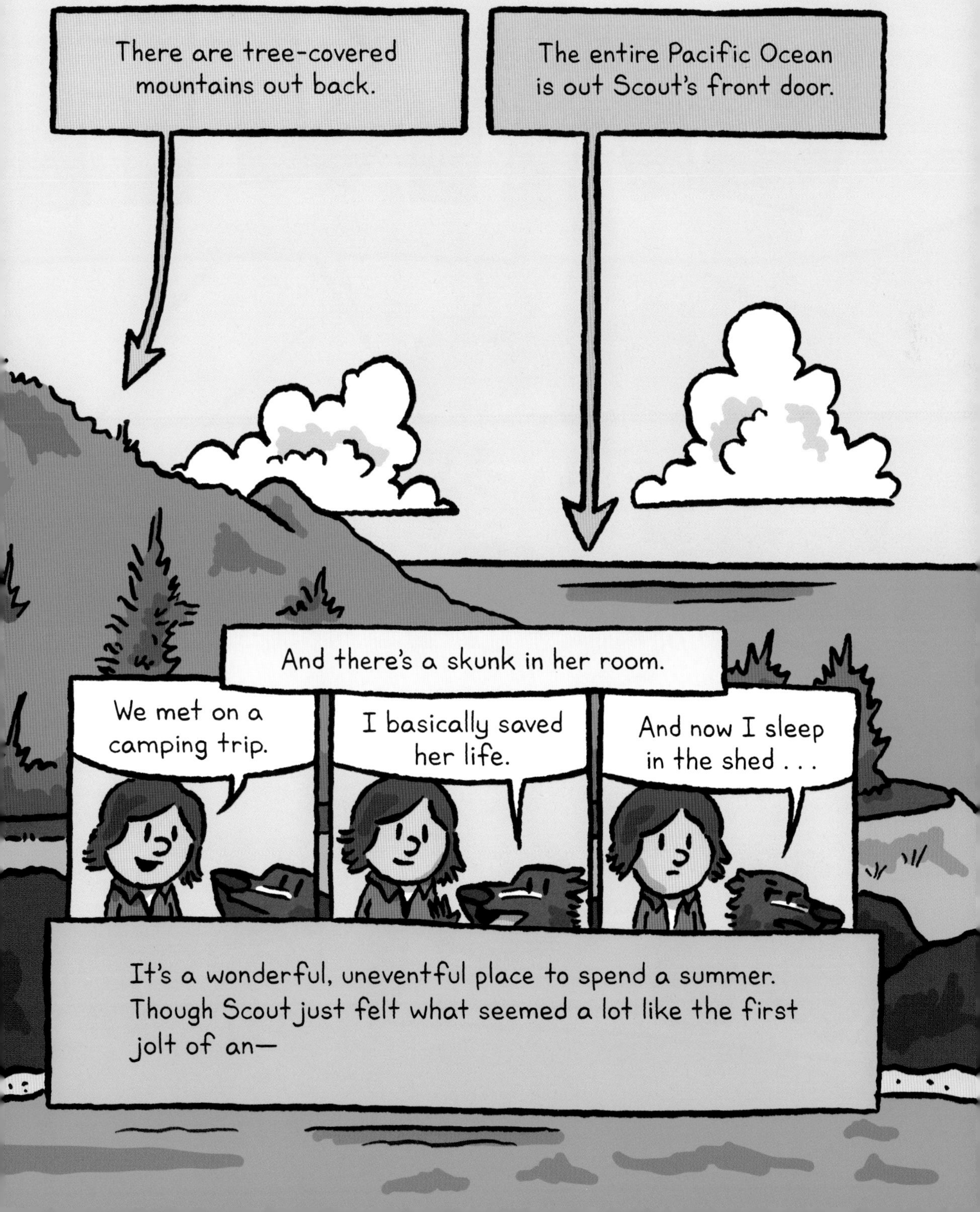
There are tree-covered mountains out back.
The entire Pacific Ocean is out Scout's front door.
And there's a skunk in her room.
We met on a camping trip.
I basically saved her life.
And now I sleep in the shed . . .
It's a wonderful, uneventful place to spend a summer. Though Scout just felt what seemed a lot like the first jolt of an—

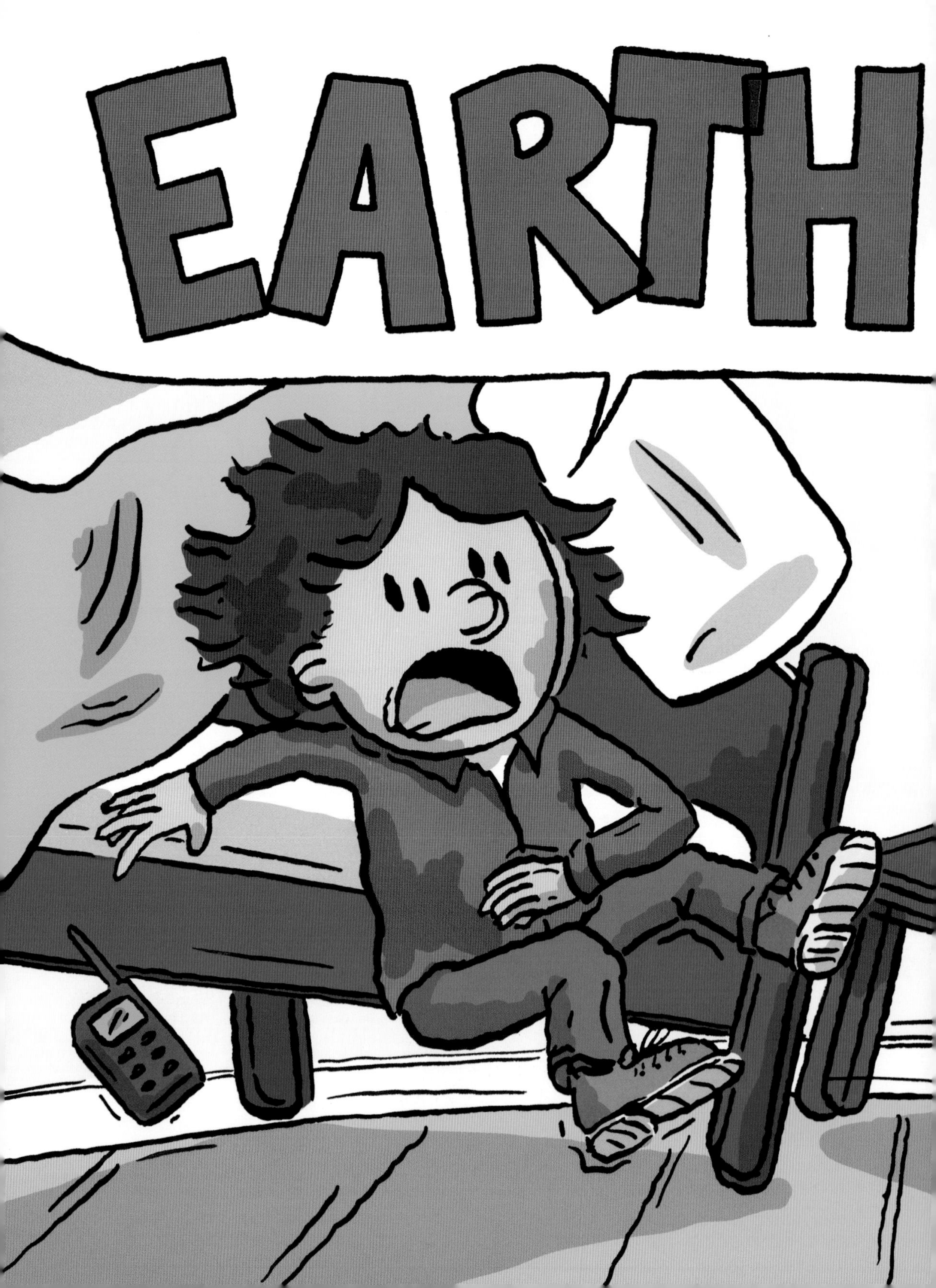
EARTH

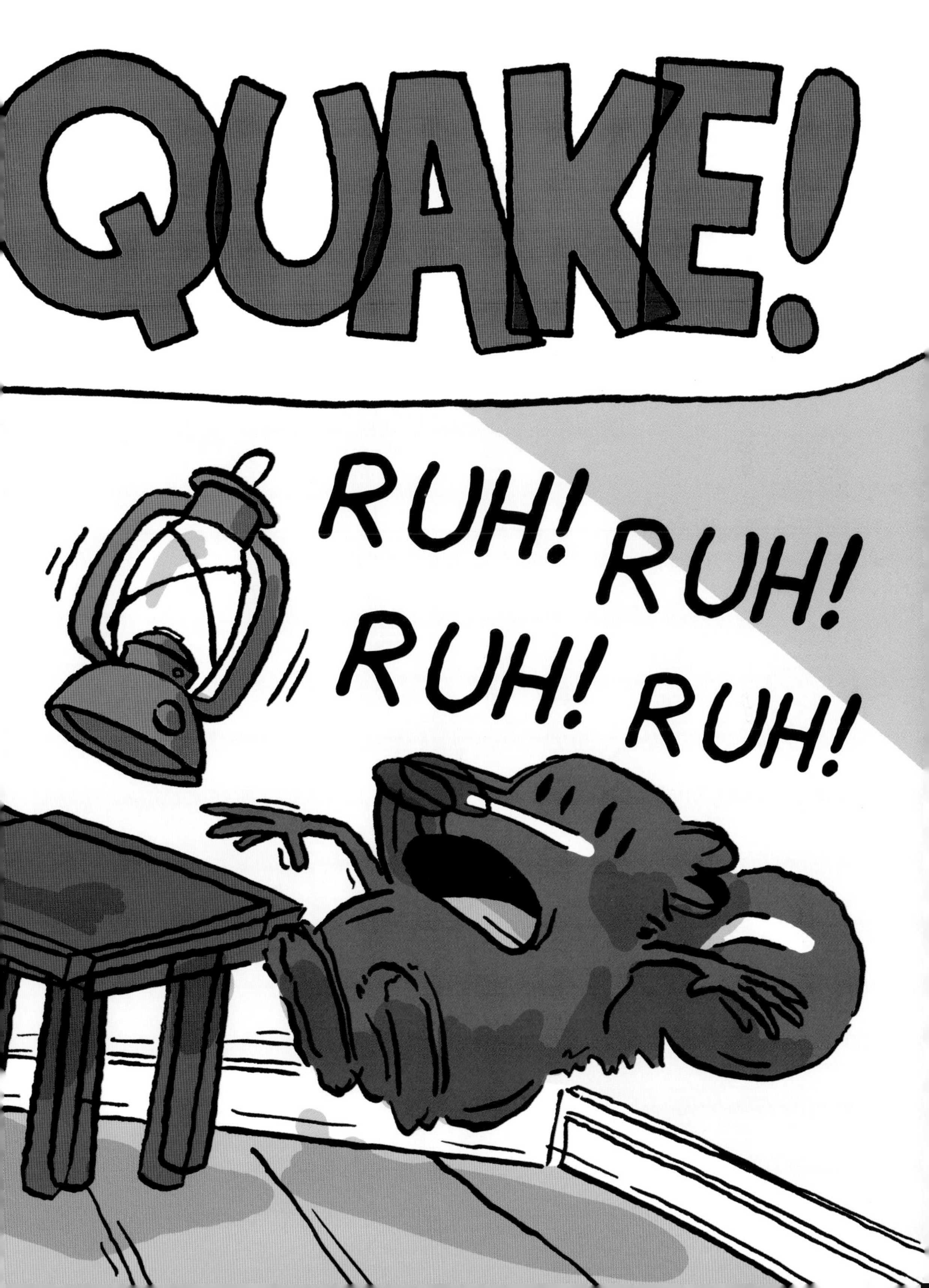
QUAKE!
RUH! RUH! RUH! RUH!

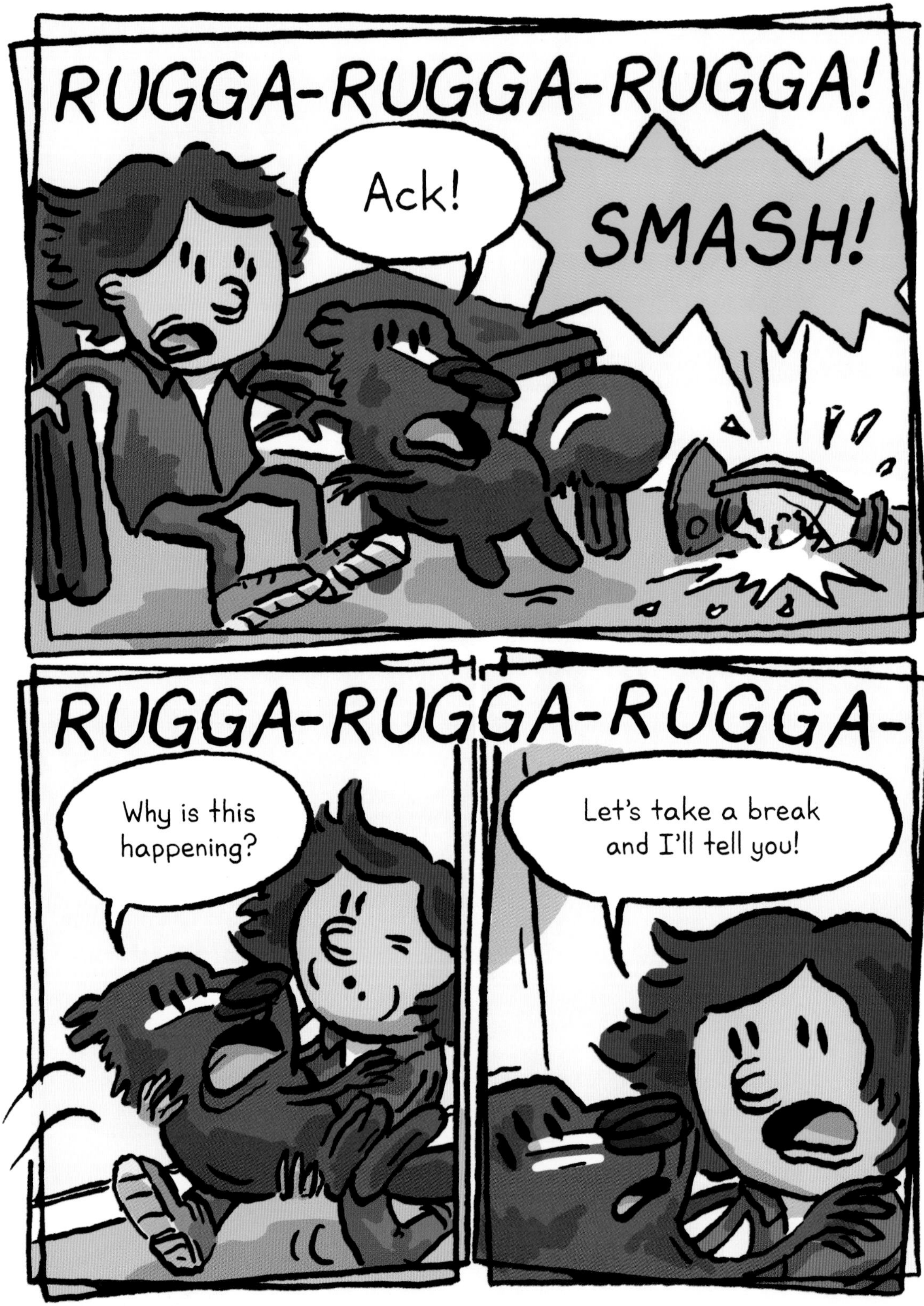
RUGGA-RUGGA-RUGGA!
Ack!
SMASH!
RUGGA-RUGGA-RUGGA-
Why is this happening?
Let's take a break and I'll tell you!

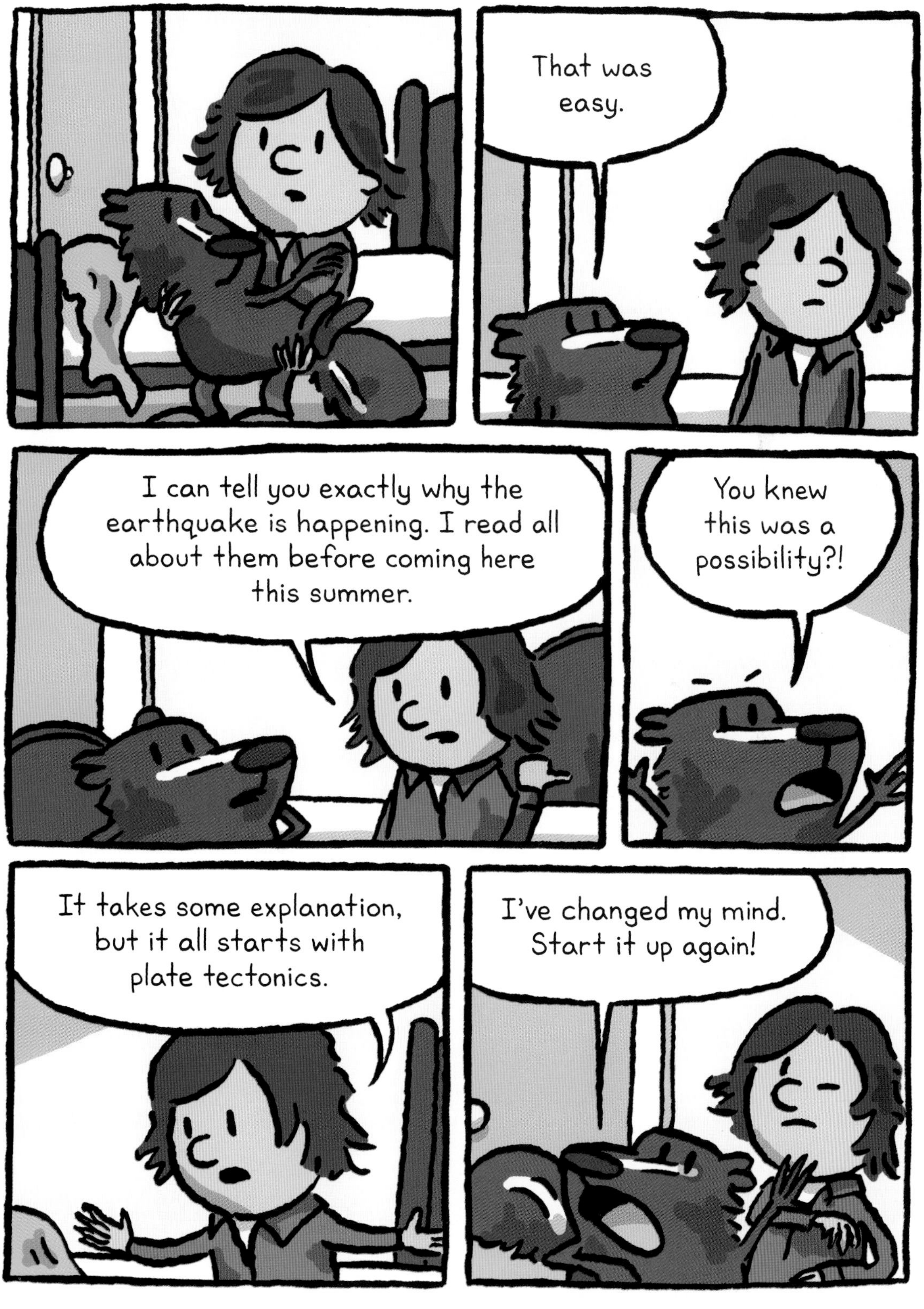
That was easy.
I can tell you exactly why the earthquake is happening. I read all about them before coming here this summer.
You knew this was a possibility?!
It takes some explanation, but it all starts with plate tectonics.
I've changed my mind. Start it up again!

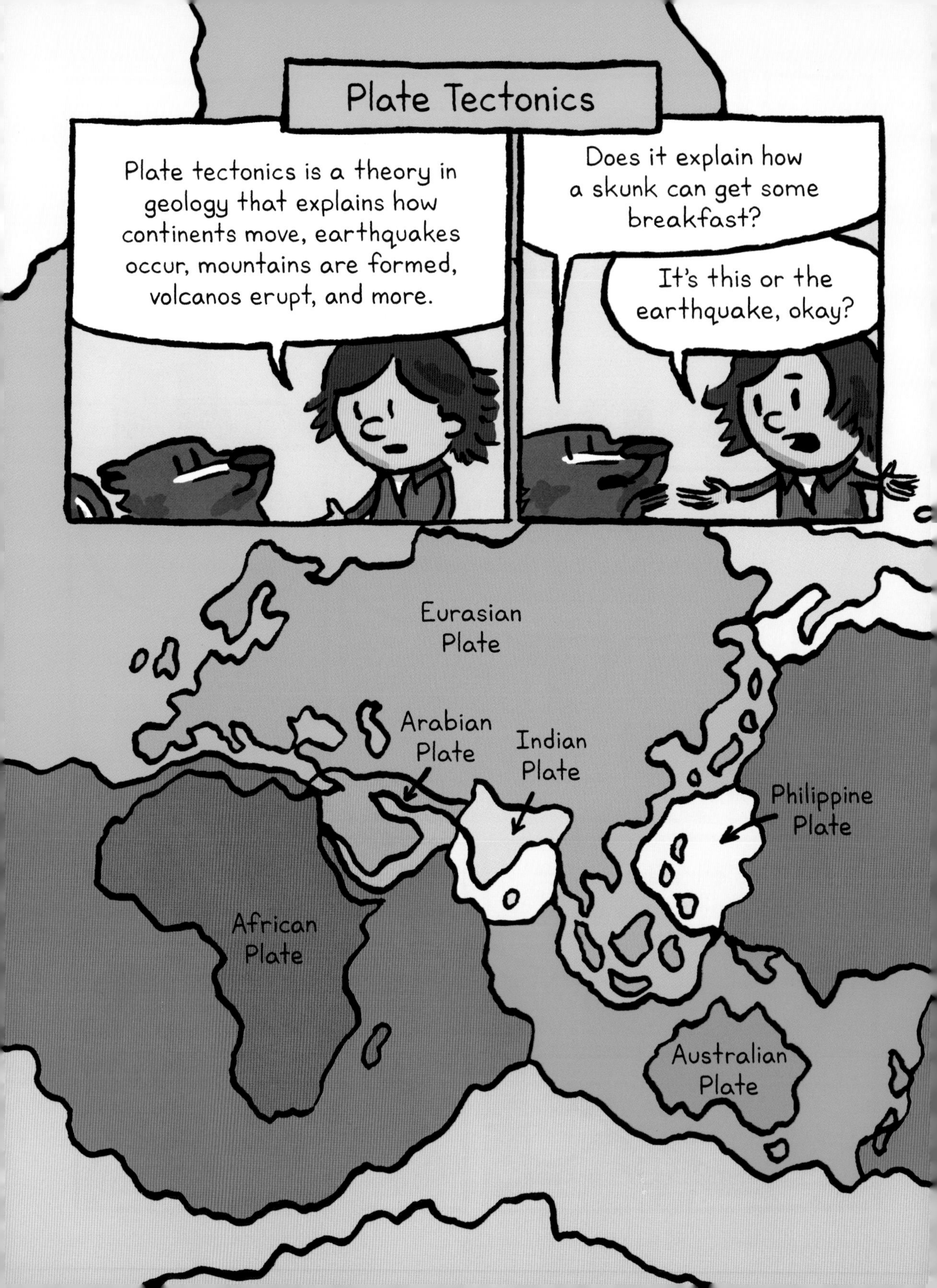
Plate Tectonics
Plate tectonics is a theory in geology that explains how continents move, earthquakes occur, mountains are formed, volcanos erupt, and more.
Does it explain how a skunk can get some breakfast?
It's this or the earthquake, okay?
Eurasian Plate
Arabian Plate
Indian Plate
Philippine Plate
African Plate
Australian Plate

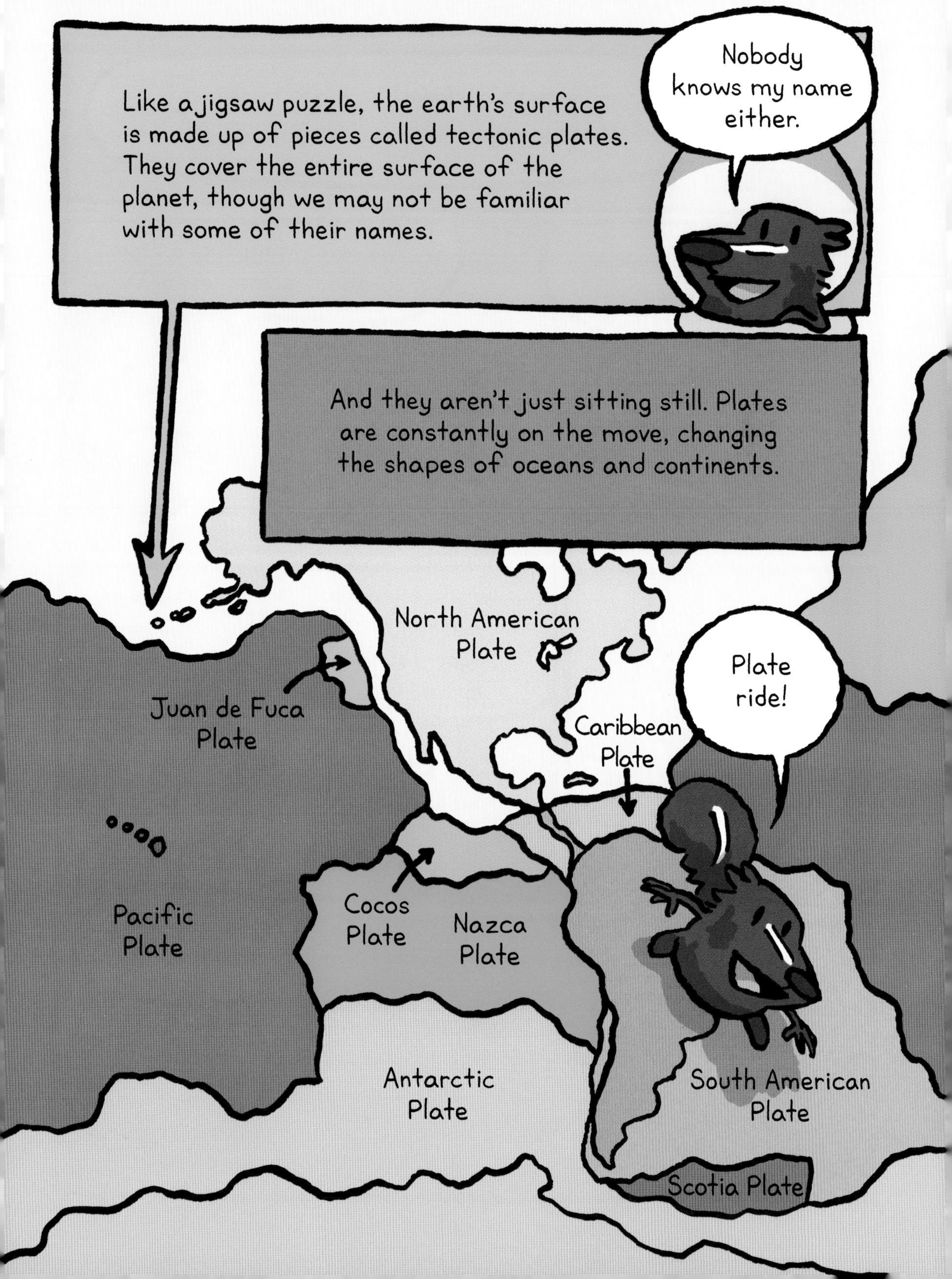
Like a jigsaw puzzle, the earth's surface is made up of pieces called tectonic plates. They cover the entire surface of the planet, though we may not be familiar with some of their names.
Nobody knows my name either.
And they aren't just sitting still. Plates are constantly on the move, changing the shapes of oceans and continents.
North American Plate
Juan de Fuca Plate
Caribbean Plate
Plate ride!
Pacific Plate
Cocos Plate
Nazca Plate
Antarctic Plate
South American Plate
Scotia Plate

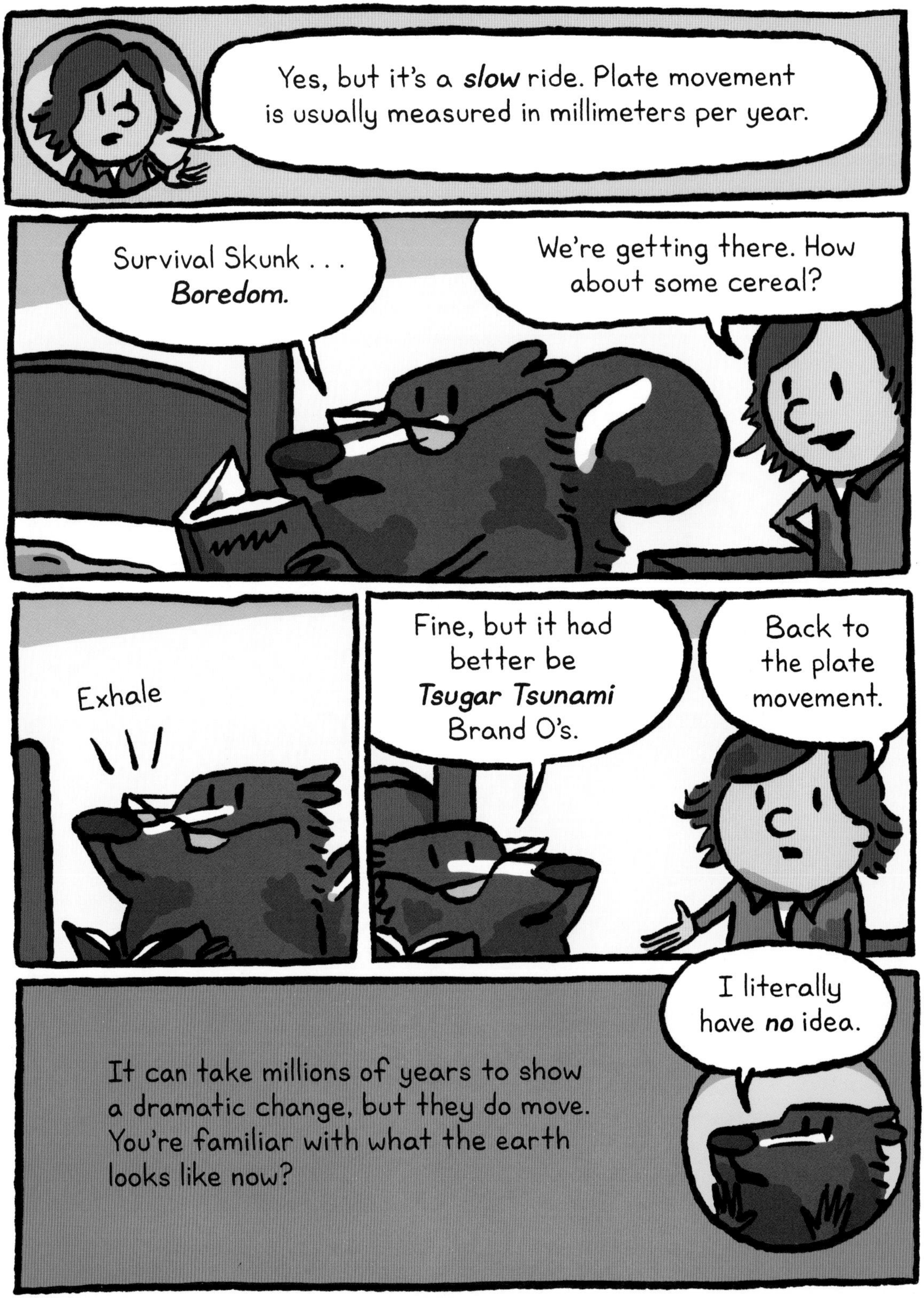

Yes, but it's a slow ride. Plate movement is usually measured in millimeters per year.
Survival Skunk . . . Boredom.
We're getting there. How about some cereal?
Exhale
Fine, but it had better be Tsugar Tsunami Brand O's.
Back to the plate movement.
It can take millions of years to show a dramatic change, but they do move. You're familiar with what the earth looks like now?
I literally have no idea.

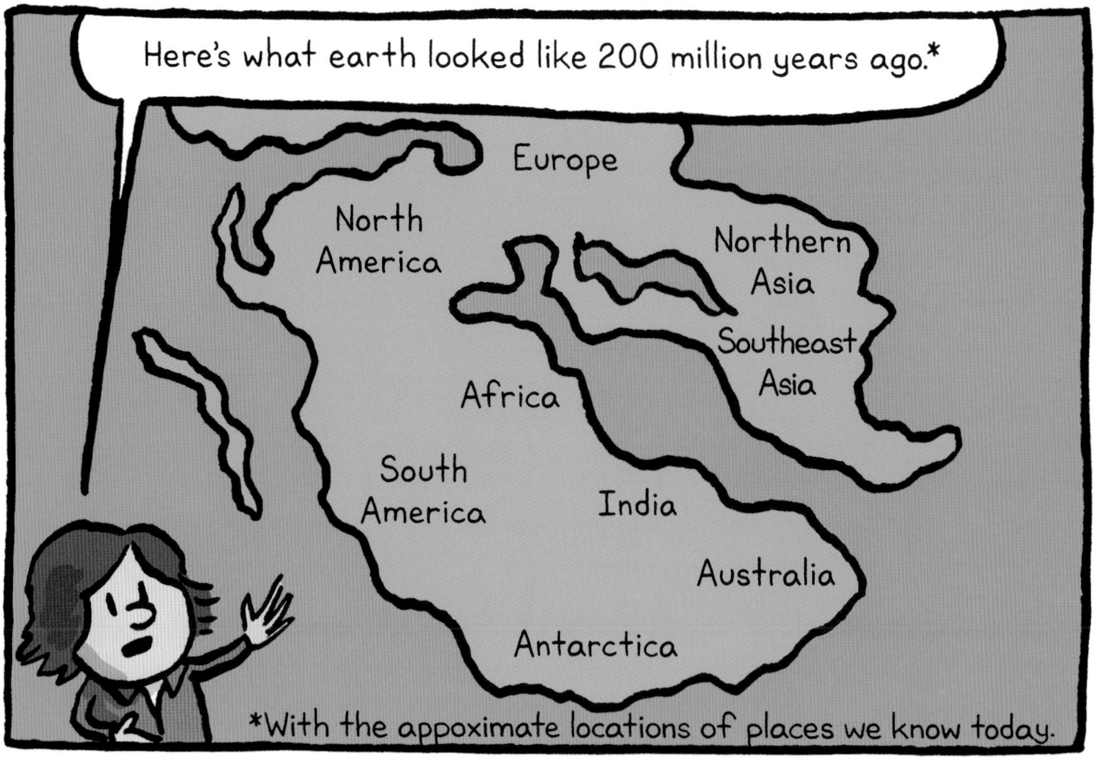
Here's what earth looked like 200 million years ago.*
Europe
North America
Northern Asia
Southeast Asia
Africa
South America
India
Australia
Antarctica
*With the appoximate locations of places we know today.

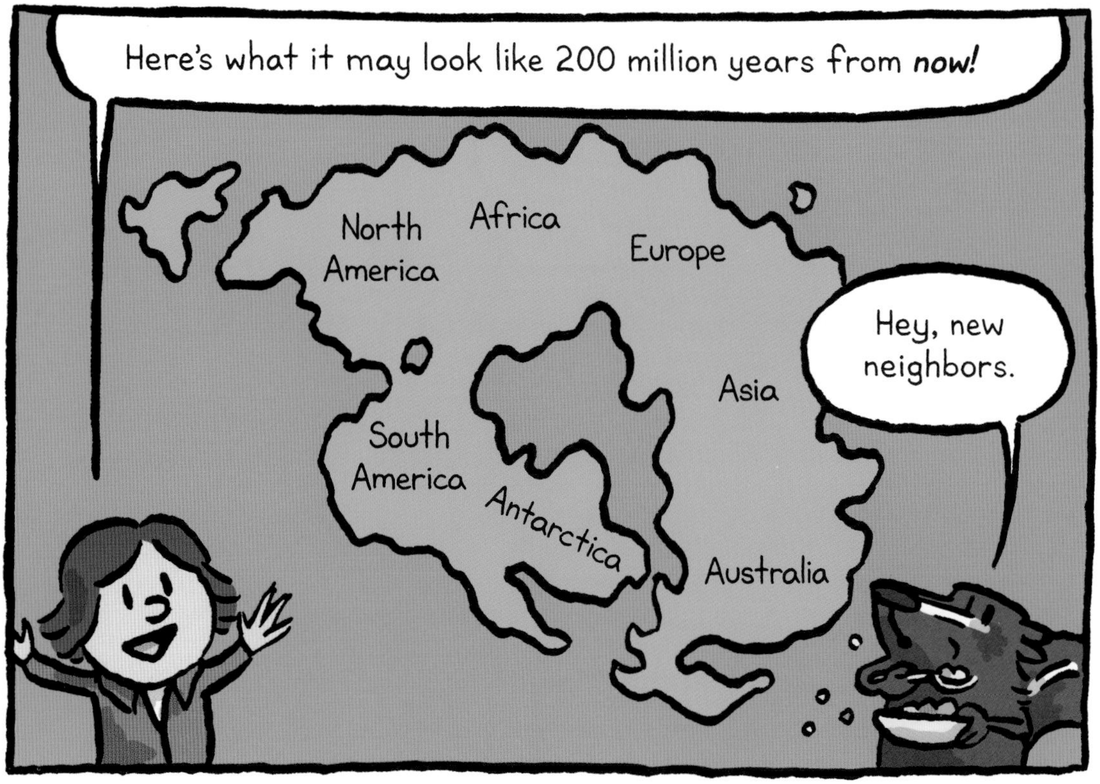
Here's what it may look like 200 million years from **now!**
North America
Africa
Europe
Hey, new neighbors.
Asia
South America
Antarctica
Australia

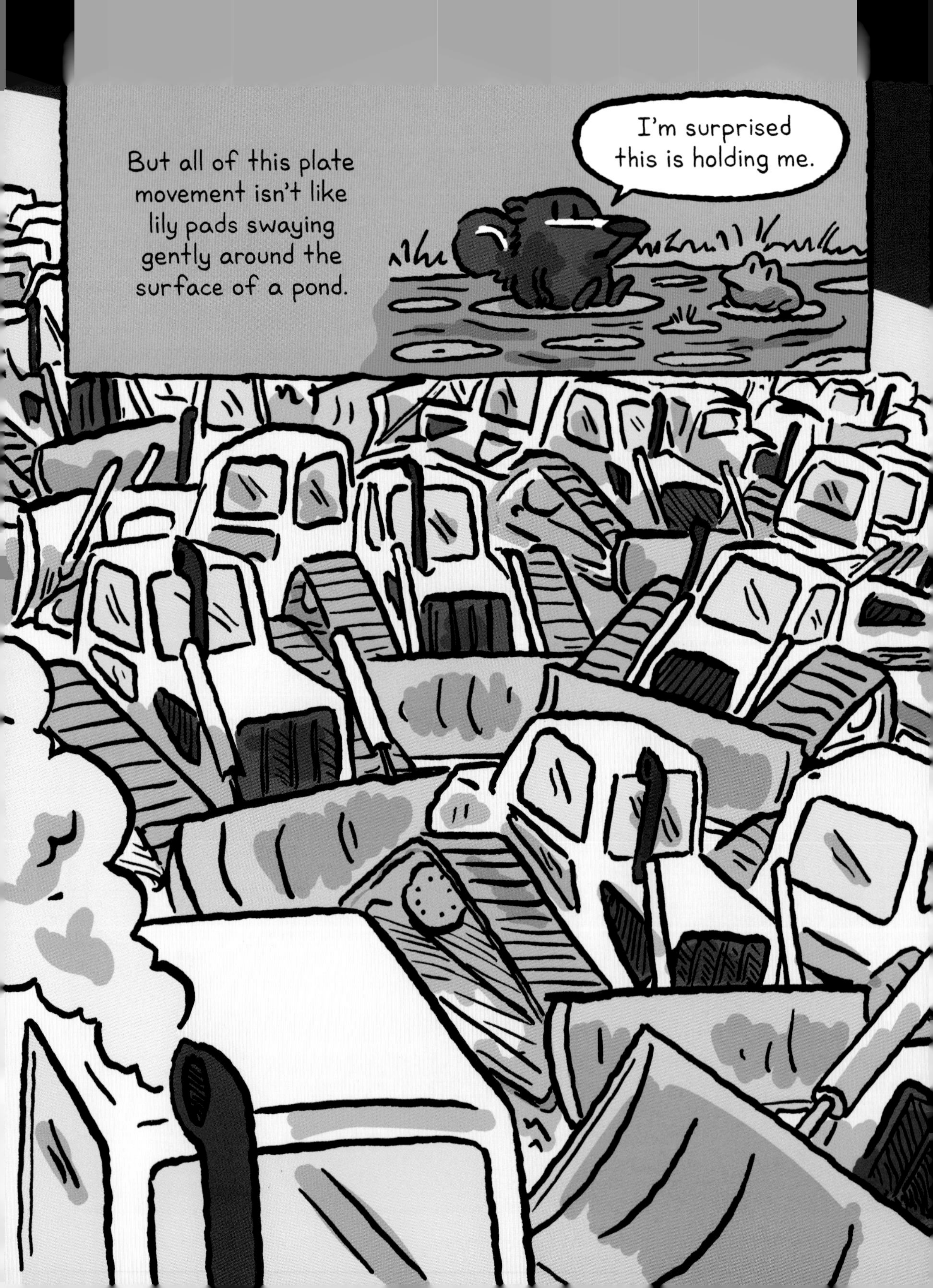
But all of this plate movement isn't like lily pads swaying gently around the surface of a pond.
I'm surprised this is holding me.

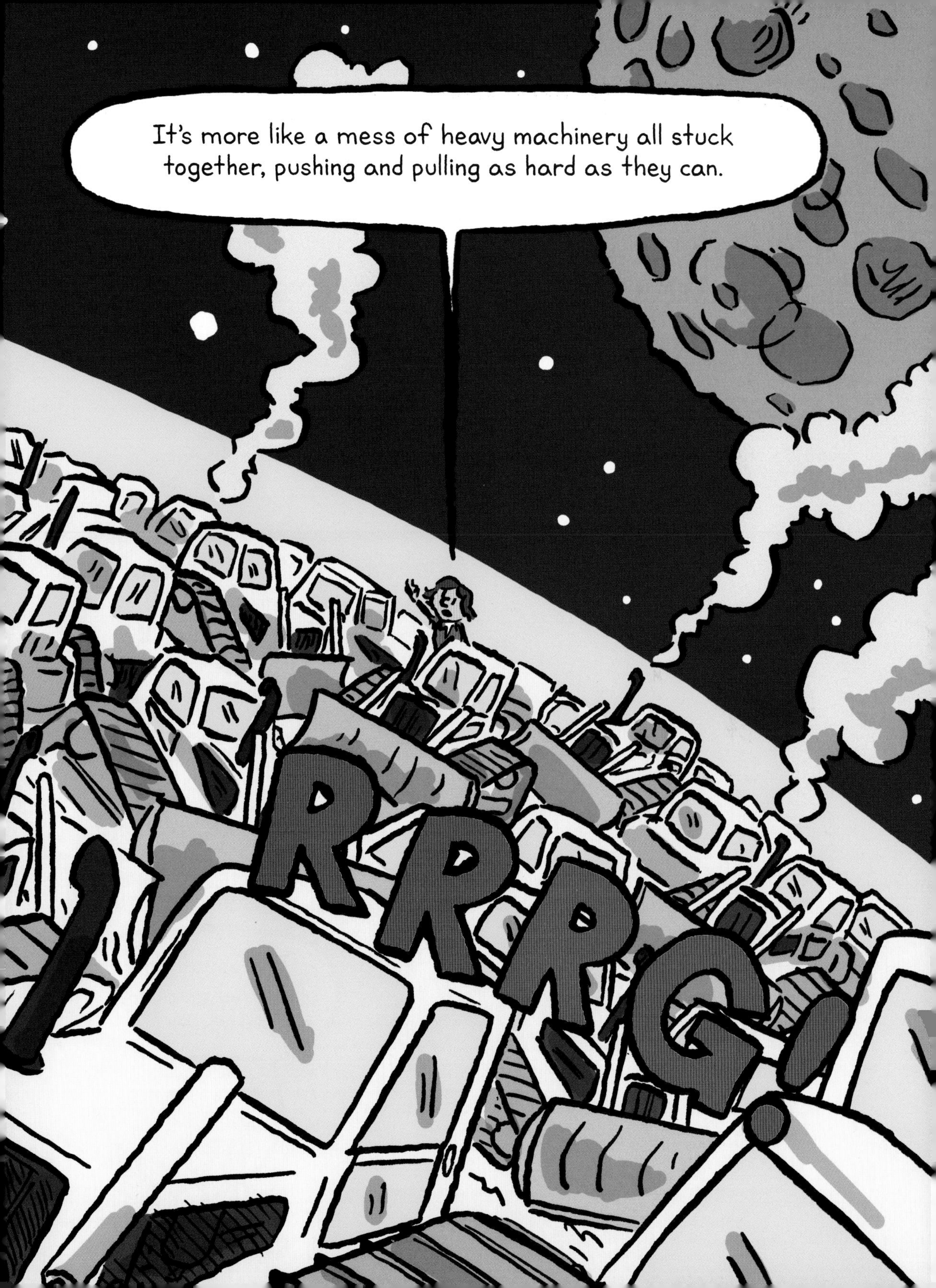
It's more like a mess of heavy machinery all stuck together, pushing and pulling as hard as they can.
RRRG!

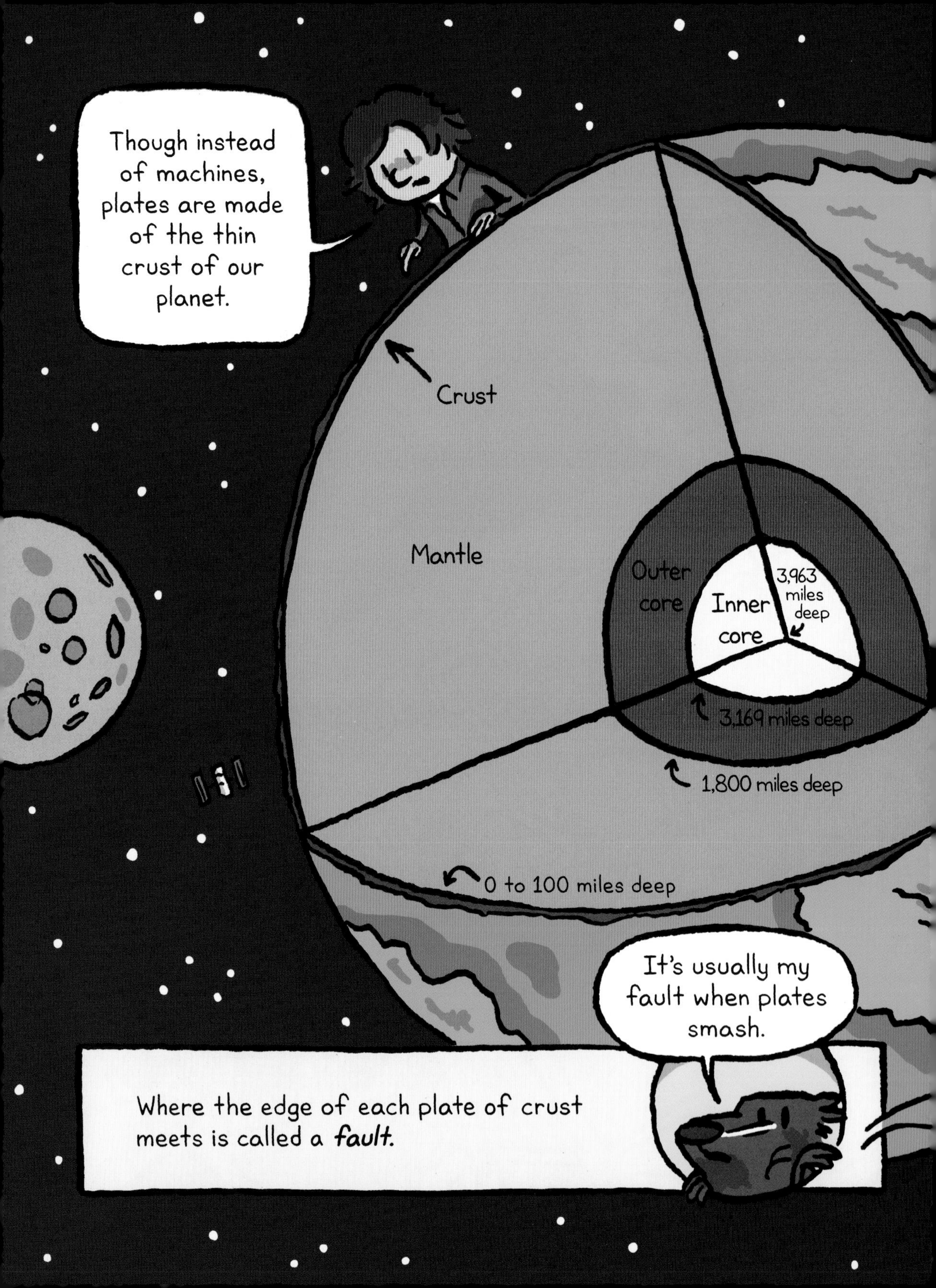
Though instead of machines, plates are made of the thin crust of our planet.
Crust
Mantle
Outer core
Inner core
3,963 miles deep
3,169 miles deep
1,800 miles deep
0 to 100 miles deep
It's usually my fault when plates smash.
Where the edge of each plate of crust meets is called a *fault*.

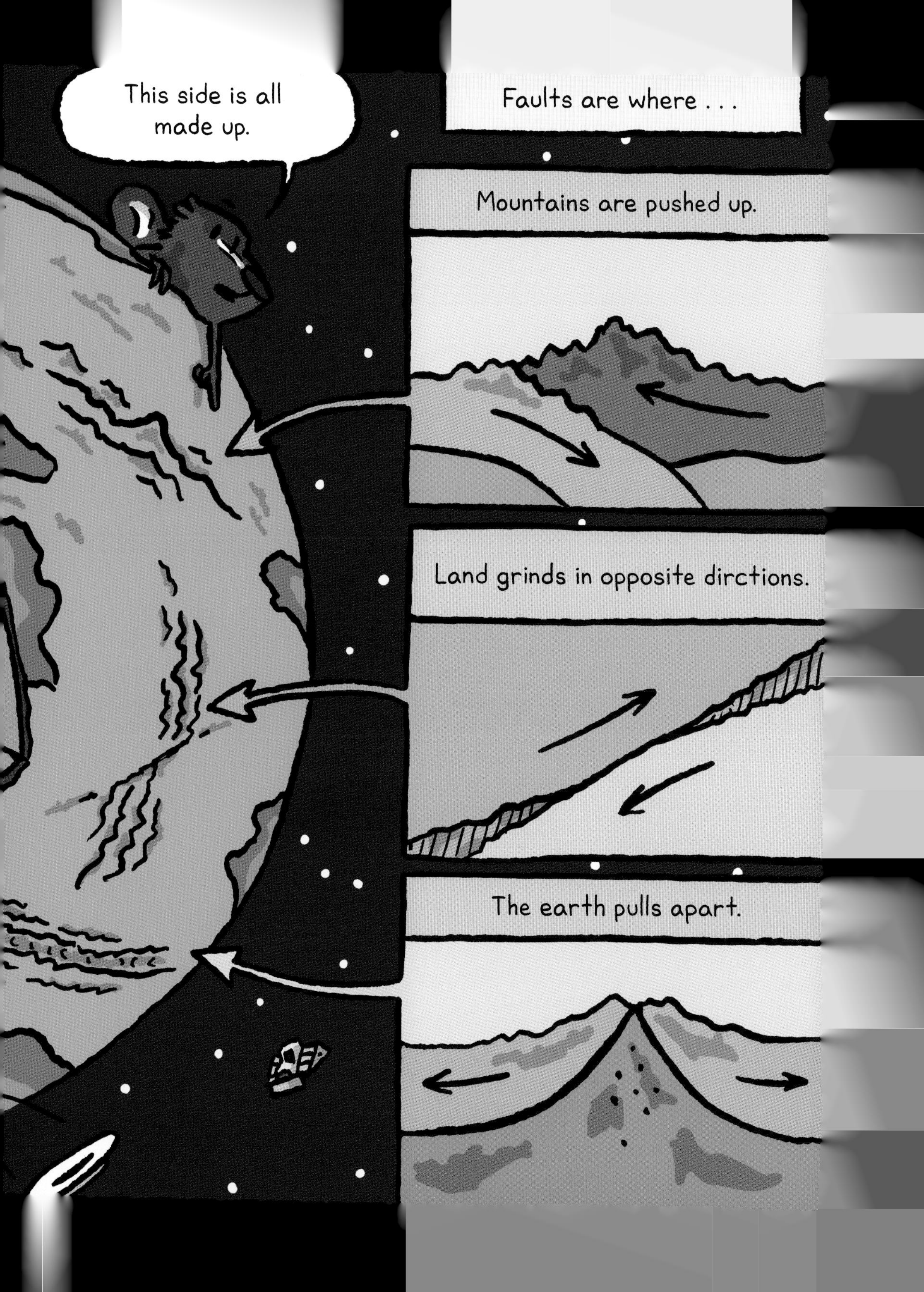
This side is all made up.
Faults are where . . .
Mountains are pushed up.
Land grinds in opposite dirctions.
The earth pulls apart.

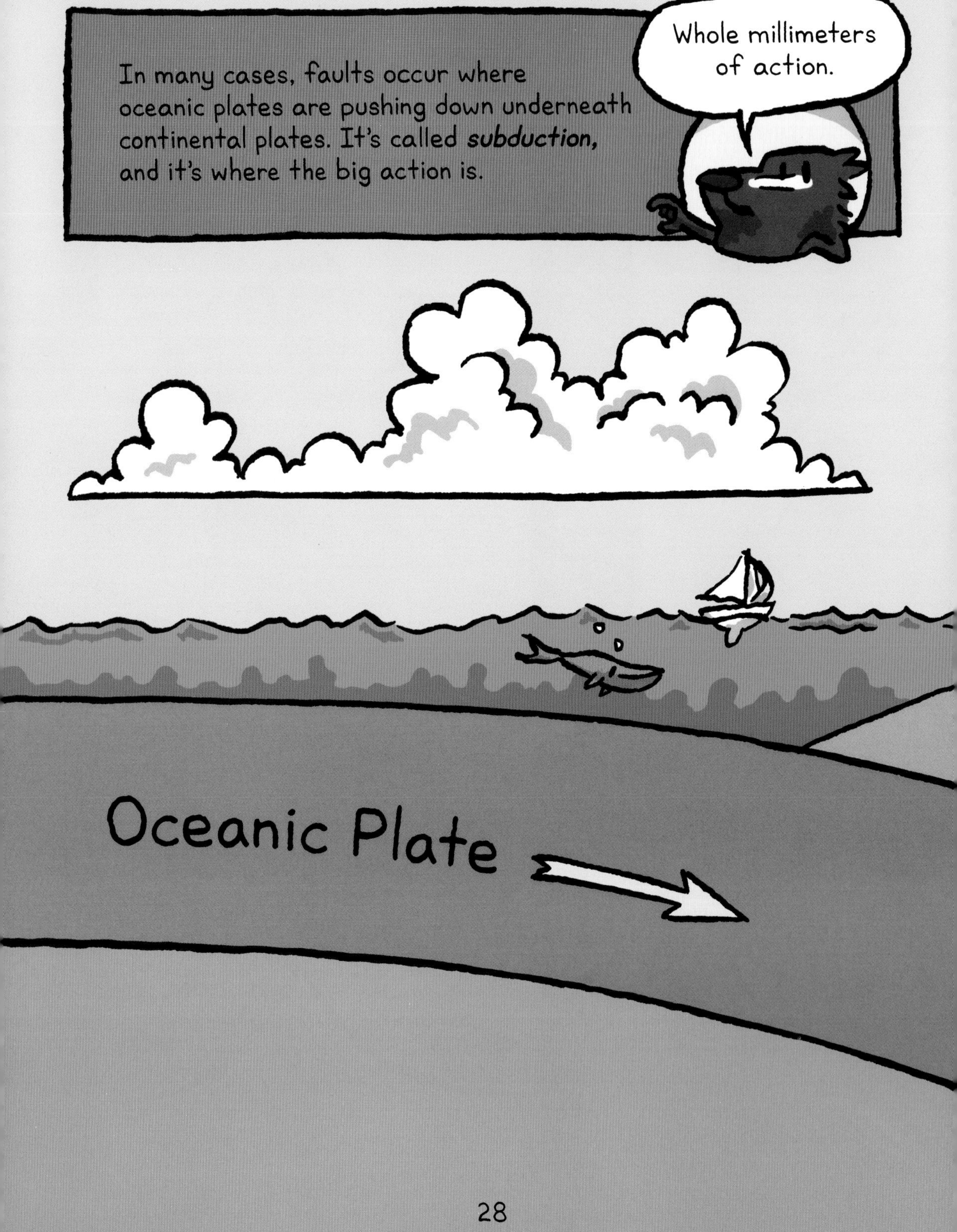
In many cases, faults occur where oceanic plates are pushing down underneath continental plates. It's called ***subduction,*** and it's where the big action is.
Whole millimeters of action.
Oceanic Plate

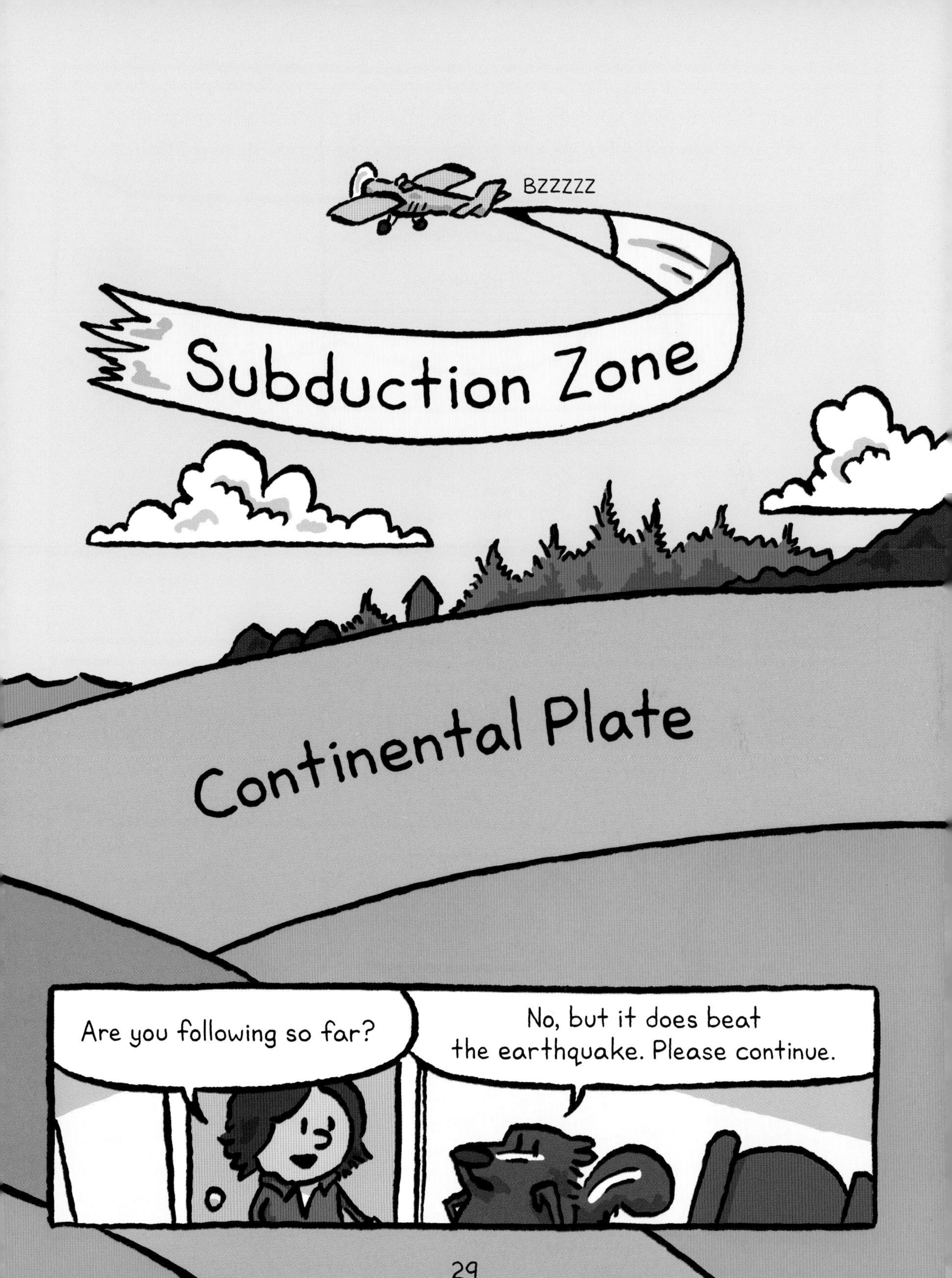
BZZZZZ
Subduction Zone
Continental Plate
Are you following so far?
No, but it does beat the earthquake. Please continue.

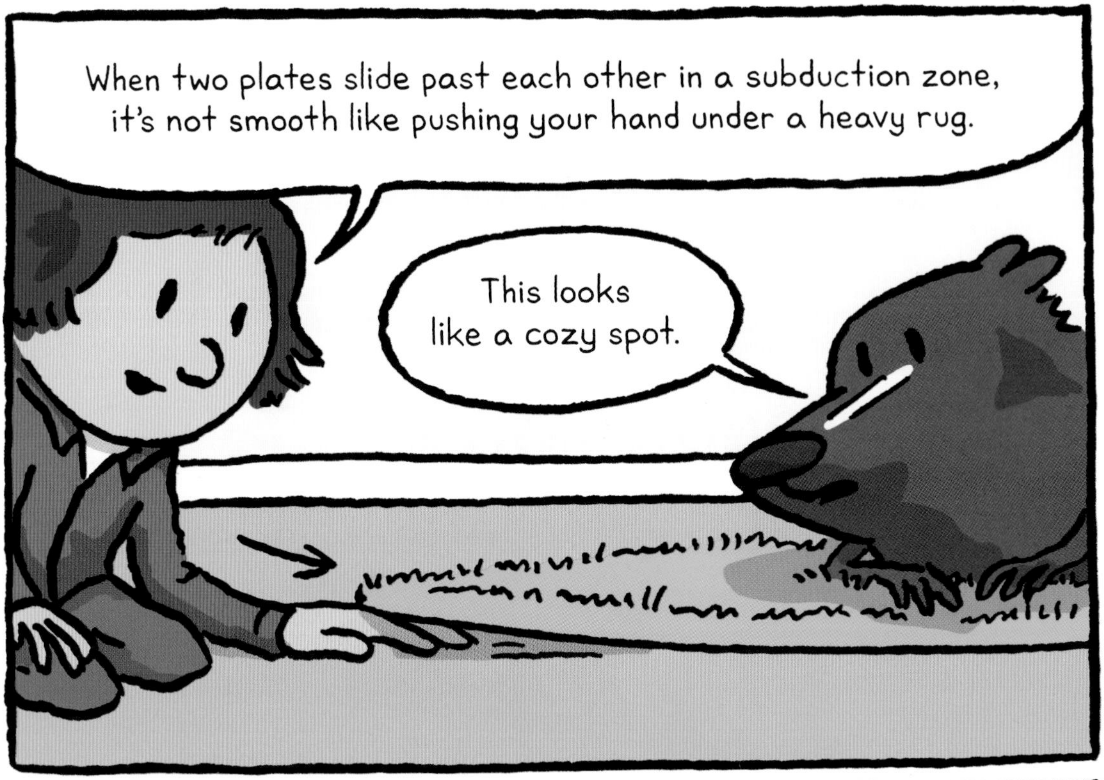
When two plates slide past each other in a subduction zone, it's not smooth like pushing your hand under a heavy rug.
This looks like a cozy spot.

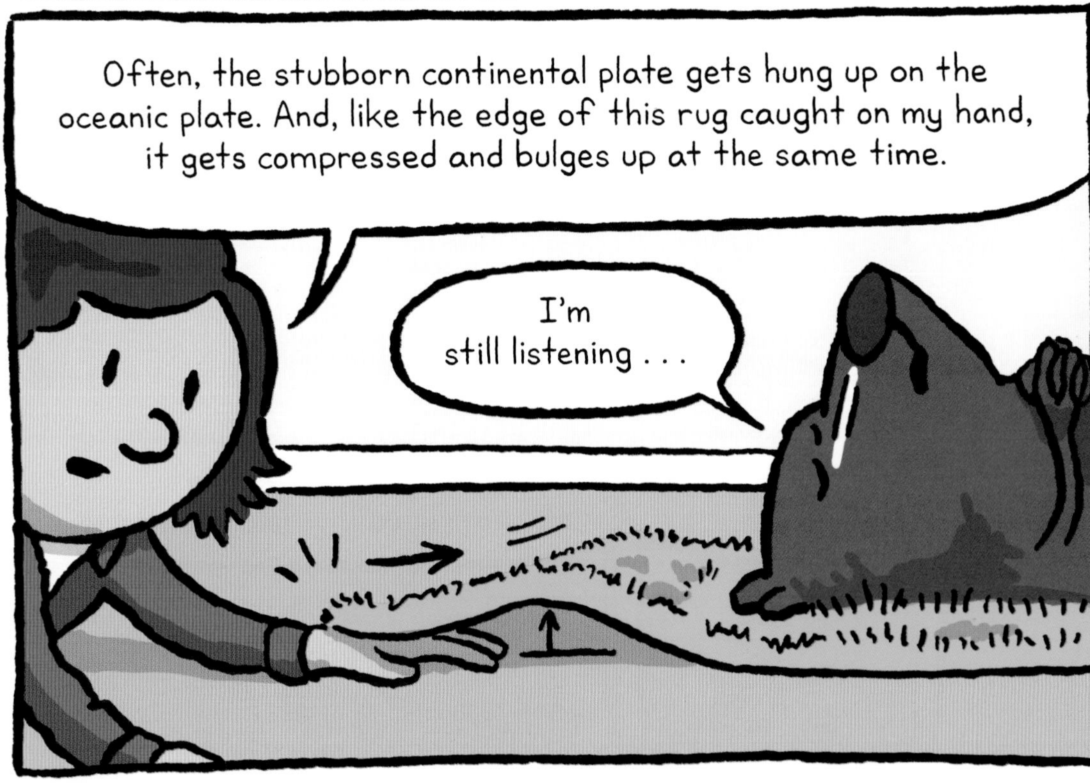
Often, the stubborn continental plate gets hung up on the oceanic plate. And, like the edge of this rug caught on my hand, it gets compressed and bulges up at the same time.
I'm still listening . . .

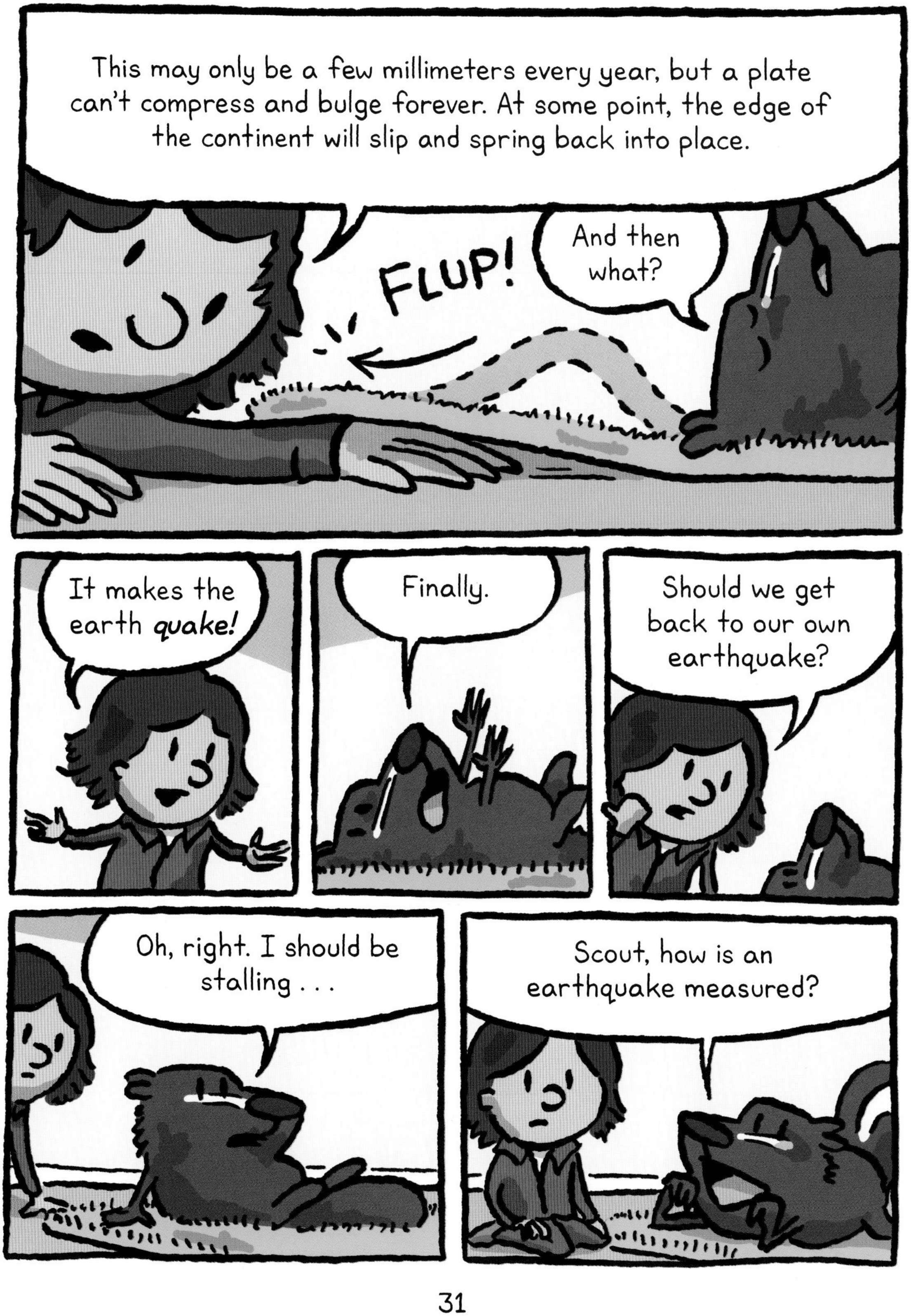
This may only be a few millimeters every year, but a plate can't compress and bulge forever. At some point, the edge of the continent will slip and spring back into place.
FLUP!
And then what?
It makes the earth *quake!*
Finally.
Should we get back to our own earthquake?
Oh, right. I should be stalling . . .
Scout, how is an earthquake measured?

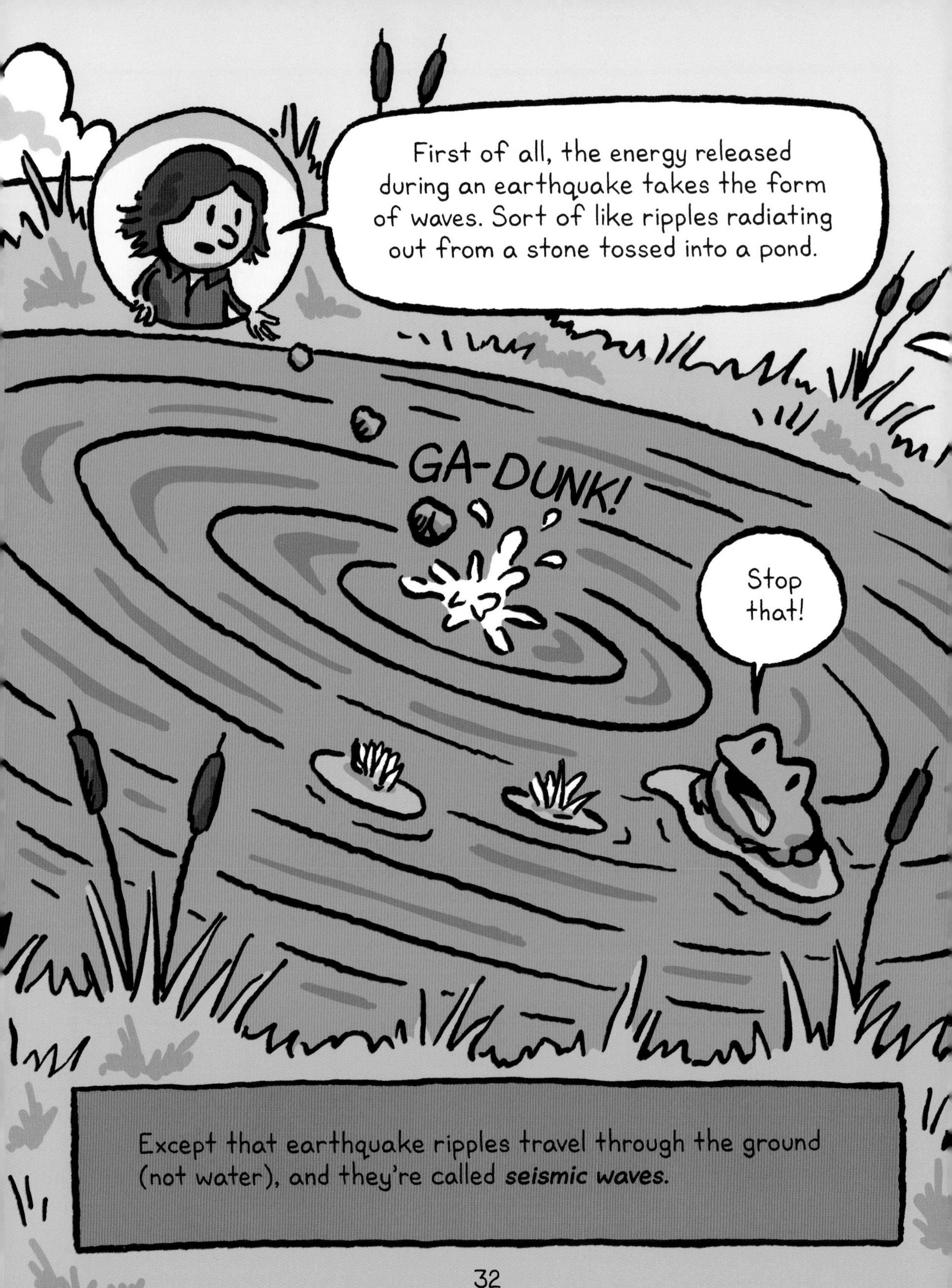
First of all, the energy released during an earthquake takes the form of waves. Sort of like ripples radiating out from a stone tossed into a pond.
GA-DUNK!
Stop that!
Except that earthquake ripples travel through the ground (not water), and they're called *seismic waves.*

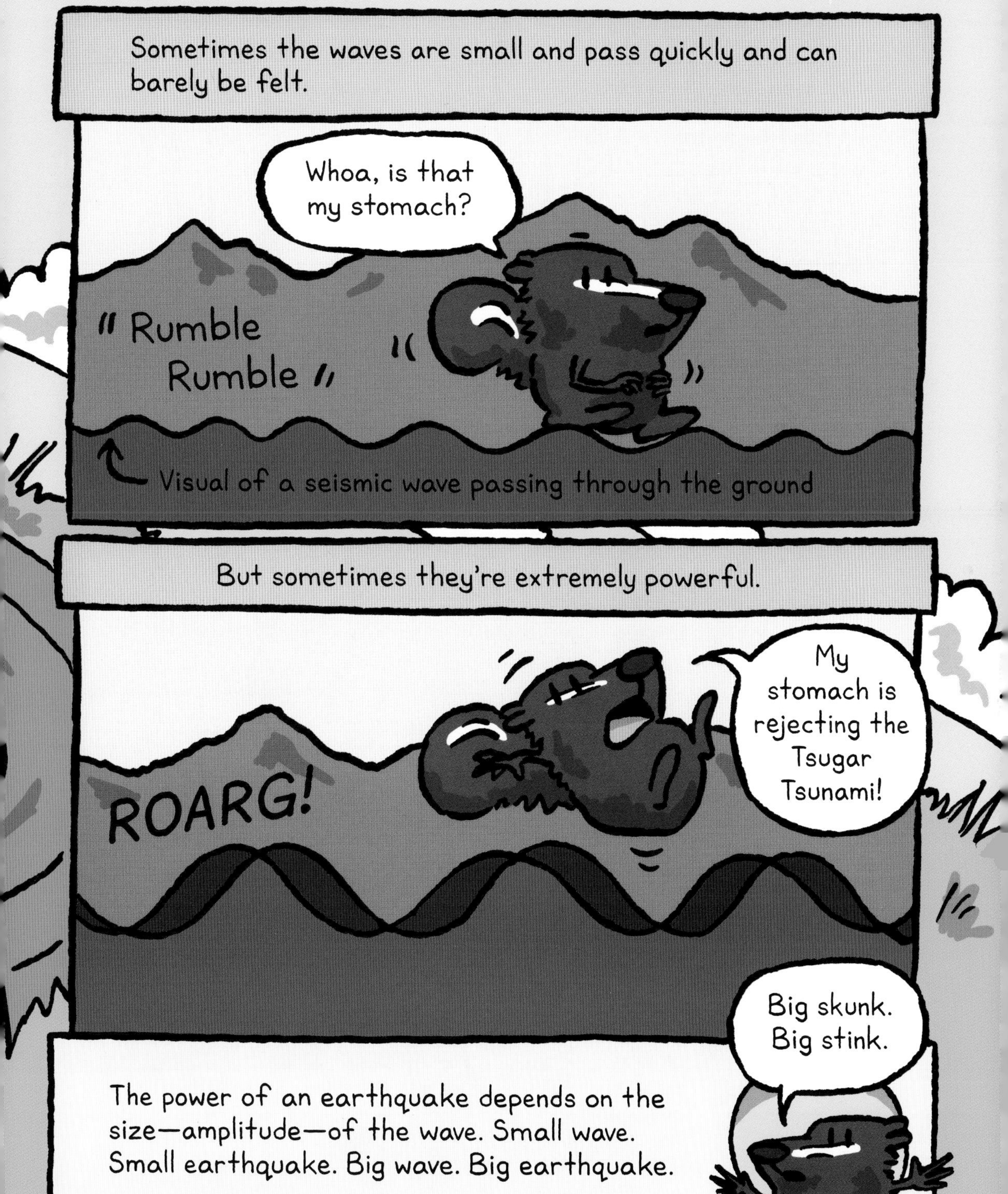
Sometimes the waves are small and pass quickly and can barely be felt.
Whoa, is that my stomach?
" Rumble Rumble "
Visual of a seismic wave passing through the ground
But sometimes they're extremely powerful.
ROARG!
My stomach is rejecting the Tsugar Tsunami!
The power of an earthquake depends on the size—amplitude—of the wave. Small wave. Small earthquake. Big wave. Big earthquake.
Big skunk. Big stink.

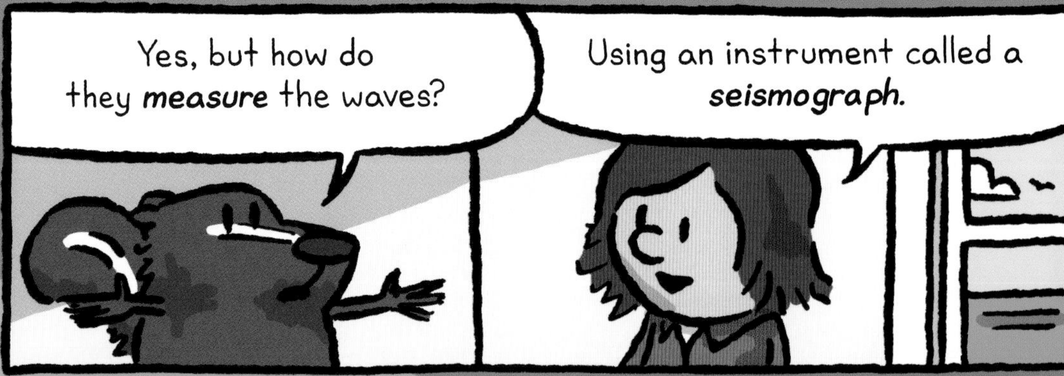
Yes, but how do they **measure** the waves?
Using an instrument called a ***seismograph.***

Modern versions are all sensors and electronics, but here's how the old ones worked.

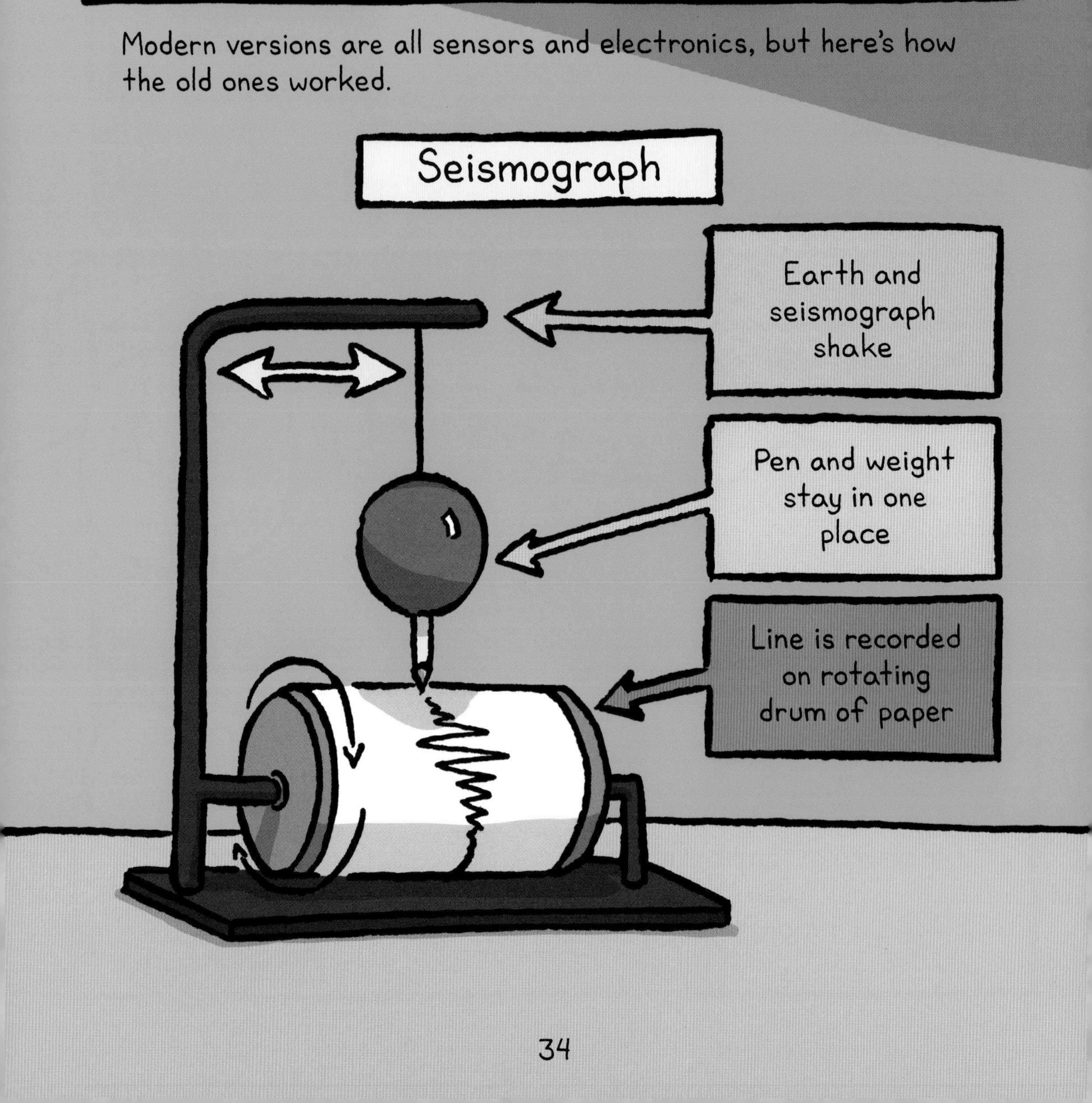
Seismograph
Earth and seismograph shake
Pen and weight stay in one place
Line is recorded on rotating drum of paper

Seismogram

Made by the seismograph, this is the written record of the ground movement.

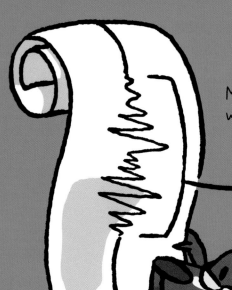

An earthquake

Squiggly lines. Very interesting.

With this information they can determine the size of an earthquake.

Now tell me who *they* are.

Seismologists are scientists who study earthquakes.

And *seismology* is the science of earthquakes.

It's a shaky field of study.

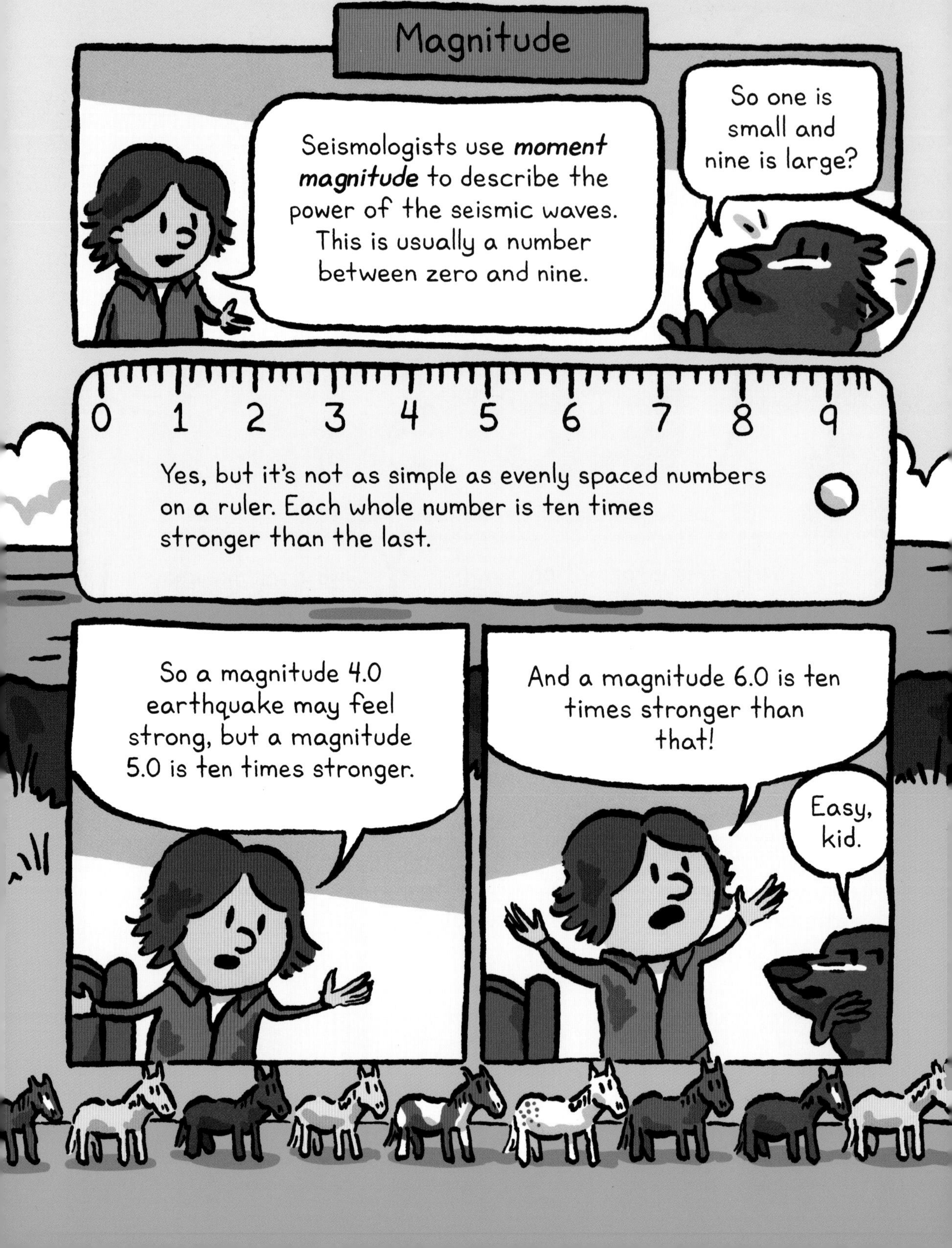
Magnitude
Seismologists use ***moment magnitude*** to describe the power of the seismic waves. This is usually a number between zero and nine.
So one is small and nine is large?
0 1 2 3 4 5 6 7 8 9
Yes, but it's not as simple as evenly spaced numbers on a ruler. Each whole number is ten times stronger than the last.
So a magnitude 4.0 earthquake may feel strong, but a magnitude 5.0 is ten times stronger.
And a magnitude 6.0 is ten times stronger than that!
Easy, kid.

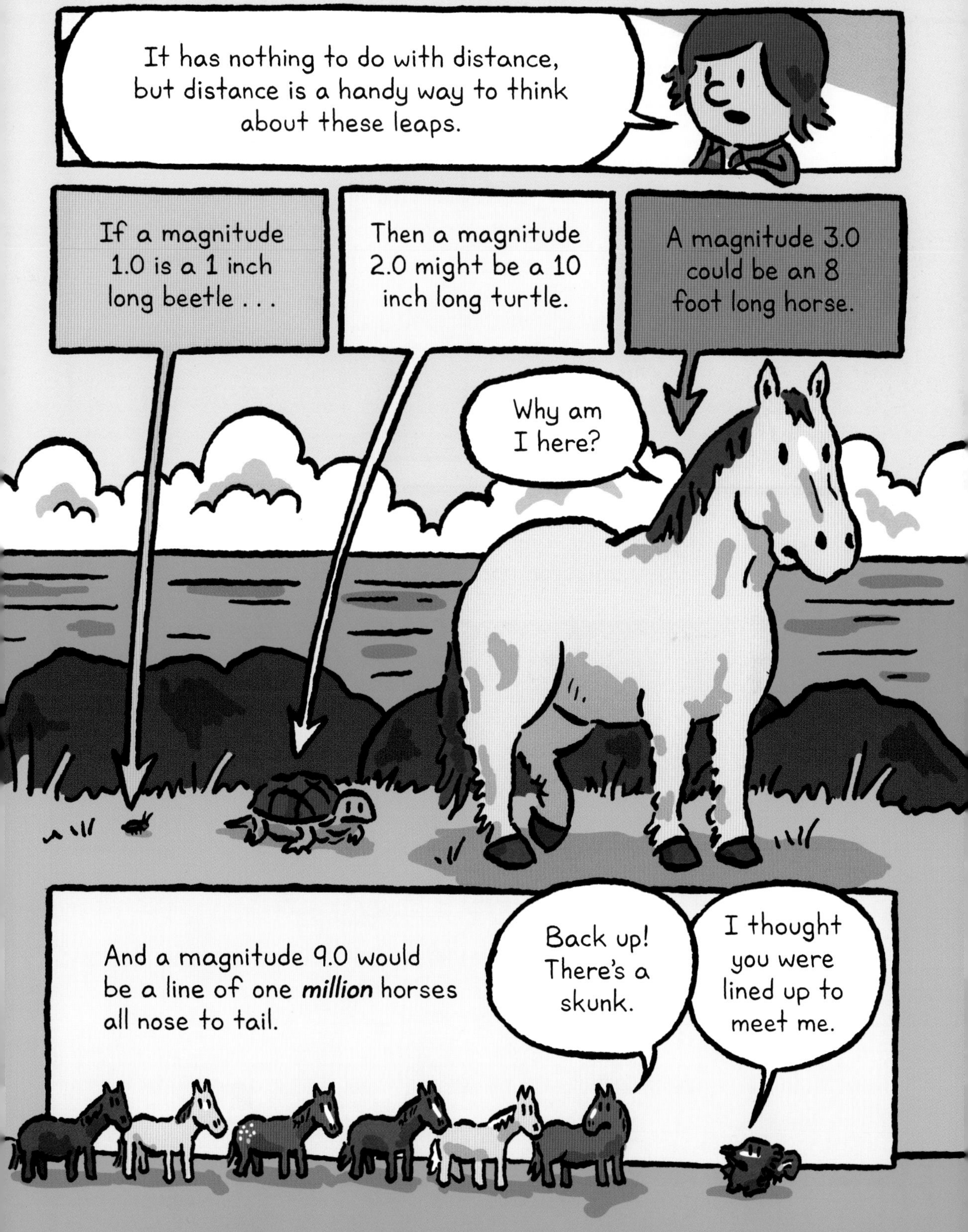
It has nothing to do with distance, but distance is a handy way to think about these leaps.
If a magnitude 1.0 is a 1 inch long beetle . . .
Then a magnitude 2.0 might be a 10 inch long turtle.
A magnitude 3.0 could be an 8 foot long horse.
Why am I here?
And a magnitude 9.0 would be a line of one *million* horses all nose to tail.
Back up! There's a skunk.
I thought you were lined up to meet me.

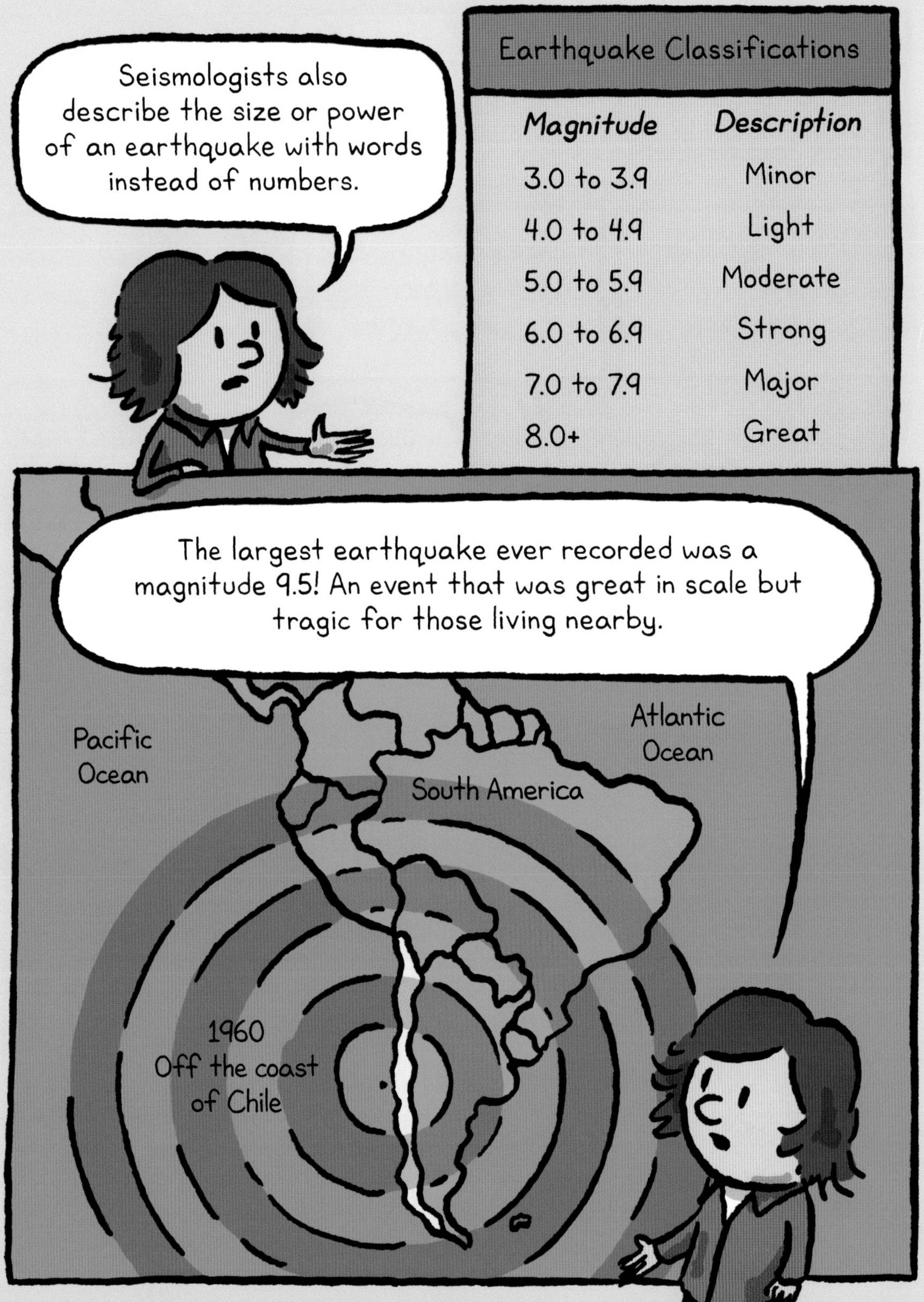
Seismologists also describe the size or power of an earthquake with words instead of numbers.
Earthquake Classifications
Magnitude Description
3.0 to 3.9 Minor
4.0 to 4.9 Light
5.0 to 5.9 Moderate
6.0 to 6.9 Strong
7.0 to 7.9 Major
8.0+ Great
The largest earthquake ever recorded was a magnitude 9.5! An event that was great in scale but tragic for those living nearby.
Pacific Ocean
Atlantic Ocean
South America
1960 Off the coast of Chile

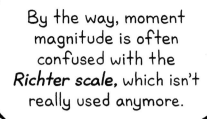
By the way, moment magnitude is often confused with the *Richter scale,* which isn't really used anymore.

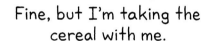
Also not to be confused with Richter Scale, our summer exchange student.

Guten Tag.
[Good day.]

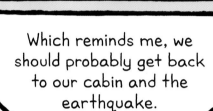
Which reminds me, we should probably get back to our cabin and the earthquake.

Fine, but I'm taking the cereal with me.

And Richter.

Nein!
[No!]

Here we go . . .

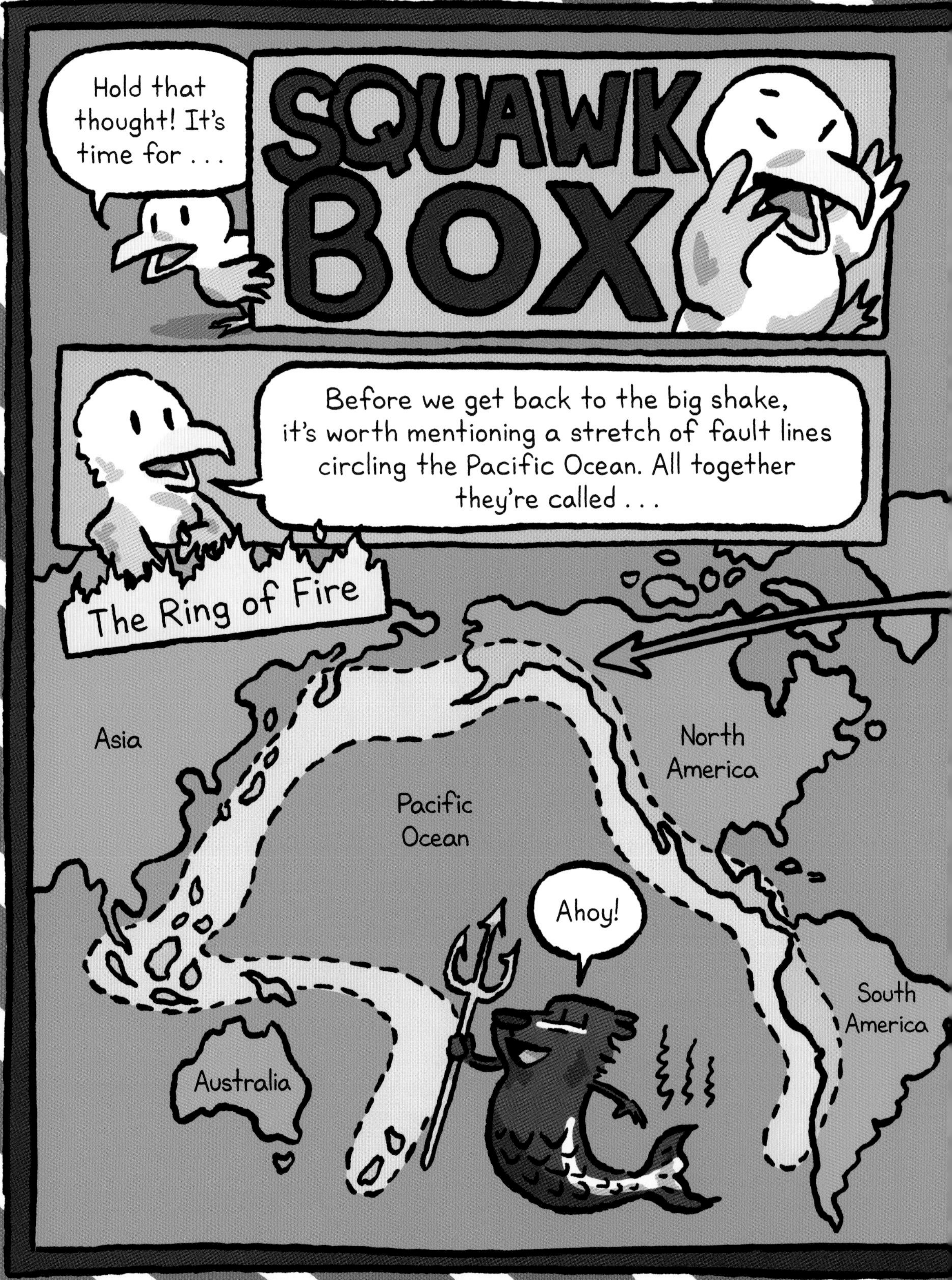
Hold that thought! It's time for . . .
SQUAWK BOX
Before we get back to the big shake, it's worth mentioning a stretch of fault lines circling the Pacific Ocean. All together they're called . . .
The Ring of Fire
Asia
North America
Pacific Ocean
Ahoy!
South America
Australia

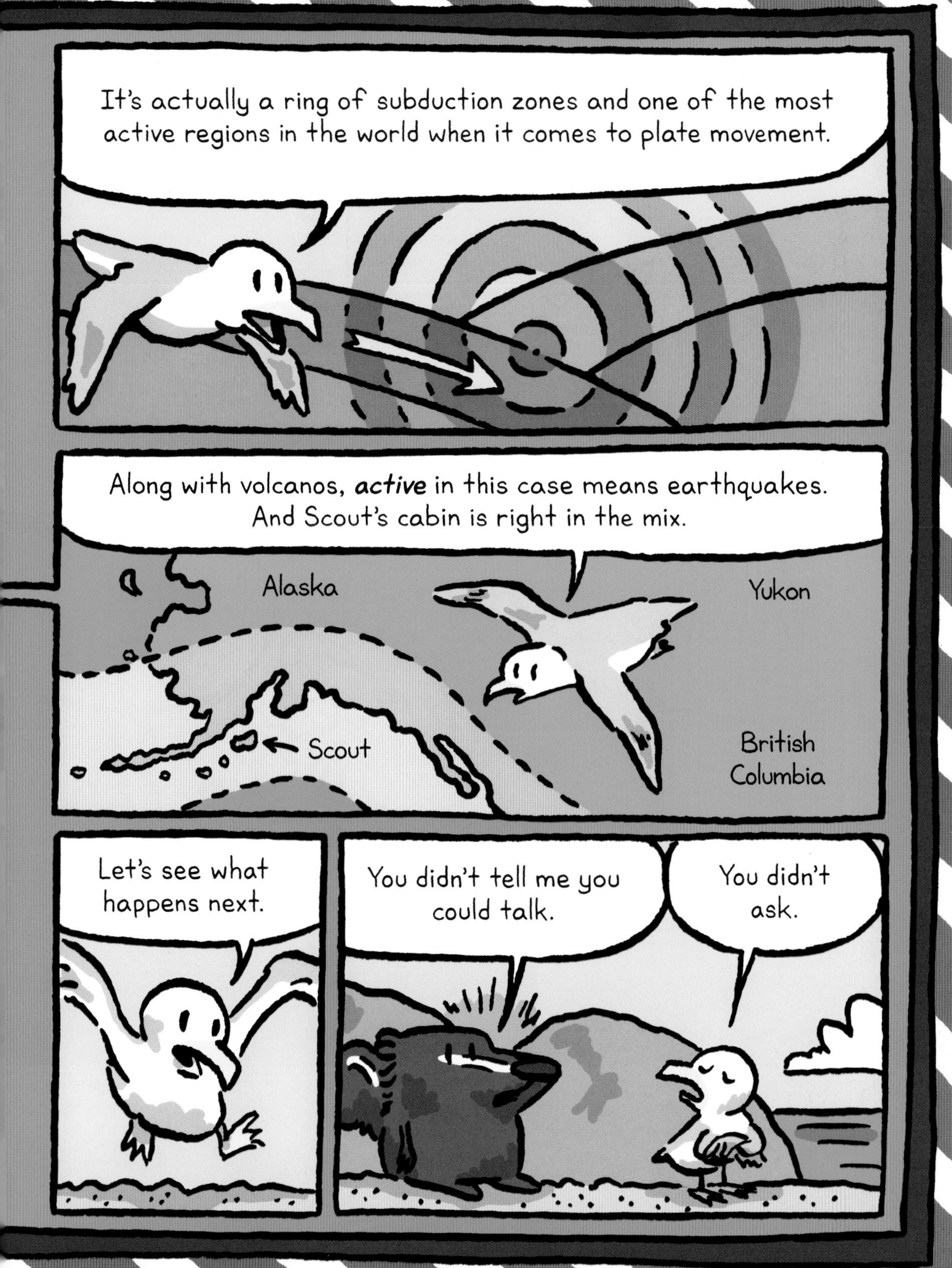

It's actually a ring of subduction zones and one of the most active regions in the world when it comes to plate movement.
Along with volcanos, ***active*** in this case means earthquakes. And Scout's cabin is right in the mix.
Alaska
Yukon
Scout
British Columbia
Let's see what happens next.
You didn't tell me you could talk.
You didn't ask.

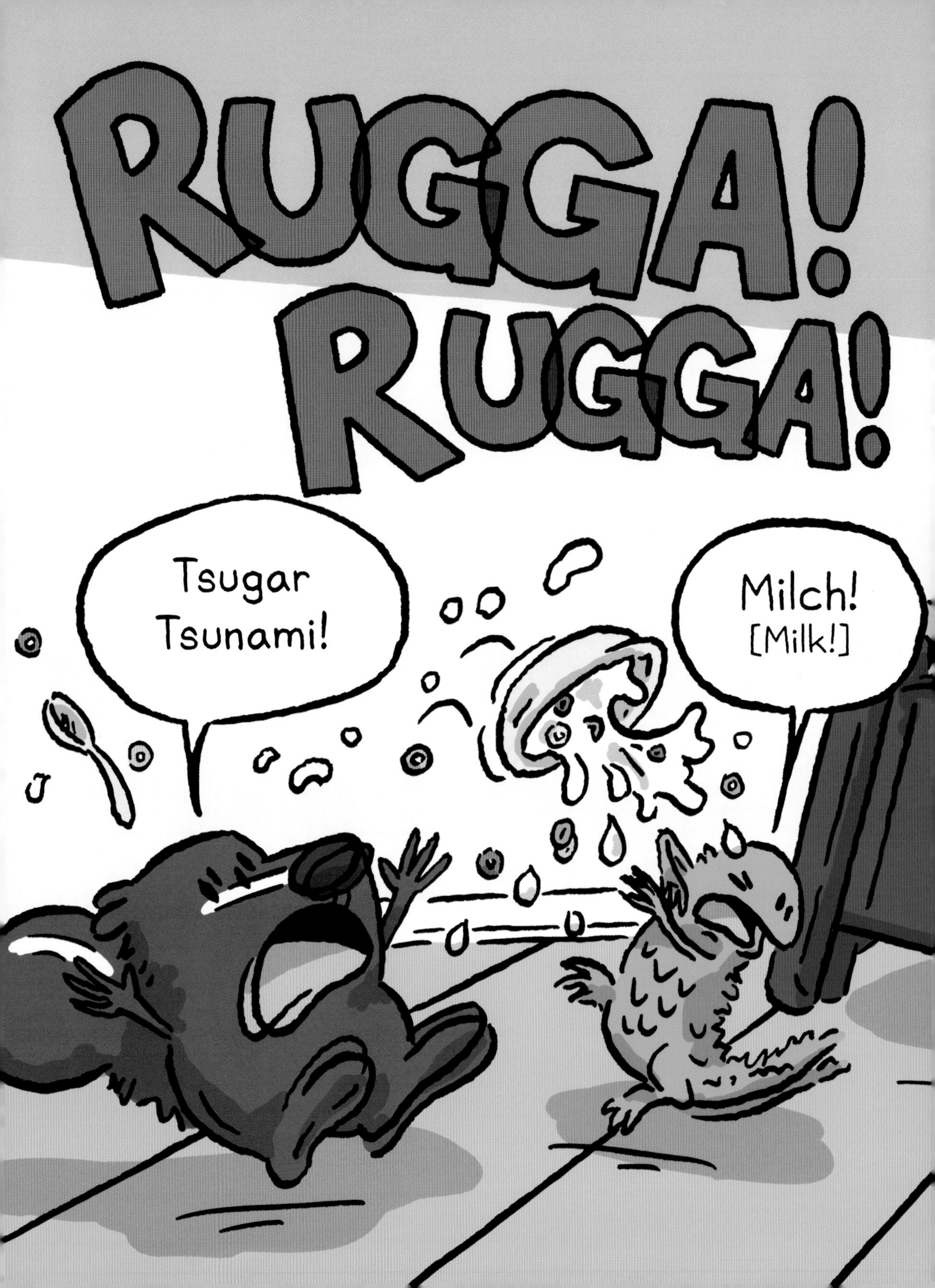
RUGGA!
RUGGA!
Tsugar Tsunami!
Milch!
[Milk!]

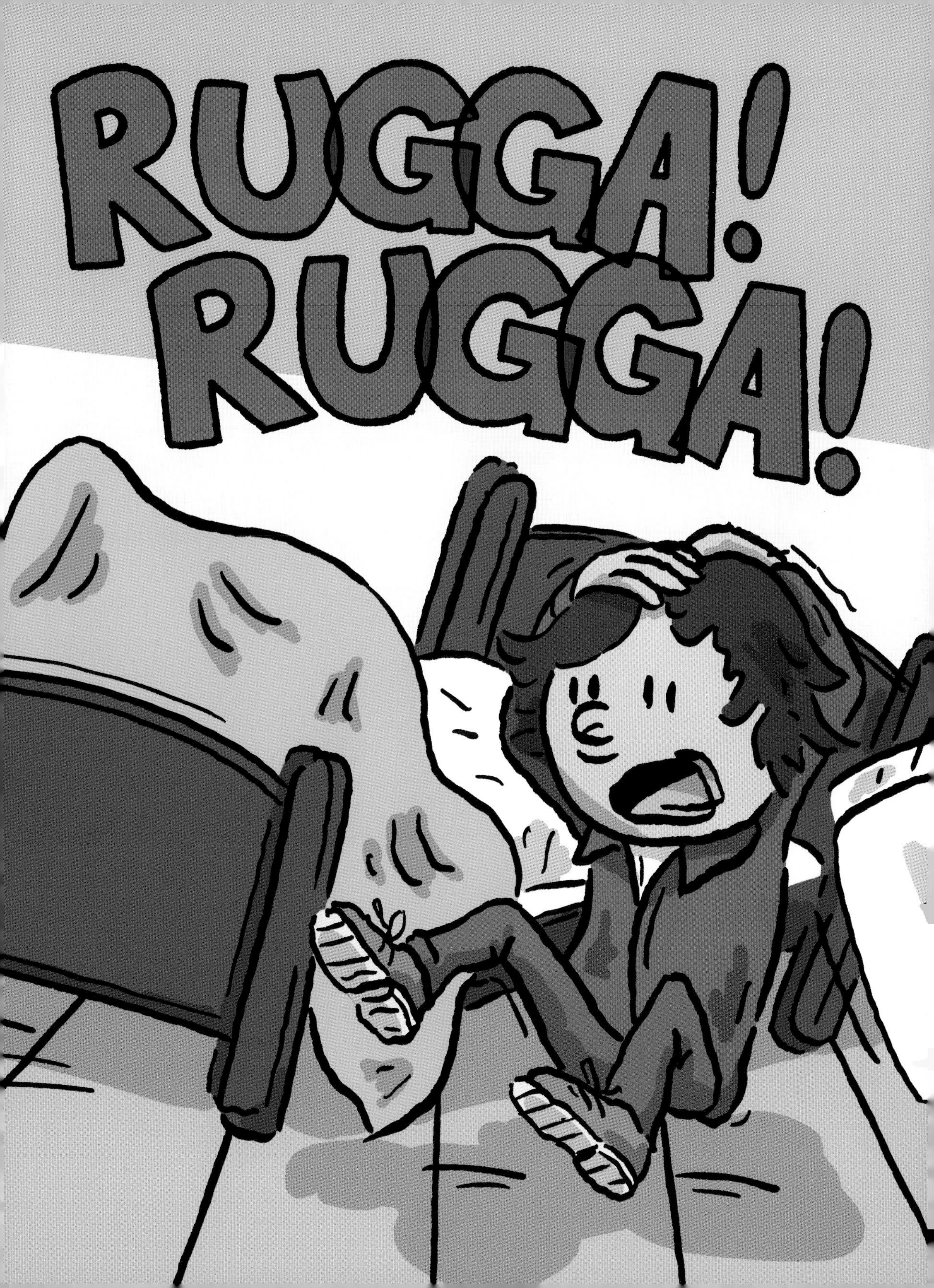
RUGGA! RUGGA!

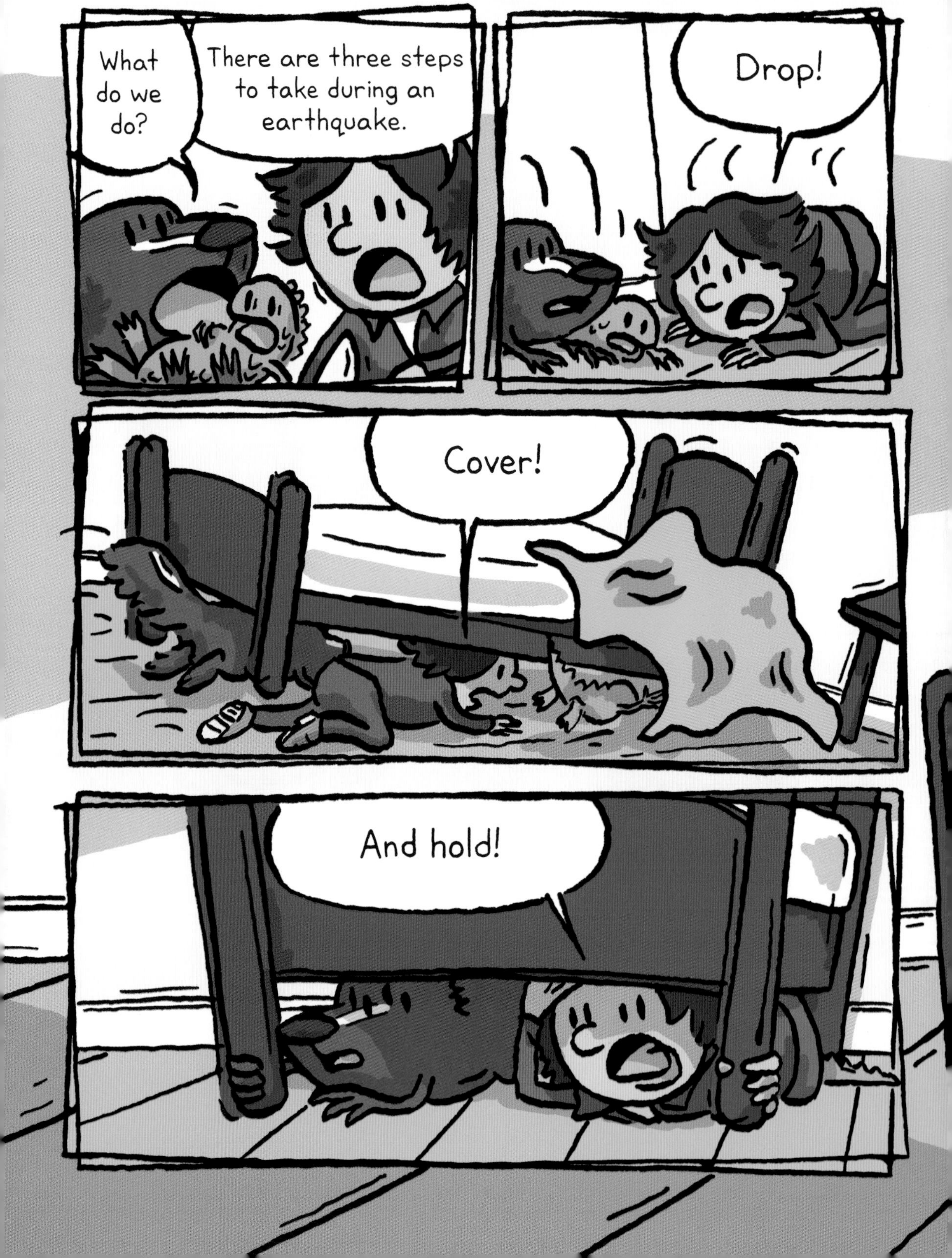
What do we do?
There are three steps to take during an earthquake.
Drop!
Cover!
And hold!

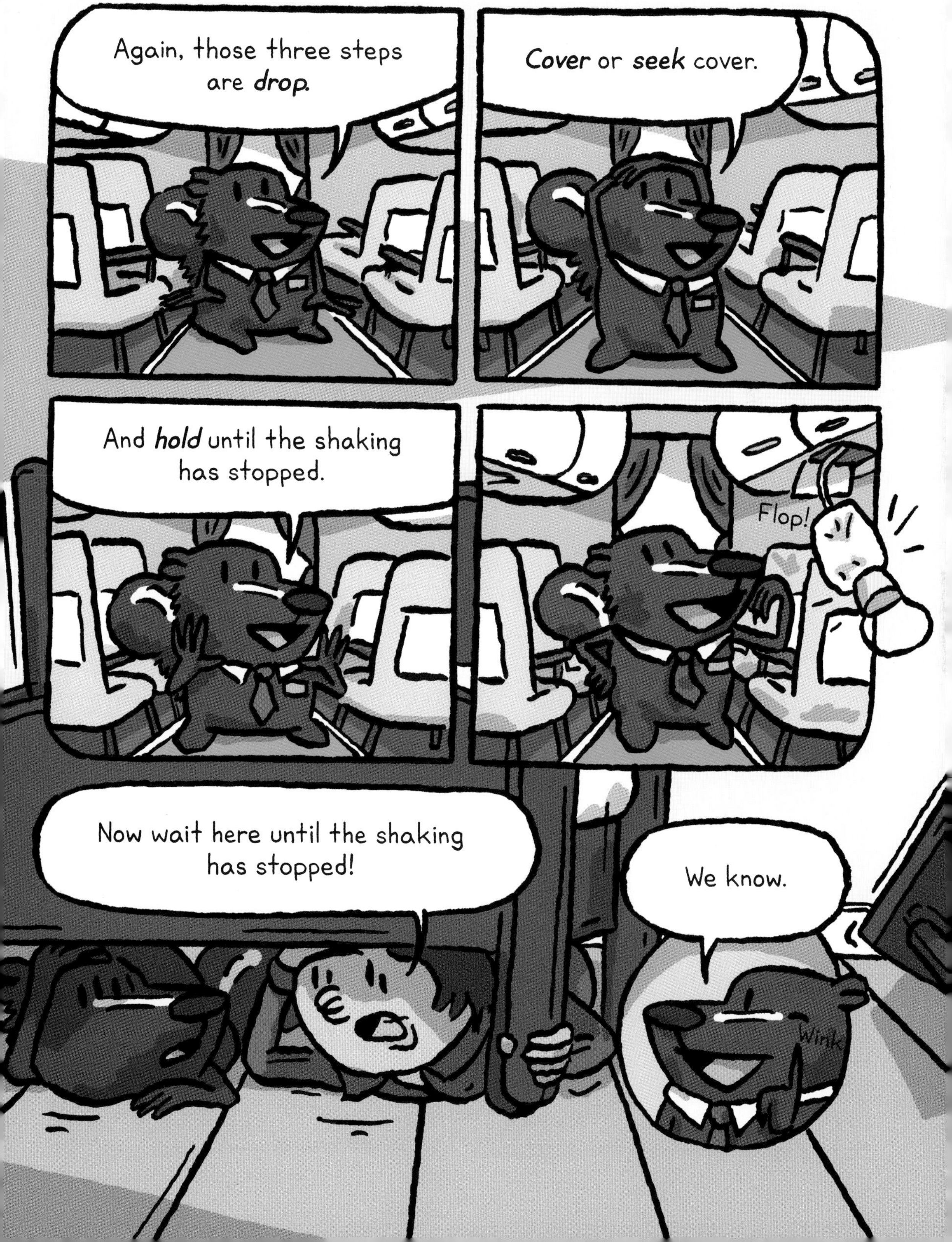
Again, those three steps are *drop*.
Cover or *seek* cover.
And *hold* until the shaking has stopped.
Flop!
Now wait here until the shaking has stopped!
We know.
Wink

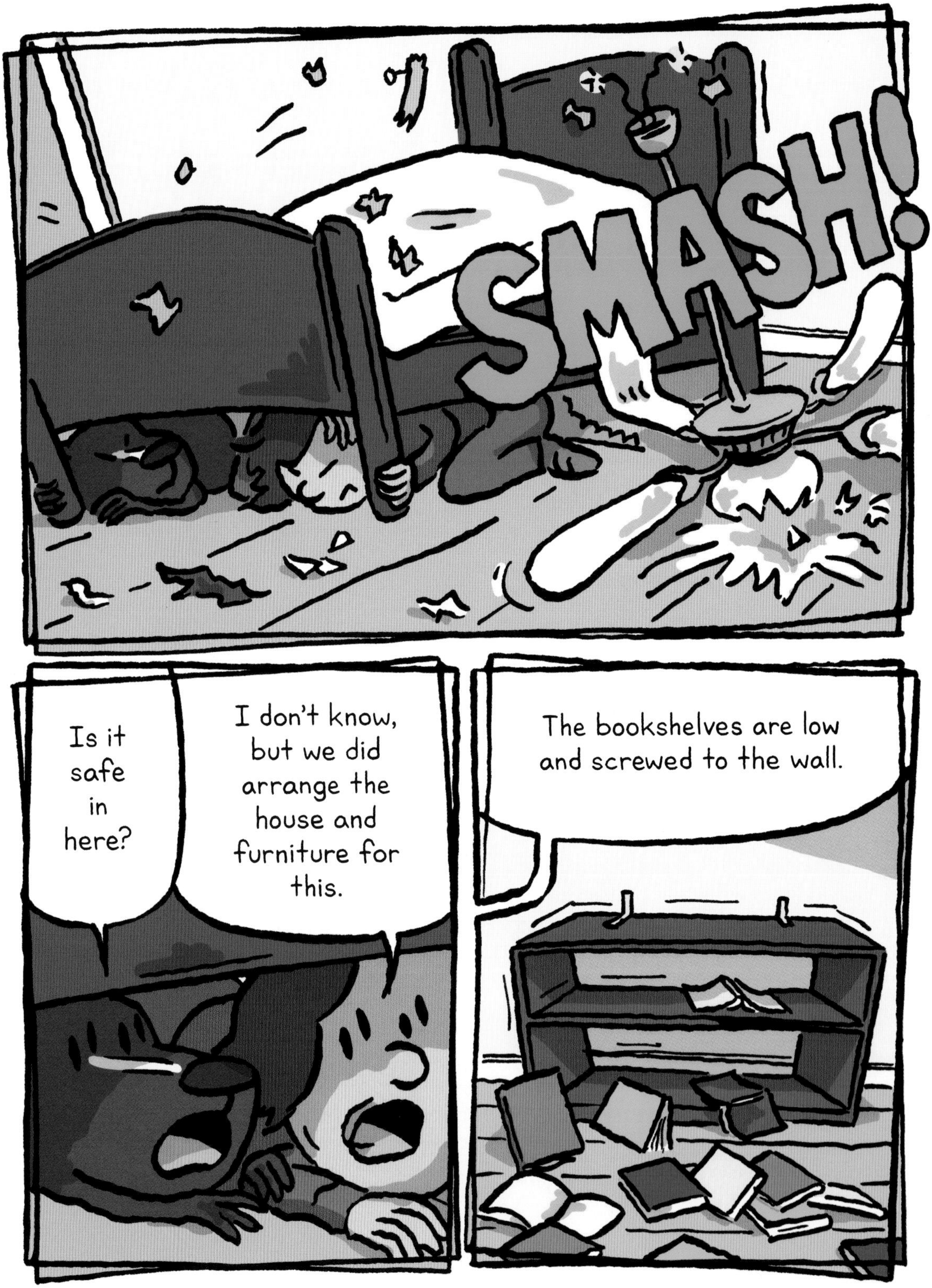
SMASH!
Is it safe in here?
I don't know, but we did arrange the house and furniture for this.
The bookshelves are low and screwed to the wall.

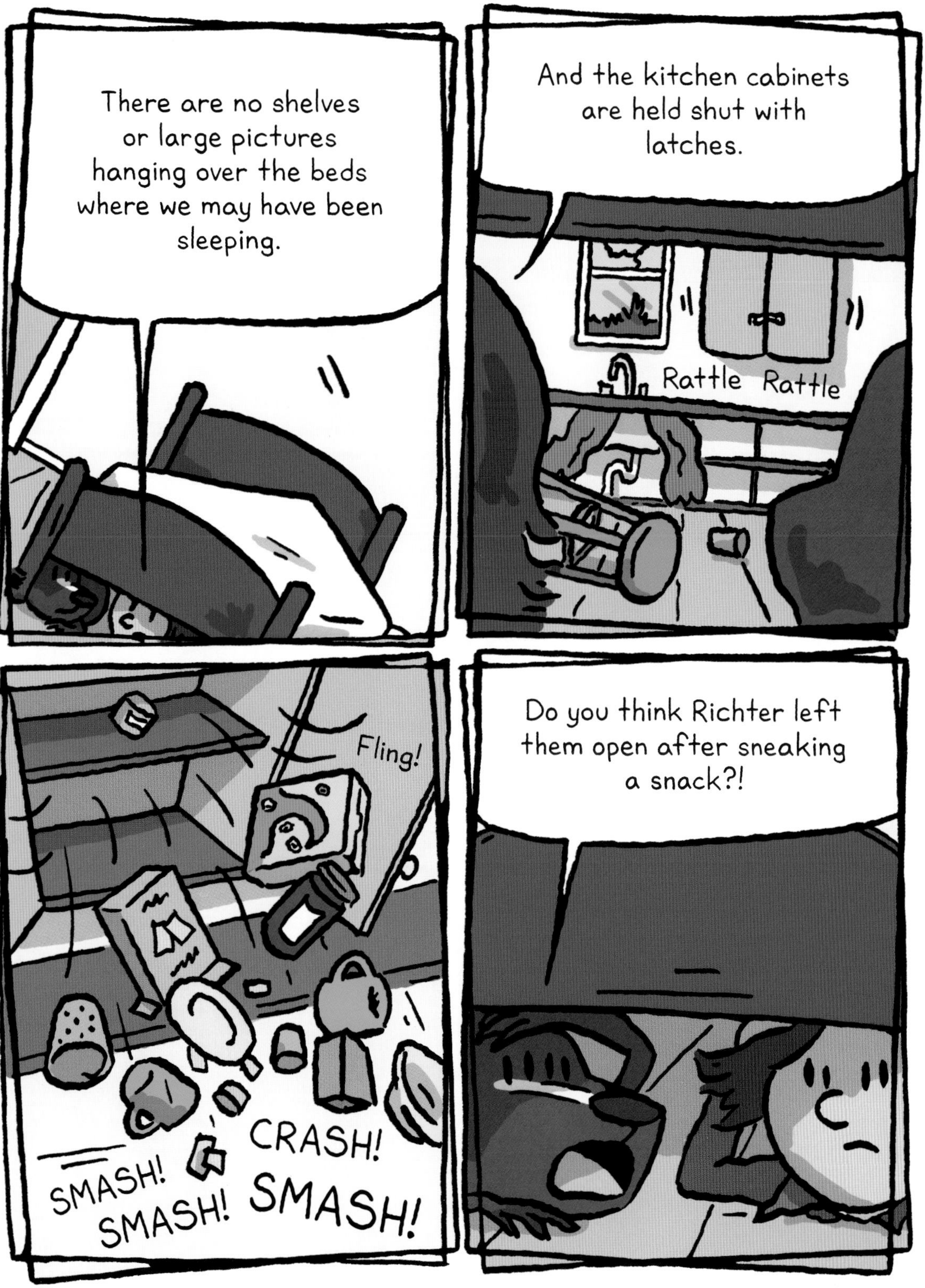
There are no shelves or large pictures hanging over the beds where we may have been sleeping.
And the kitchen cabinets are held shut with latches.
Rattle Rattle
Fling!
CRASH!
SMASH! SMASH! SMASH!
Do you think Richter left them open after sneaking a snack?!

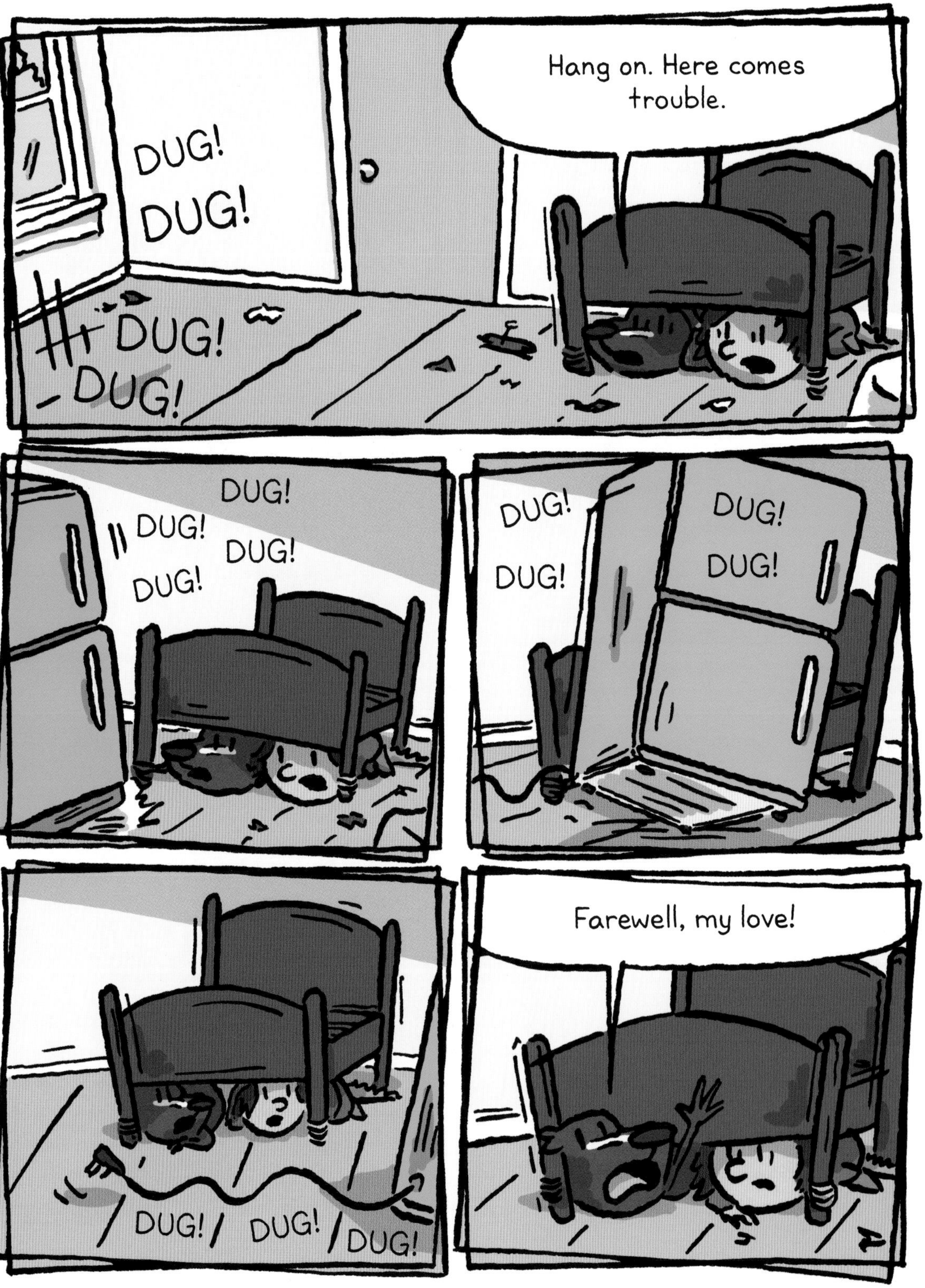
Hang on. Here comes trouble.
DUG!
DUG!
DUG!
DUG!
DUG!
DUG!
DUG!
DUG!
DUG!
DUG!
DUG!
DUG!
DUG!
DUG!
DUG!
Farewell, my love!

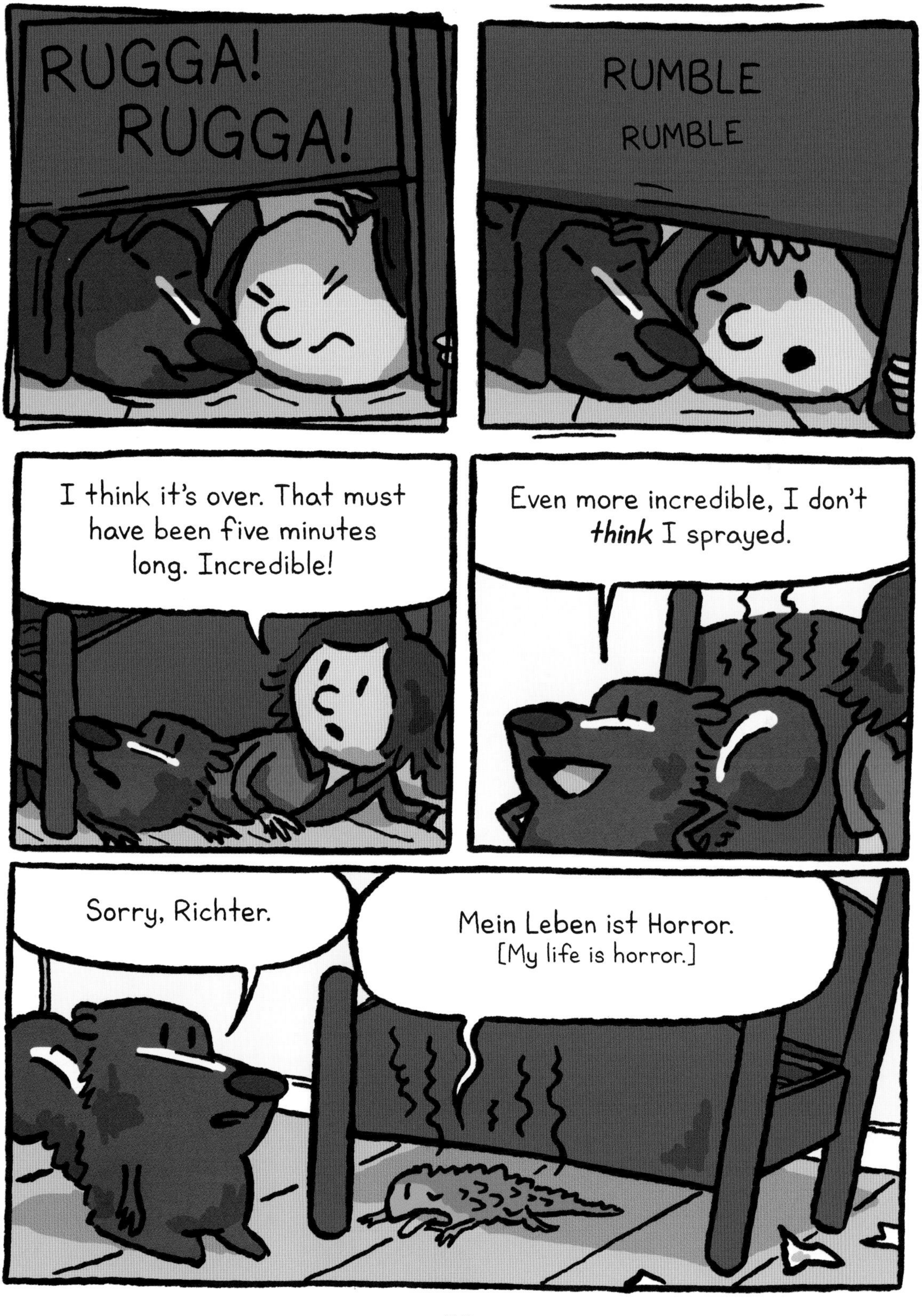
RUGGA! RUGGA!
RUMBLE RUMBLE
I think it's over. That must have been five minutes long. Incredible!
Even more incredible, I don't *think* I sprayed.
Sorry, Richter.
Mein Leben ist Horror.
[My life is horror.]

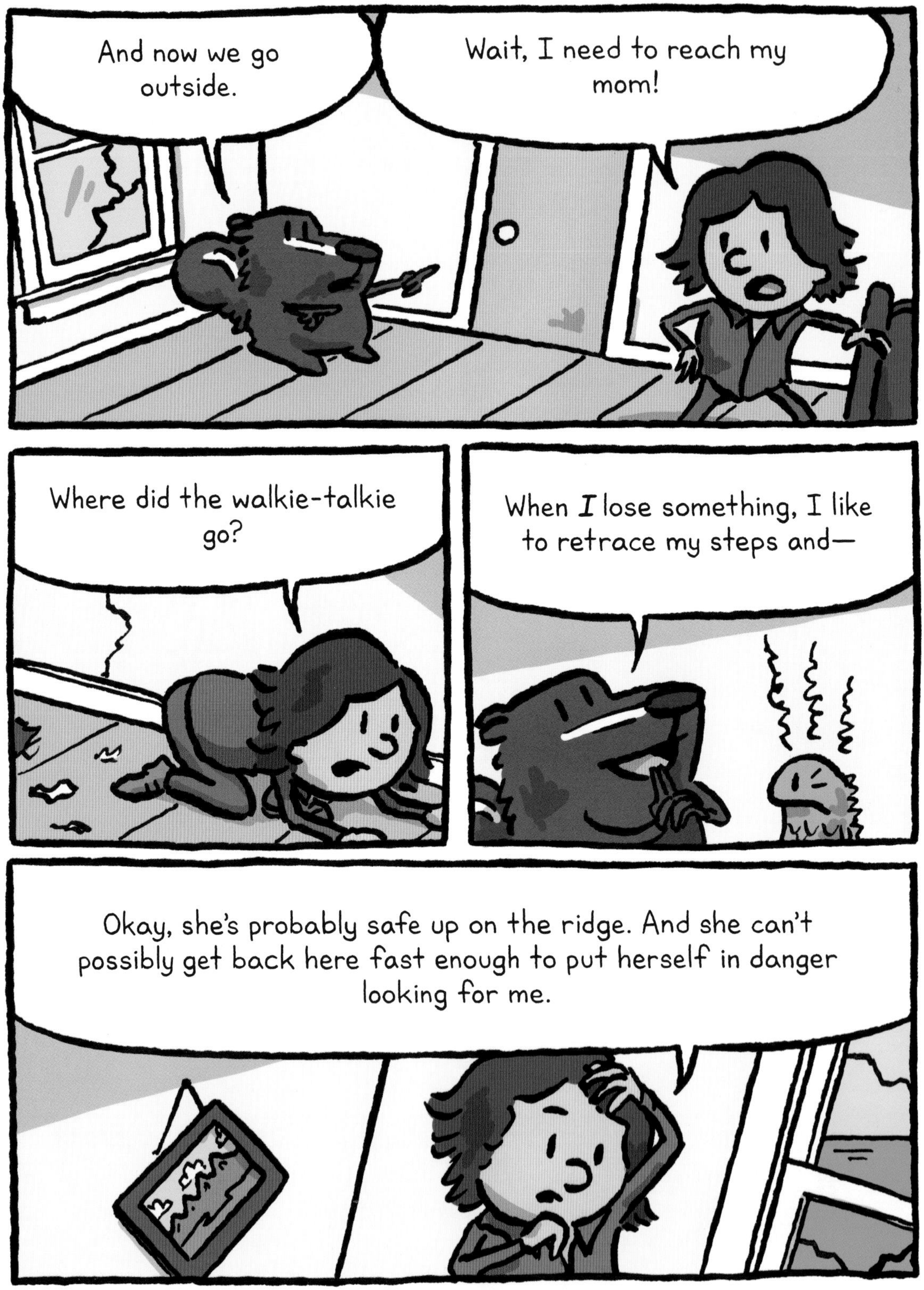
And now we go outside.
Wait, I need to reach my mom!
Where did the walkie-talkie go?
When *I* lose something, I like to retrace my steps and—
Okay, she's probably safe up on the ridge. And she can't possibly get back here fast enough to put herself in danger looking for me.

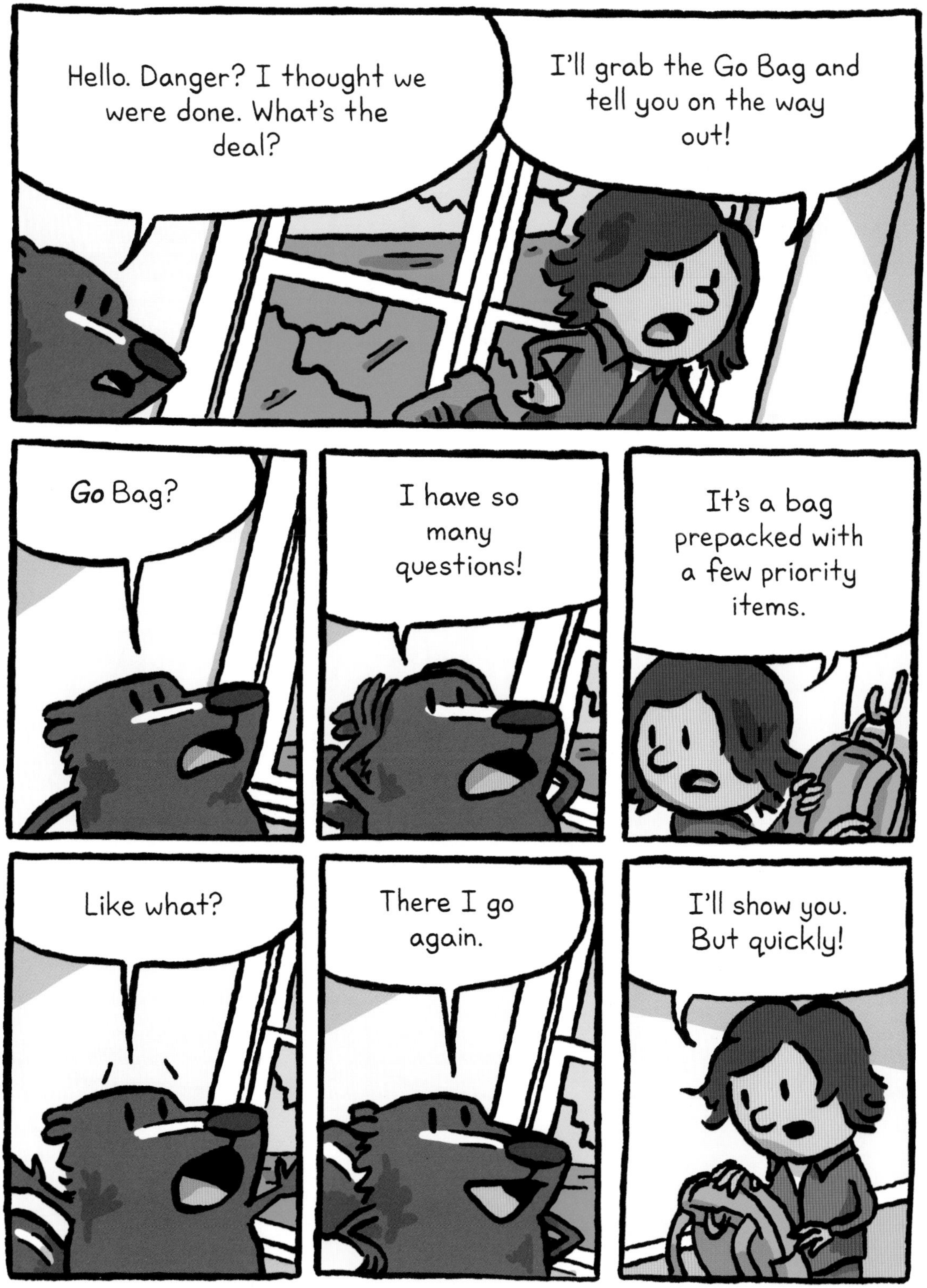
Hello. Danger? I thought we were done. What's the deal?
I'll grab the Go Bag and tell you on the way out!
Go Bag?
I have so many questions!
It's a bag prepacked with a few priority items.
Like what?
There I go again.
I'll show you. But quickly!

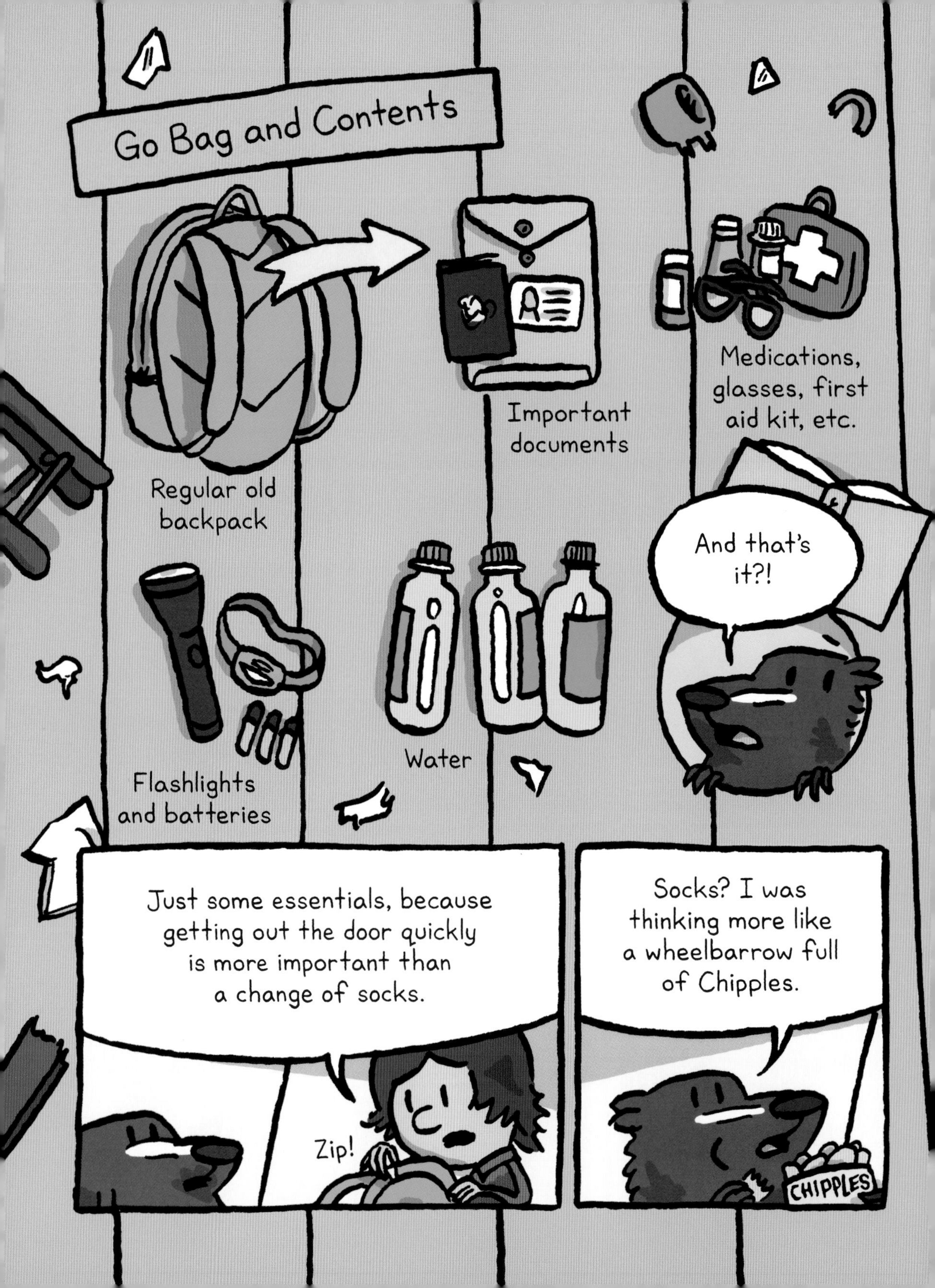
Go Bag and Contents
Regular old backpack
Important documents
Medications, glasses, first aid kit, etc.
Flashlights and batteries
Water
And that's it?!
Just some essentials, because getting out the door quickly is more important than a change of socks.
Zip!
Socks? I was thinking more like a wheelbarrow full of Chipples.
CHIPPLES

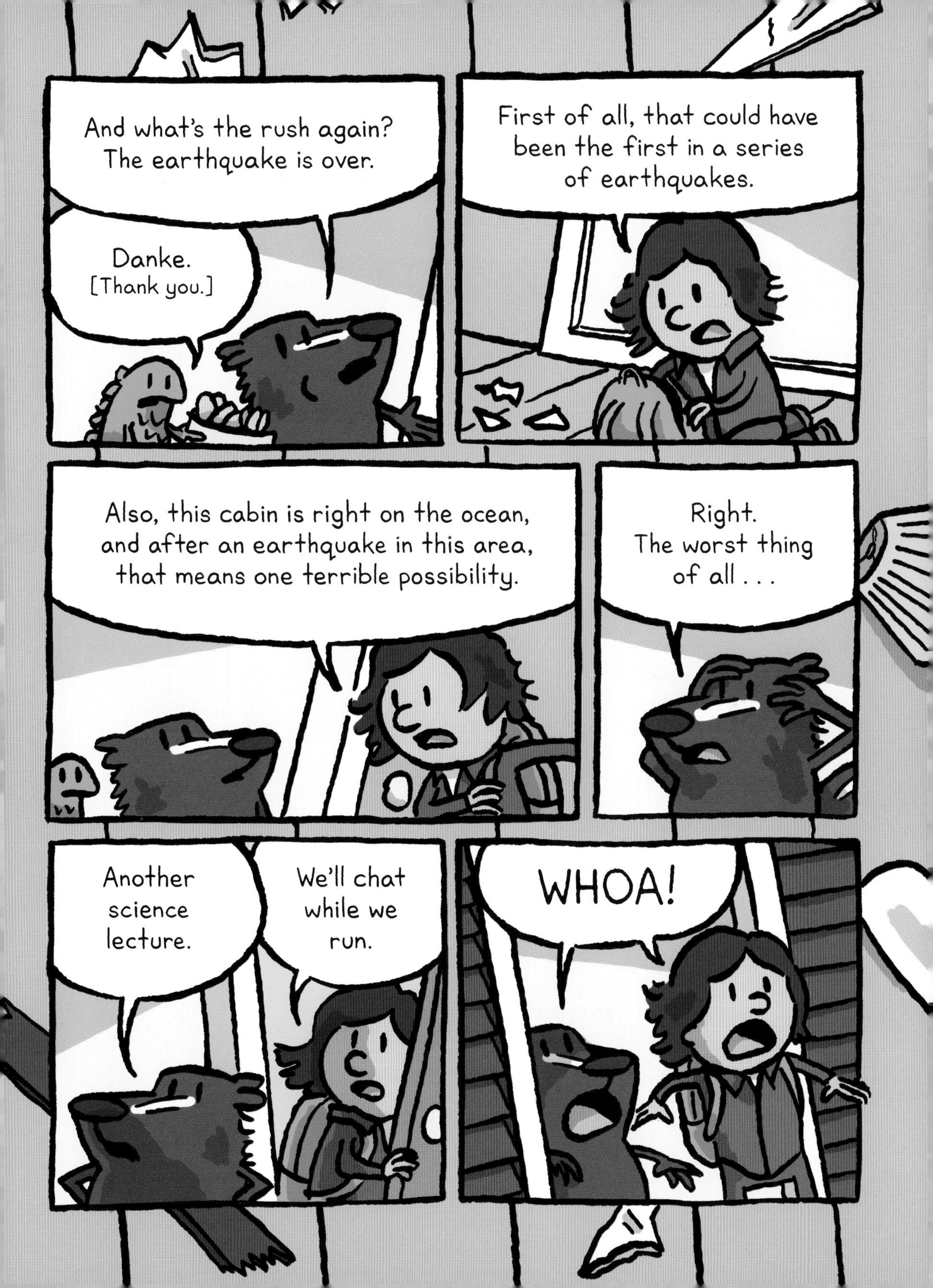
And what's the rush again? The earthquake is over.
Danke.
[Thank you.]
First of all, that could have been the first in a series of earthquakes.
Also, this cabin is right on the ocean, and after an earthquake in this area, that means one terrible possibility.
Right. The worst thing of all . . .
Another science lecture.
We'll chat while we run.
WHOA!

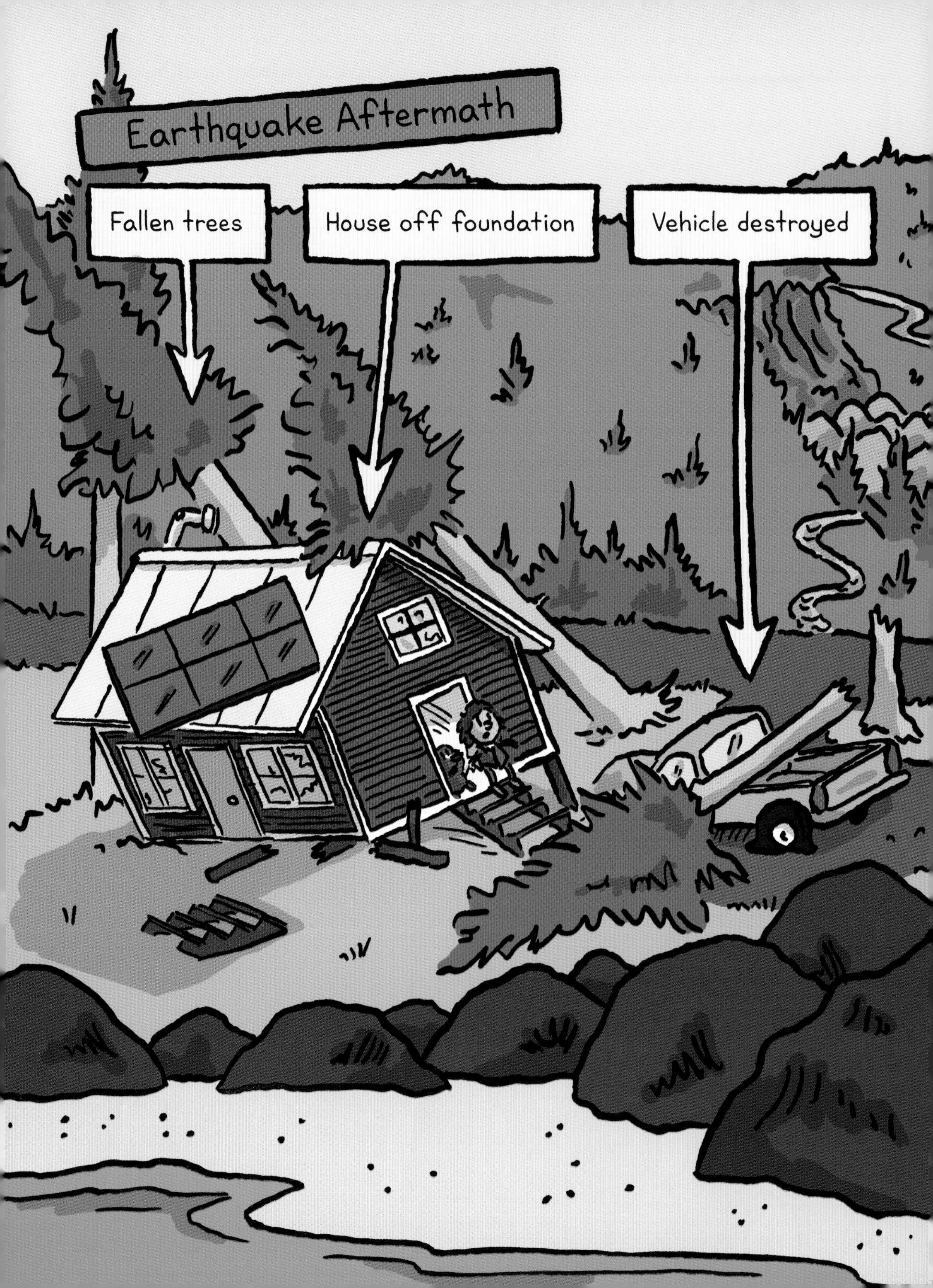
Earthquake Aftermath
Fallen trees
House off foundation
Vehicle destroyed

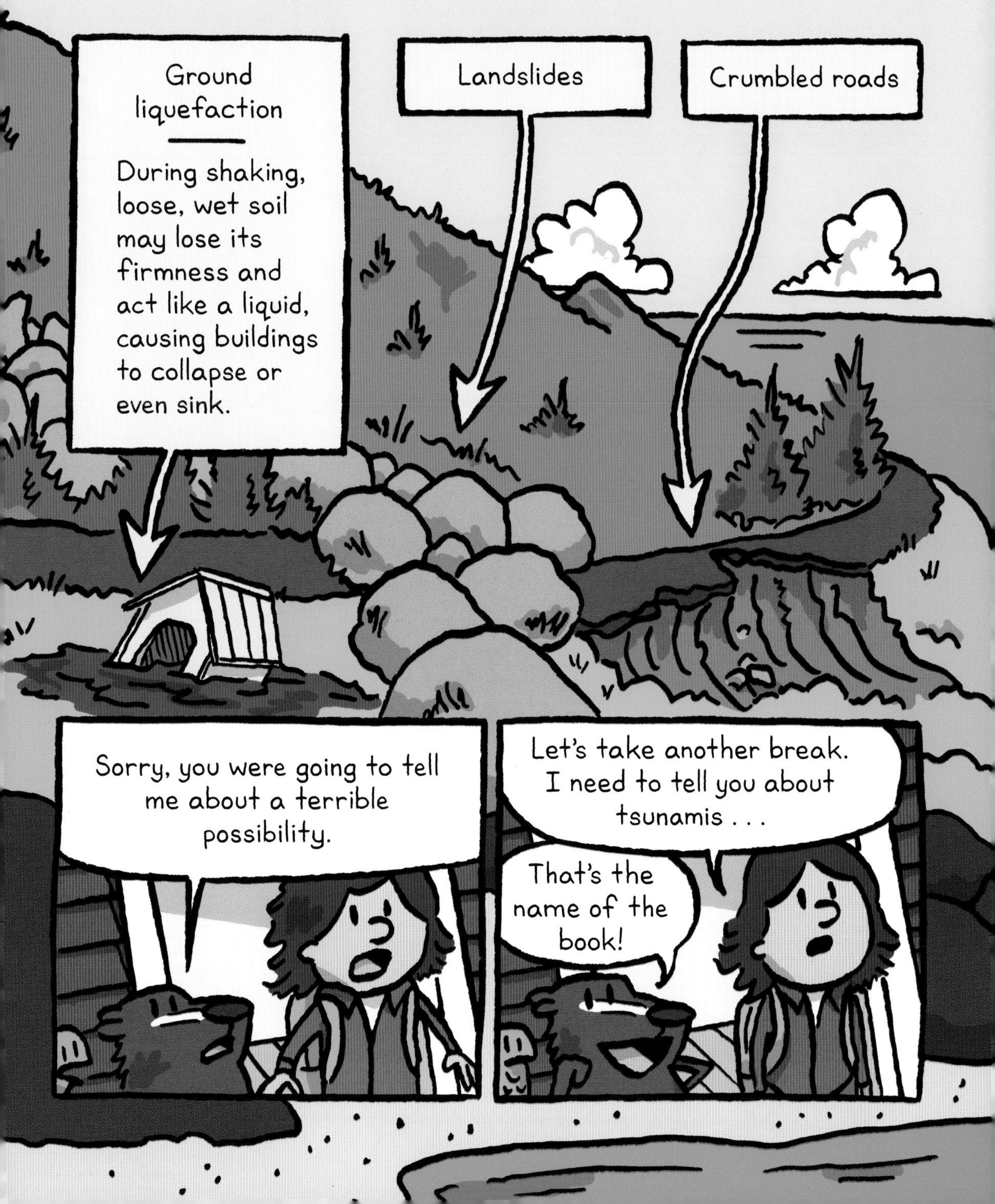
Ground liquefaction
During shaking, loose, wet soil may lose its firmness and act like a liquid, causing buildings to collapse or even sink.
Landslides
Crumbled roads
Sorry, you were going to tell me about a terrible possibility.
Let's take another break. I need to tell you about tsunamis . . .
That's the name of the book!

Tsunamis

A **tsunami** [soo-na-mee] is simply a series of incredibly long waves. Yet it's one of the most devastating, destructive, and powerful natural events on the planet.

You haven't walked behind me in a haunted Halloween corn maze.

Tsu

Nami

The name comes from the Japanese words **tsu**—for **harbor**—and **nami**— for **wave**. This is probably because tsunamis appear to spring up out of nowhere to strike harbors and shorelines, which we'll explain in a minute.

Is it the same as a tidal wave?

People sometimes call them tidal waves, but that's wrong. They have nothing to do with the tide or the gravitational pull of the moon.

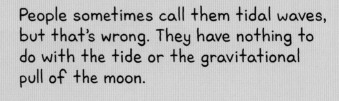

Instead, tsunamis are caused by the sudden displacement of a huge amount of water.

Like when you get into a bath and the water rises.

Wait, how did I know that?

I don't even take baths . . .

Exactly right. The body displaces the water, forcing the level to rise.

Scout, am I doing bath?

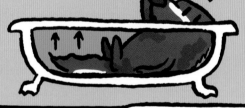

In the case of a tsunami, the sudden displacement of water is usually caused by an undersea earthquake. Let's take a step-by-step look at how an earthquake might get a tsunami going.

Does your mom mind if I borrow her towel?

Tsunami Formation

Remember, earthquakes aren't just about shaking. At their centers, the ground actually shifts and moves.

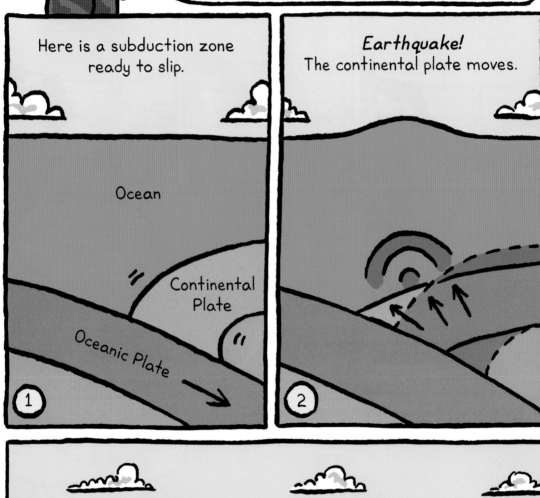

Here is a subduction zone ready to slip.

Ocean

Continental Plate

Oceanic Plate

1

Earthquake!
The continental plate moves.

2

5

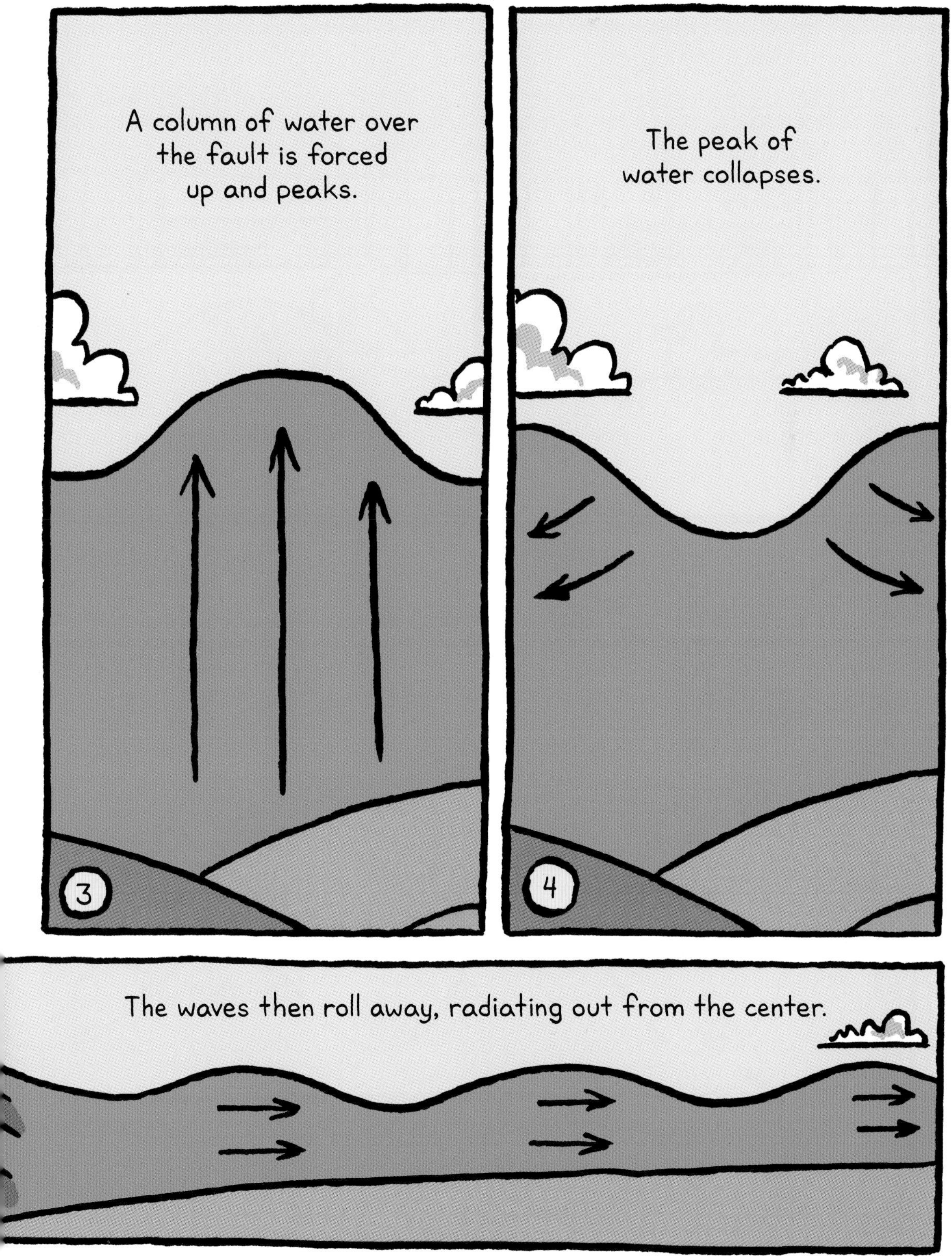
A column of water over the fault is forced up and peaks.
3
The peak of water collapses.
4
The waves then roll away, radiating out from the center.

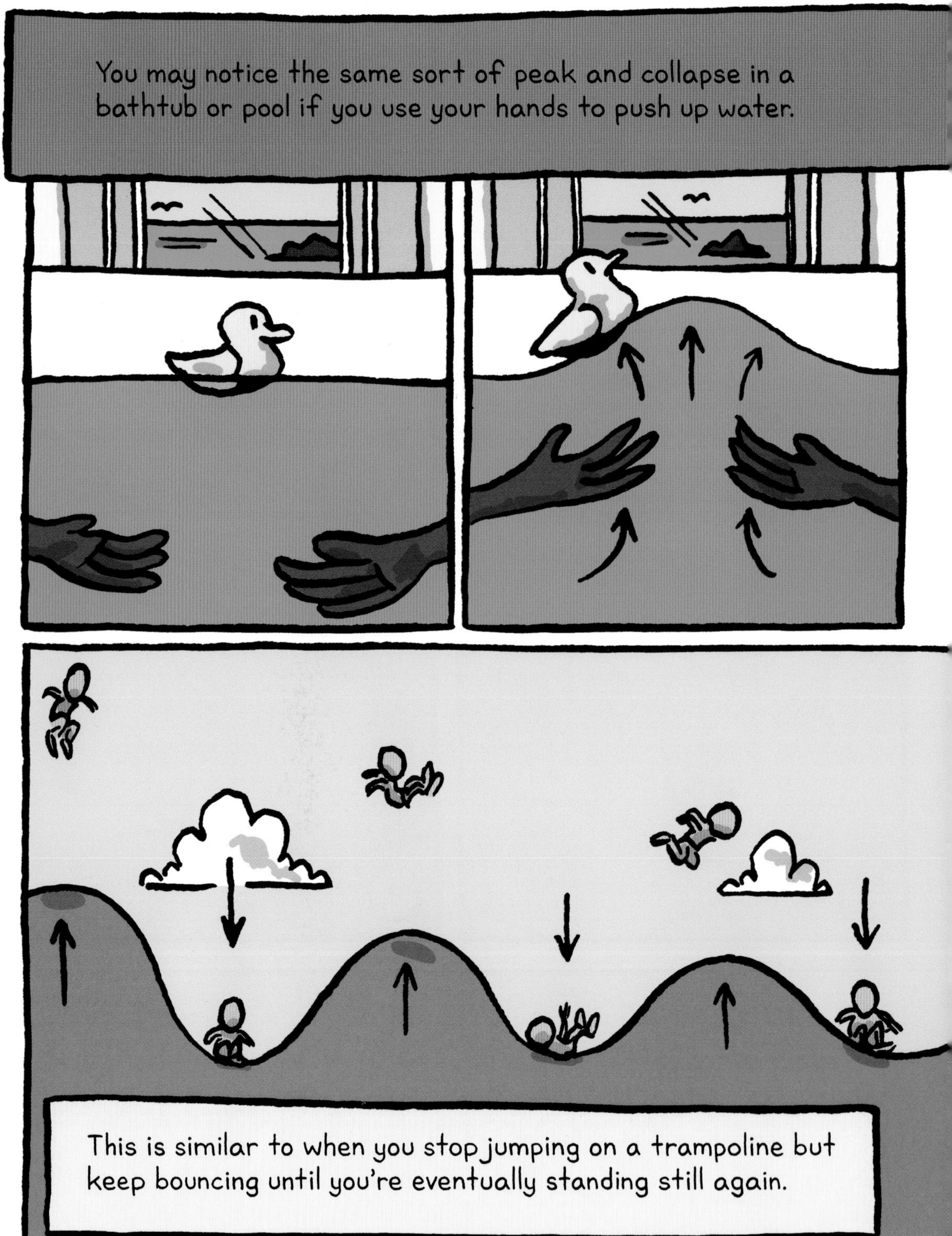
You may notice the same sort of peak and collapse in a bathtub or pool if you use your hands to push up water.
This is similar to when you stop jumping on a trampoline but keep bouncing until you're eventually standing still again.

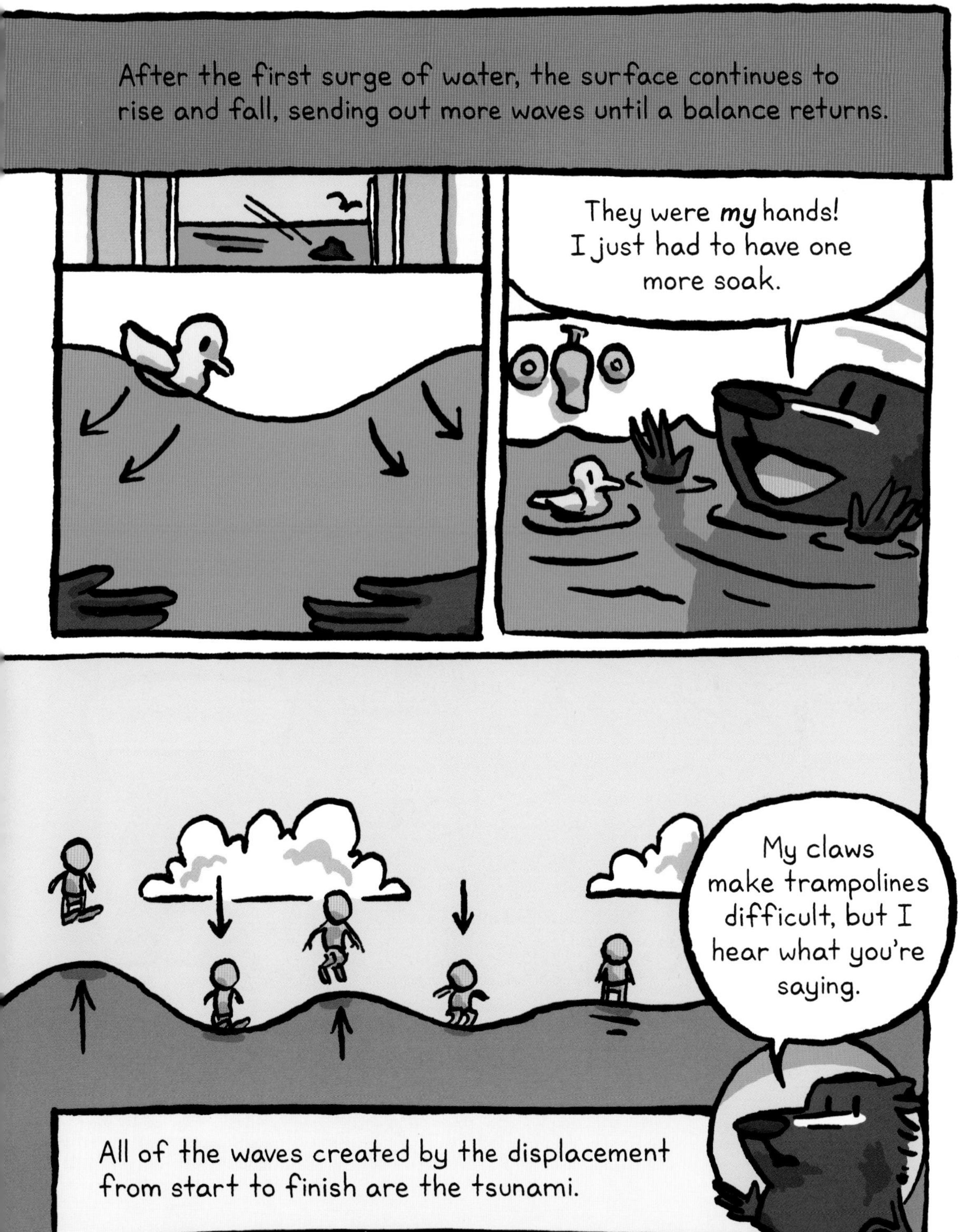
After the first surge of water, the surface continues to rise and fall, sending out more waves until a balance returns.
They were *my* hands! I just had to have one more soak.
My claws make trampolines difficult, but I hear what you're saying.
All of the waves created by the displacement from start to finish are the tsunami.

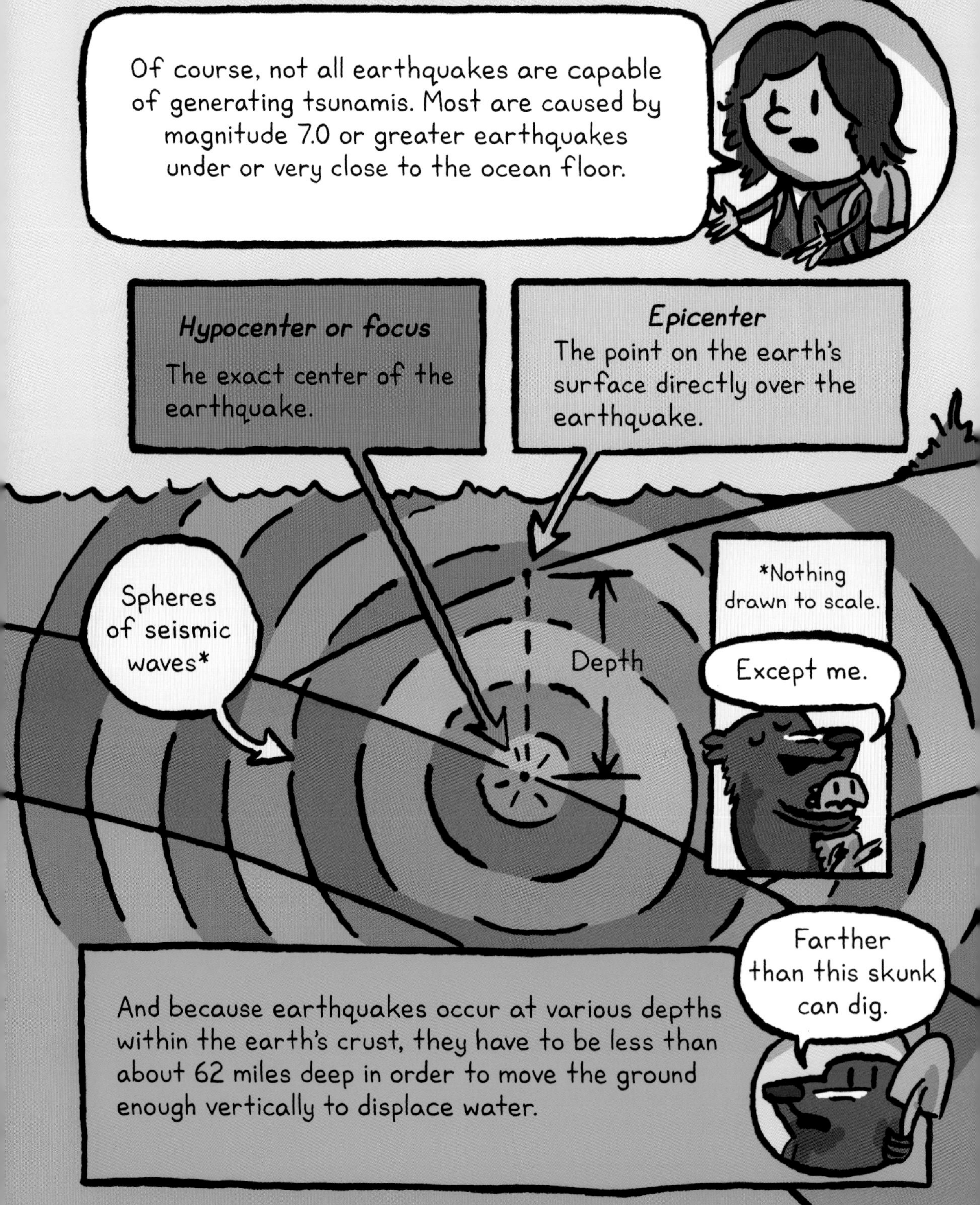
Of course, not all earthquakes are capable of generating tsunamis. Most are caused by magnitude 7.0 or greater earthquakes under or very close to the ocean floor.
Hypocenter or focus
The exact center of the earthquake.
Epicenter
The point on the earth's surface directly over the earthquake.
Spheres of seismic waves*
Depth
*Nothing drawn to scale.
Except me.
And because earthquakes occur at various depths within the earth's crust, they have to be less than about 62 miles deep in order to move the ground enough vertically to displace water.
Farther than this skunk can dig.

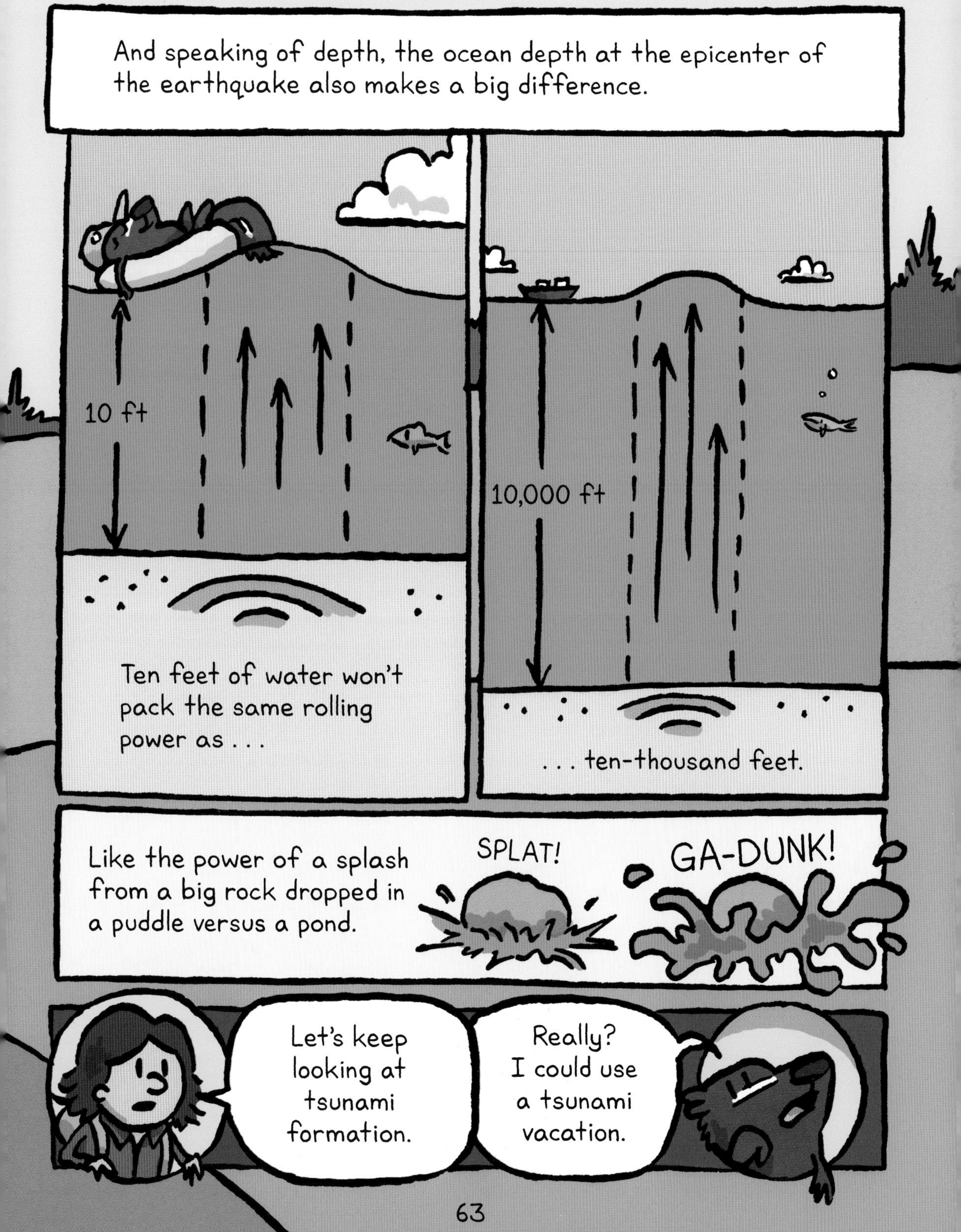

And speaking of depth, the ocean depth at the epicenter of the earthquake also makes a big difference.
10 ft
Ten feet of water won't pack the same rolling power as . . .
10,000 ft
. . . ten-thousand feet.
Like the power of a splash from a big rock dropped in a puddle versus a pond.
SPLAT!
GA-DUNK!
Let's keep looking at tsunami formation.
Really? I could use a tsunami vacation.

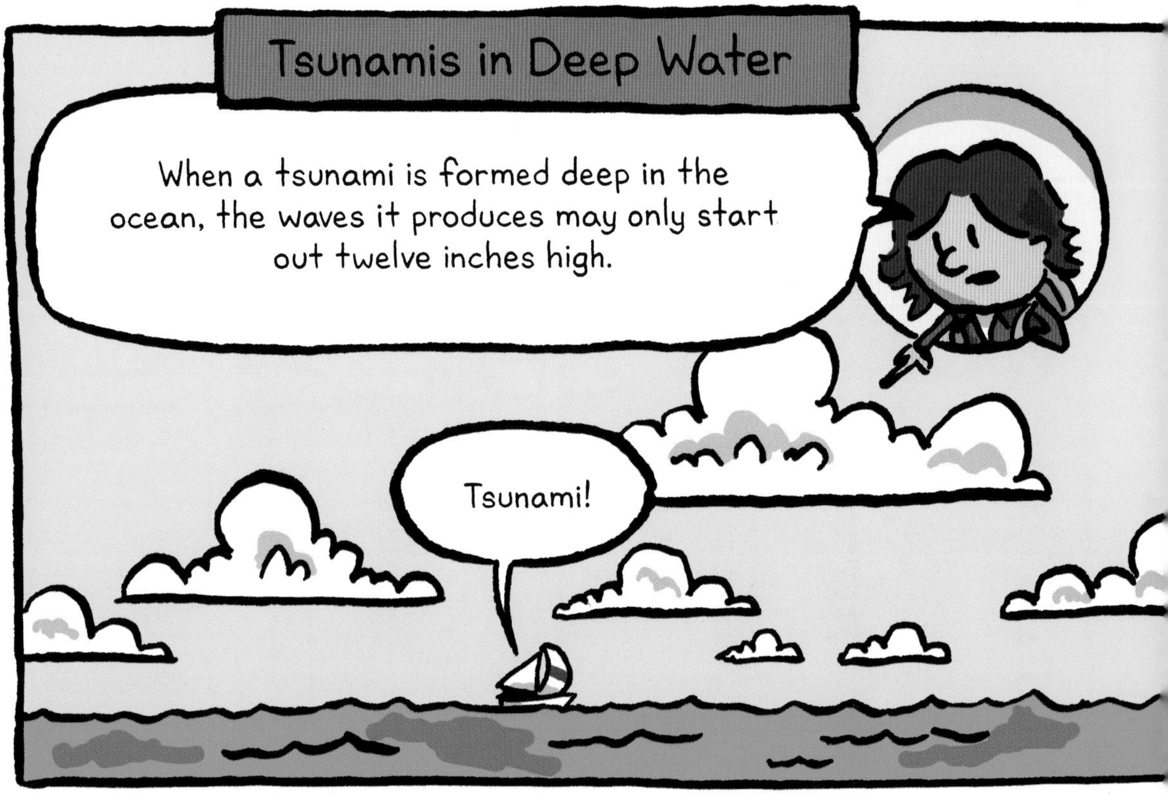
Tsunamis in Deep Water
When a tsunami is formed deep in the ocean, the waves it produces may only start out twelve inches high.
Tsunami!

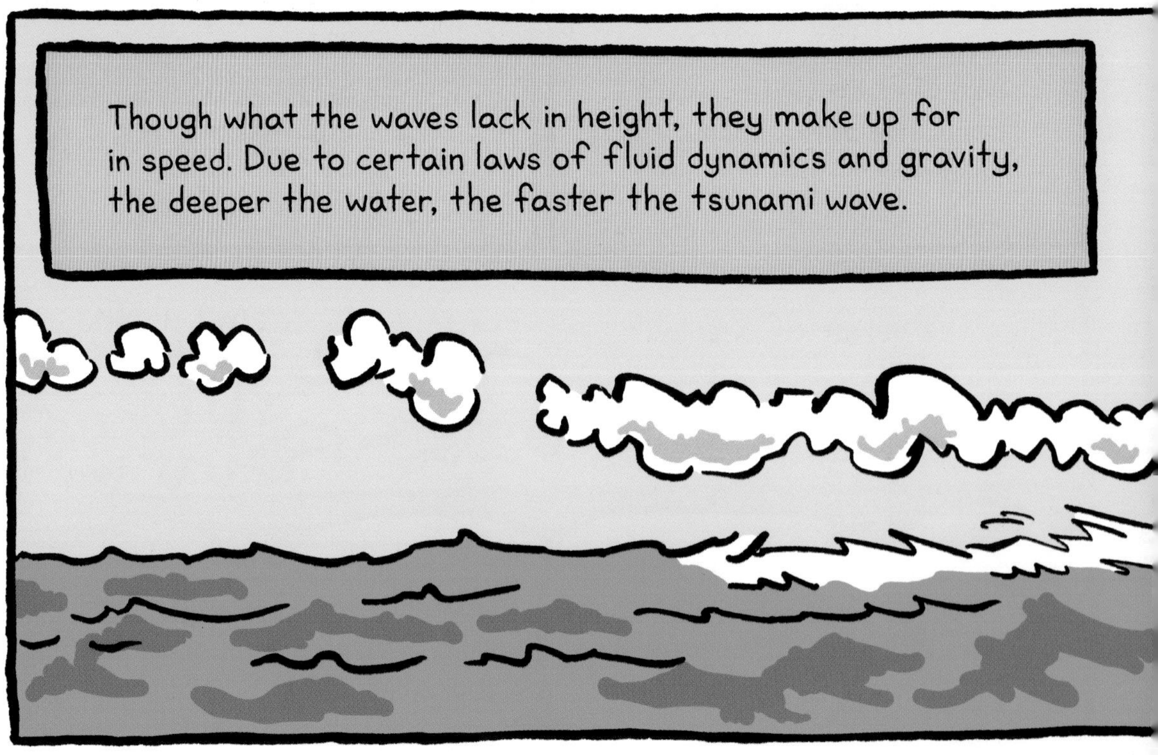
Though what the waves lack in height, they make up for in speed. Due to certain laws of fluid dynamics and gravity, the deeper the water, the faster the tsunami wave.

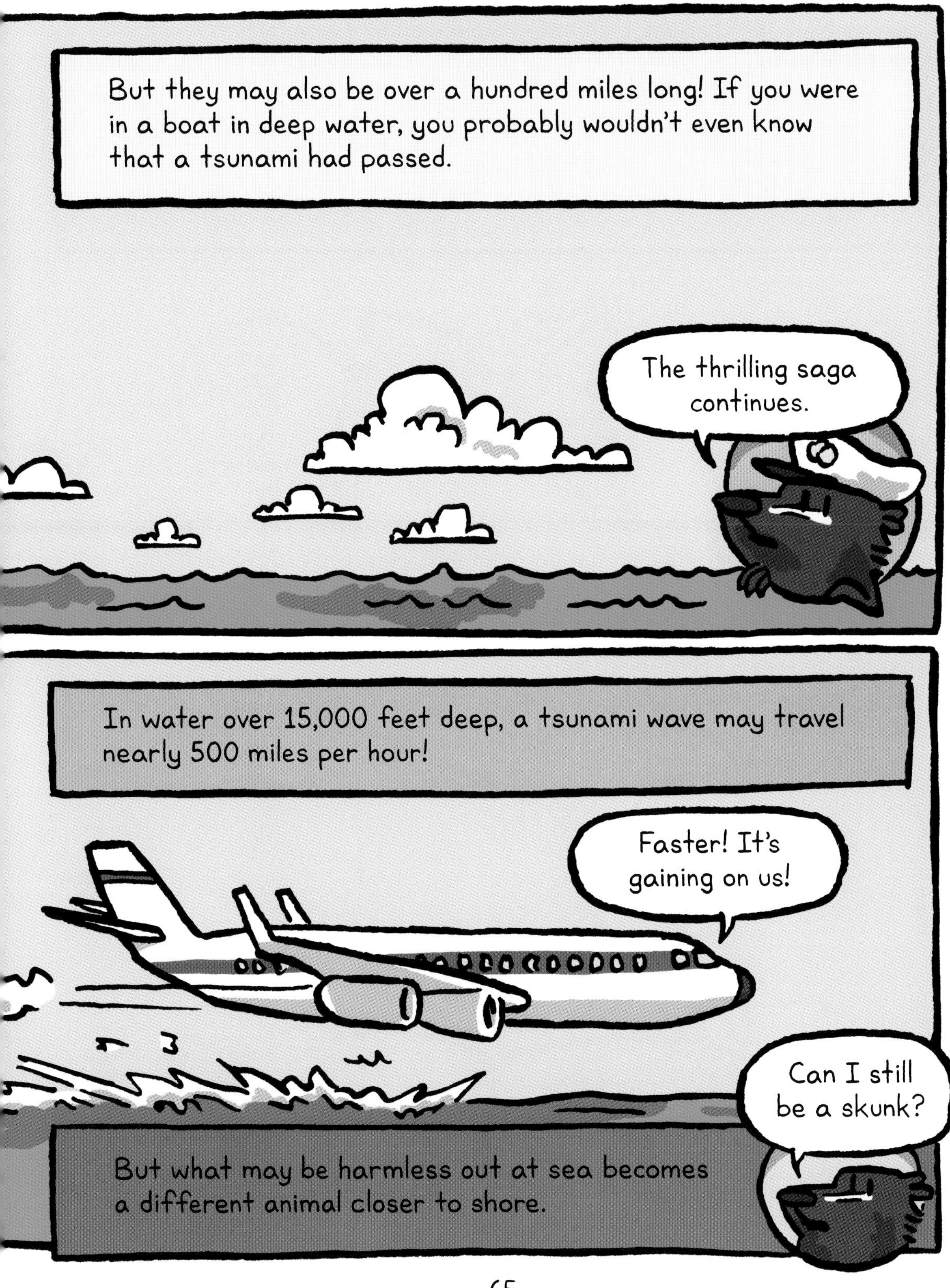
But they may also be over a hundred miles long! If you were in a boat in deep water, you probably wouldn't even know that a tsunami had passed.
The thrilling saga continues.
In water over 15,000 feet deep, a tsunami wave may travel nearly 500 miles per hour!
Faster! It's gaining on us!
Can I still be a skunk?
But what may be harmless out at sea becomes a different animal closer to shore.

Tsunamis Near Shore

As a tsunami wave approaches the coast and enters shallower water, all of that power needs somewhere to go. In this case, it's up.

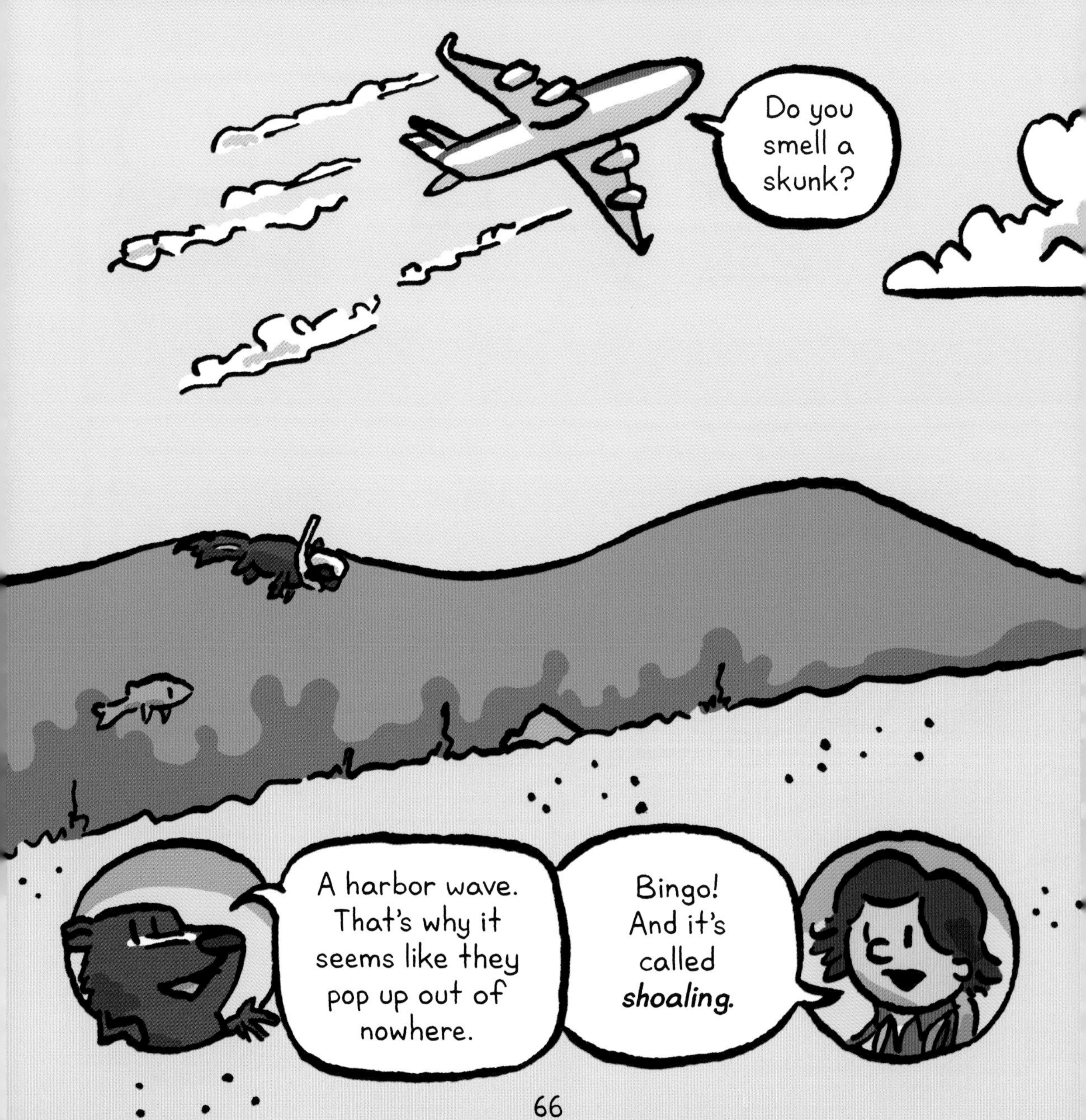
Do you smell a skunk?
A harbor wave. That's why it seems like they pop up out of nowhere.
Bingo! And it's called *shoaling*.

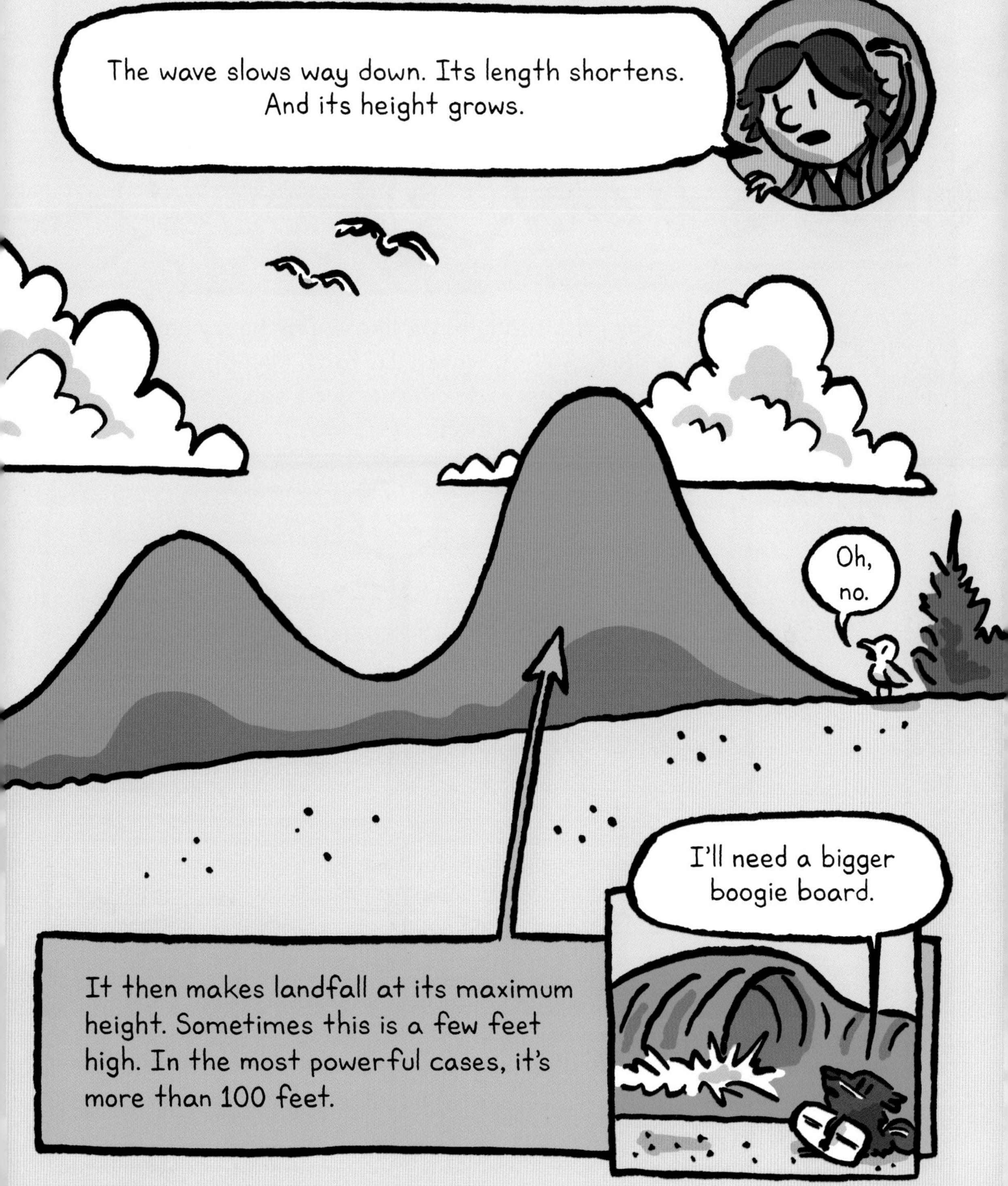
The wave slows way down. Its length shortens. And its height grows.
Oh, no.
It then makes landfall at its maximum height. Sometimes this is a few feet high. In the most powerful cases, it's more than 100 feet.
I'll need a bigger boogie board.

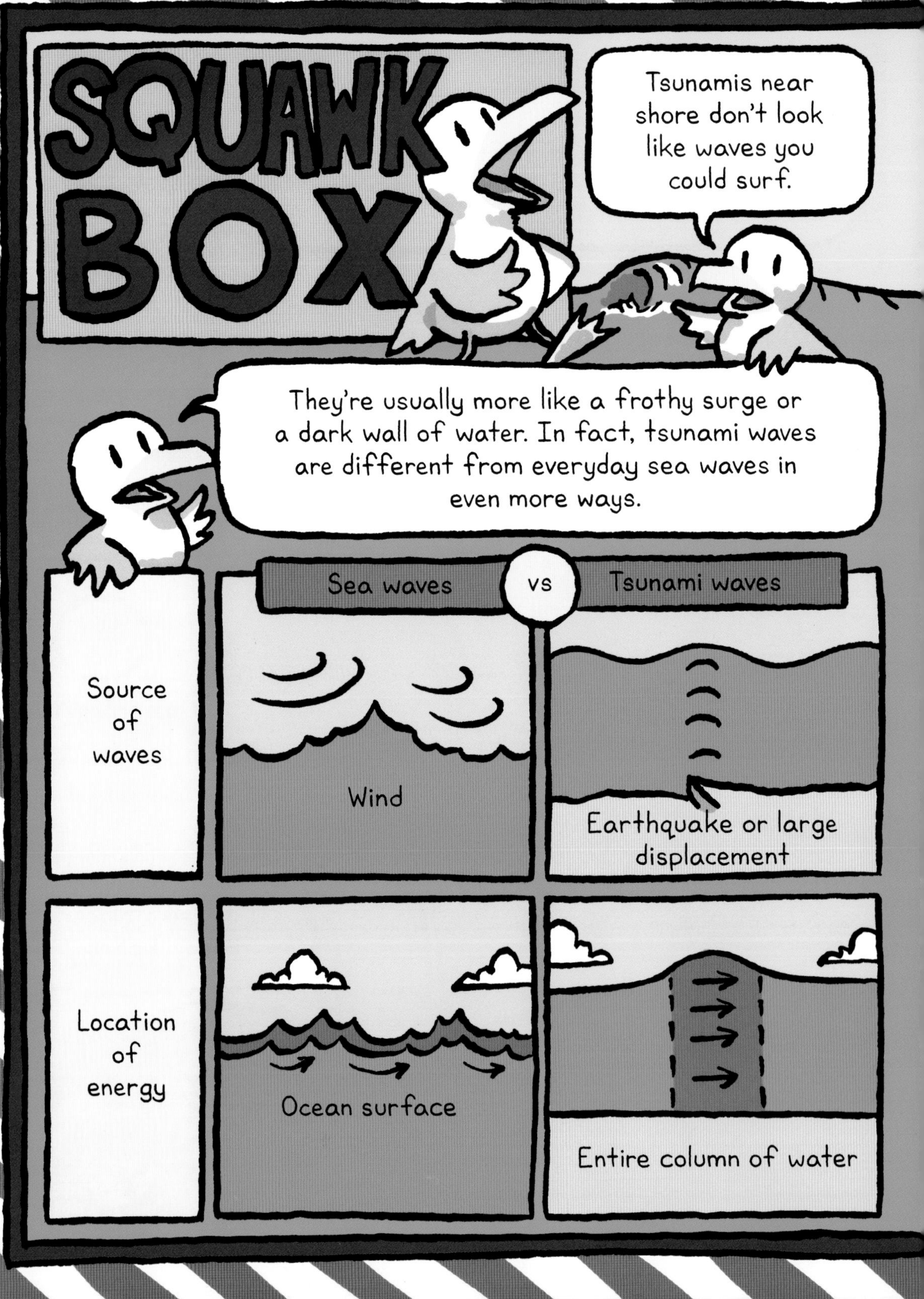
SQUAWK BOX
Tsunamis near shore don't look like waves you could surf.
They're usually more like a frothy surge or a dark wall of water. In fact, tsunami waves are different from everyday sea waves in even more ways.
Sea waves
vs
Tsunami waves
Source of waves
Wind
Earthquake or large displacement
Location of energy
Ocean surface
Entire column of water

	Sea waves	Tsunami waves
Wave length	300 to 600 feet	60 to 300 miles in deep water
Wave period (time between waves)	5 to 20 seconds	2 hours in deep ocean / As little as 5 minutes near shore
Wave speed	5 to 60 miles per hour	500 miles per hour in deep water / 20 to 30 miles per hour near shore
Wave height	6 foot average	Inches to feet in deep water / A few feet to 100 feet near shore

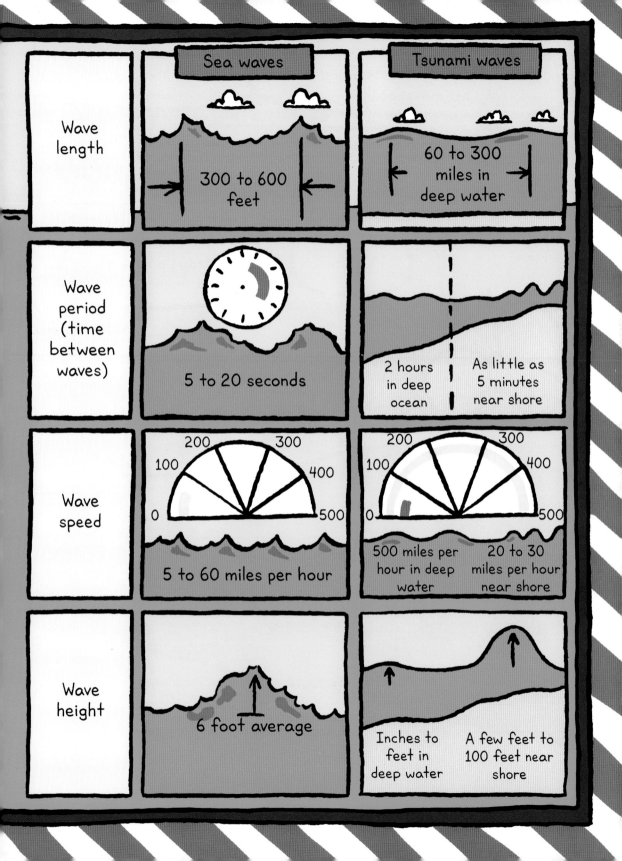

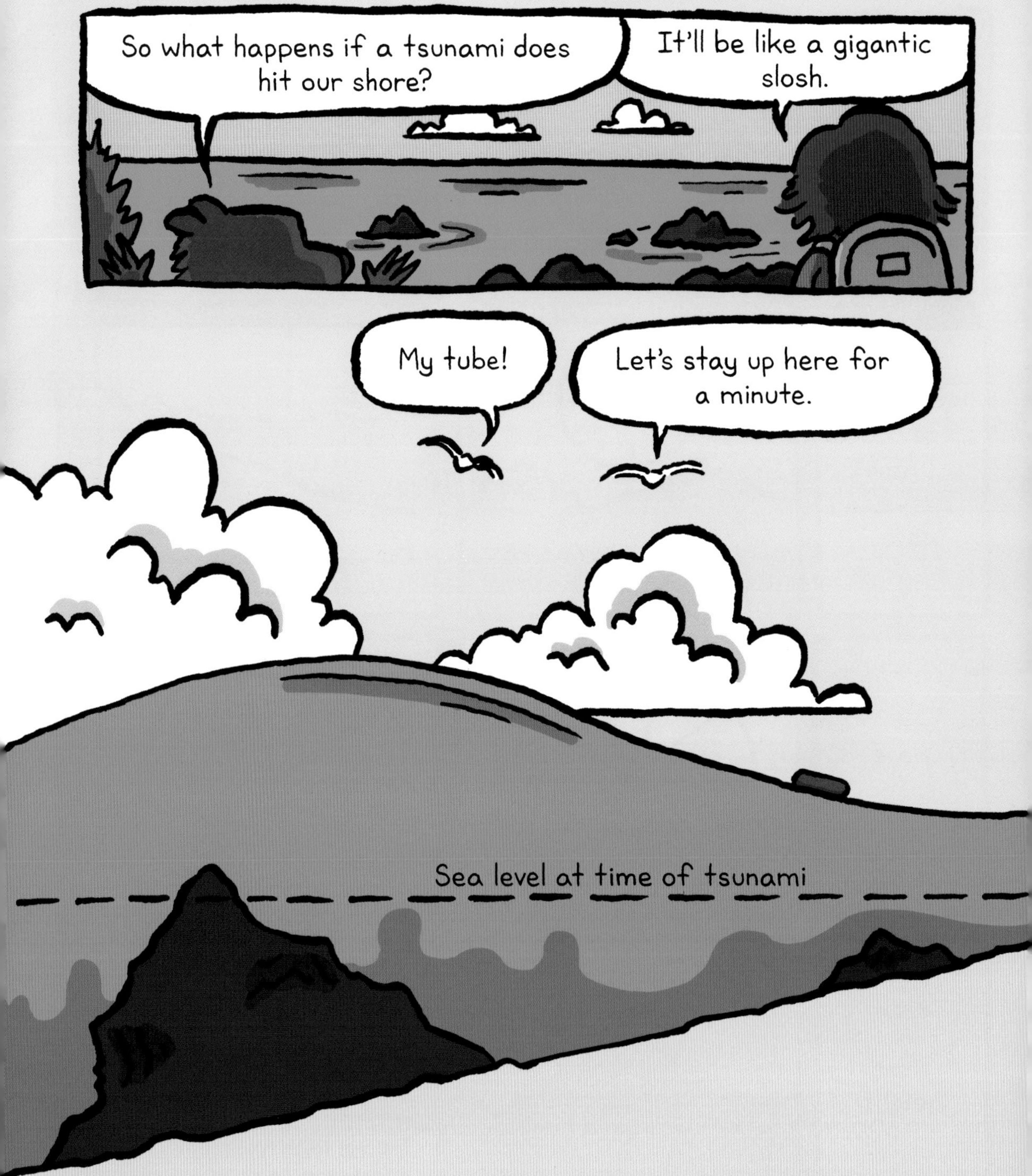
So what happens if a tsunami does hit our shore?
It'll be like a gigantic slosh.
My tube!
Let's stay up here for a minute.
Sea level at time of tsunami

Like the entire ocean suddenly moving inland.

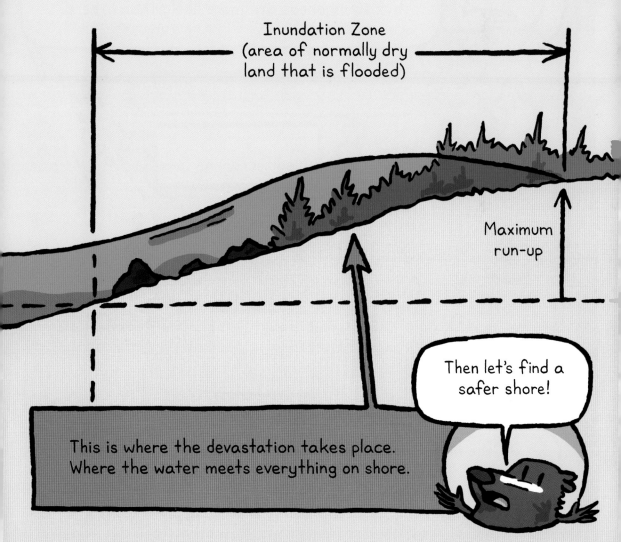

Inundation Zone
(area of normally dry land that is flooded)

Maximum run-up

This is where the devastation takes place. Where the water meets everything on shore.

Then let's find a safer shore!

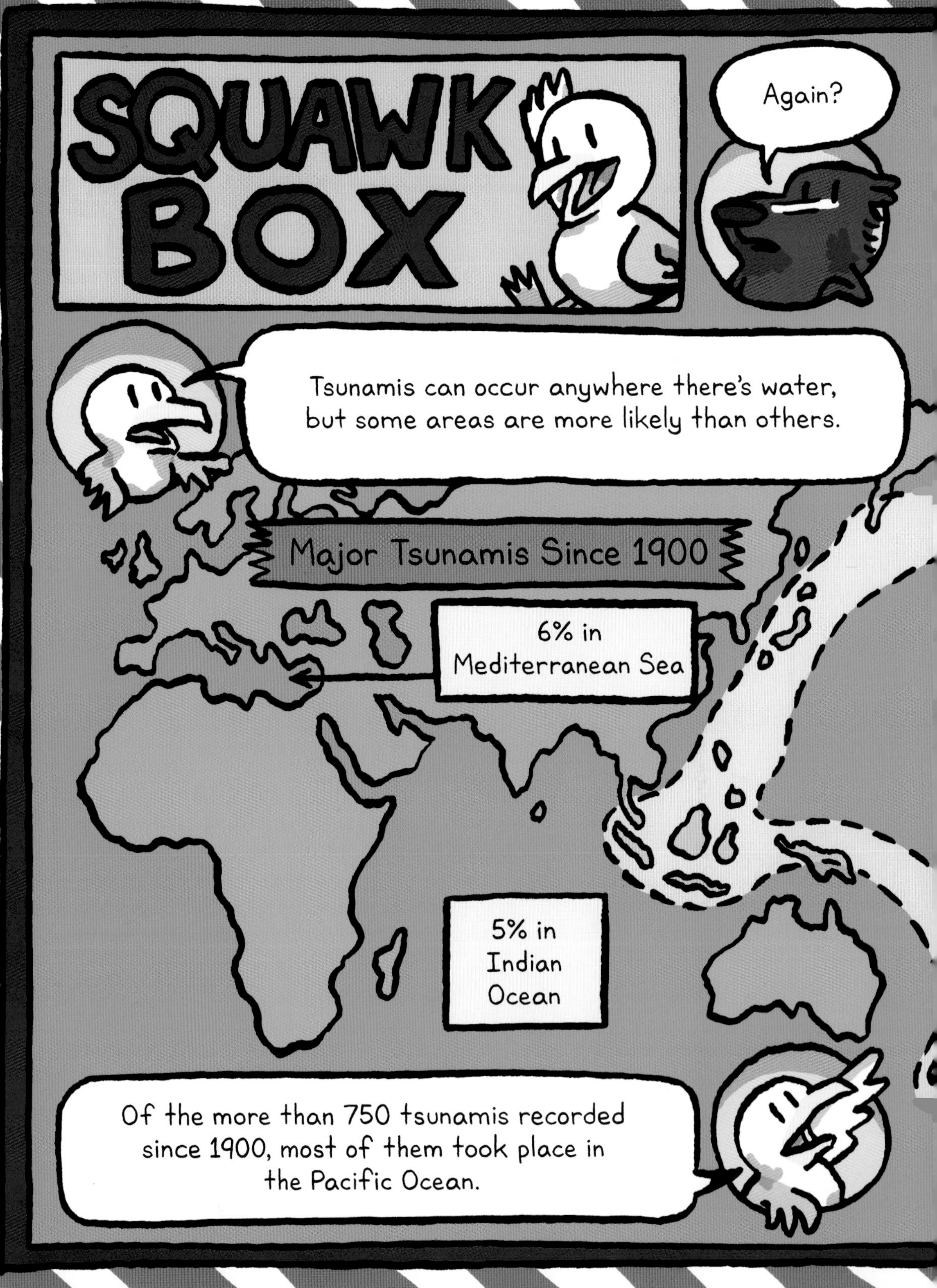
SQUAWK BOX
Again?
Tsunamis can occur anywhere there's water, but some areas are more likely than others.
Major Tsunamis Since 1900
6% in Mediterranean Sea
5% in Indian Ocean
Of the more than 750 tsunamis recorded since 1900, most of them took place in the Pacific Ocean.

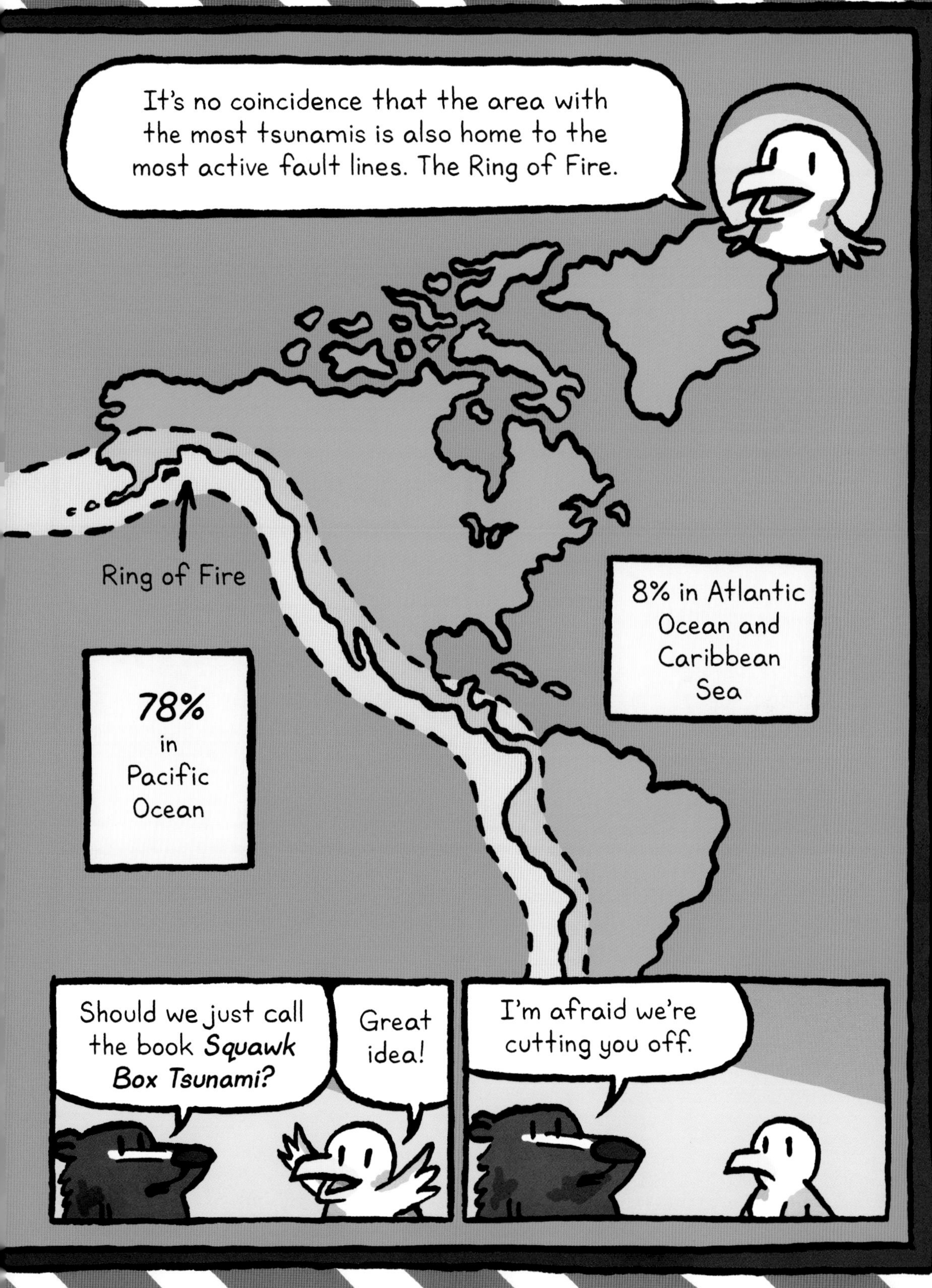
It's no coincidence that the area with the most tsunamis is also home to the most active fault lines. The Ring of Fire.
Ring of Fire
8% in Atlantic Ocean and Caribbean Sea
78% in Pacific Ocean
Should we just call the book *Squawk Box Tsunami?*
Great idea!
I'm afraid we're cutting you off.

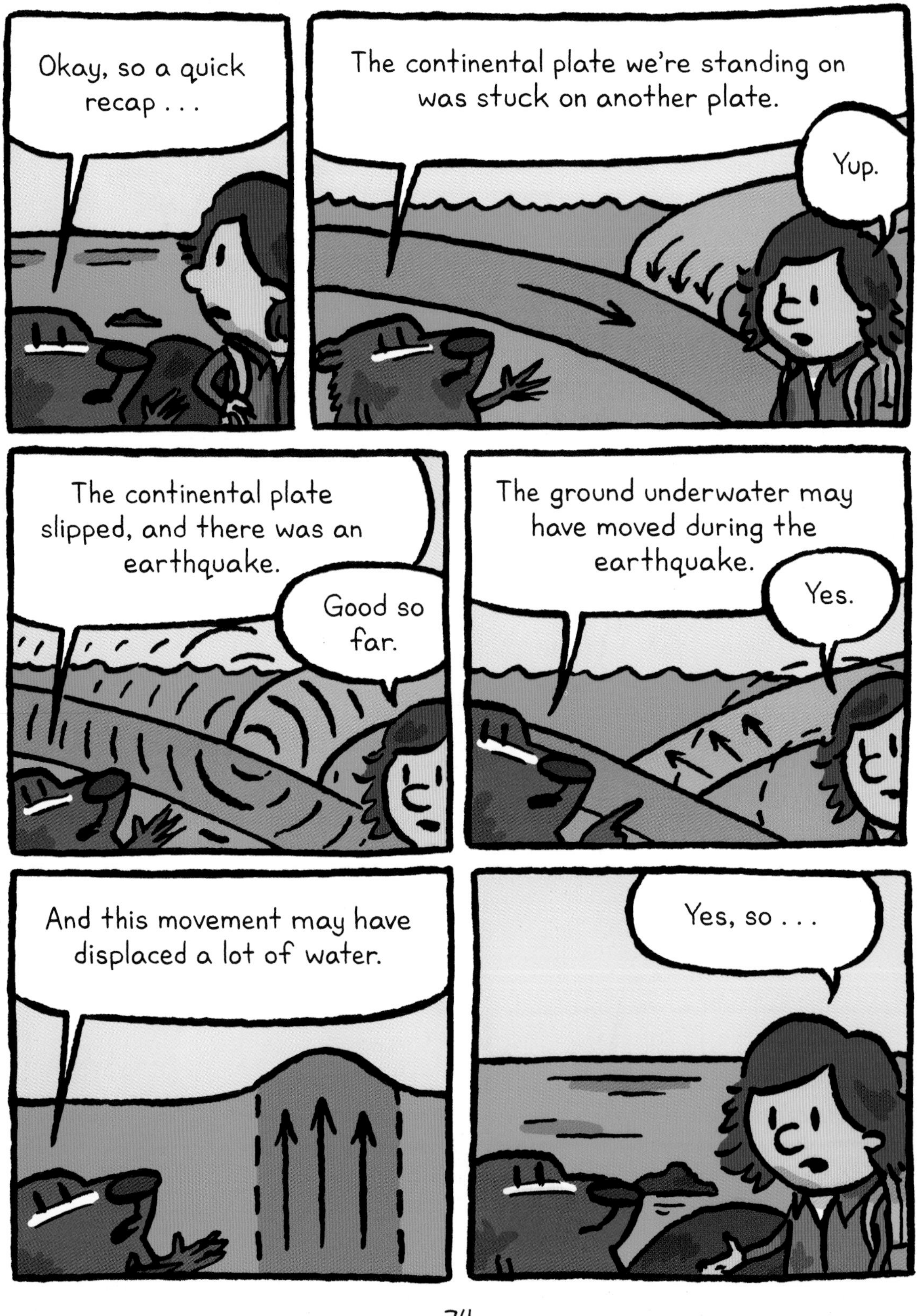
Okay, so a quick recap . . .
The continental plate we're standing on was stuck on another plate.
Yup.
The continental plate slipped, and there was an earthquake.
Good so far.
The ground underwater may have moved during the earthquake.
Yes.
And this movement may have displaced a lot of water.
Yes, so . . .

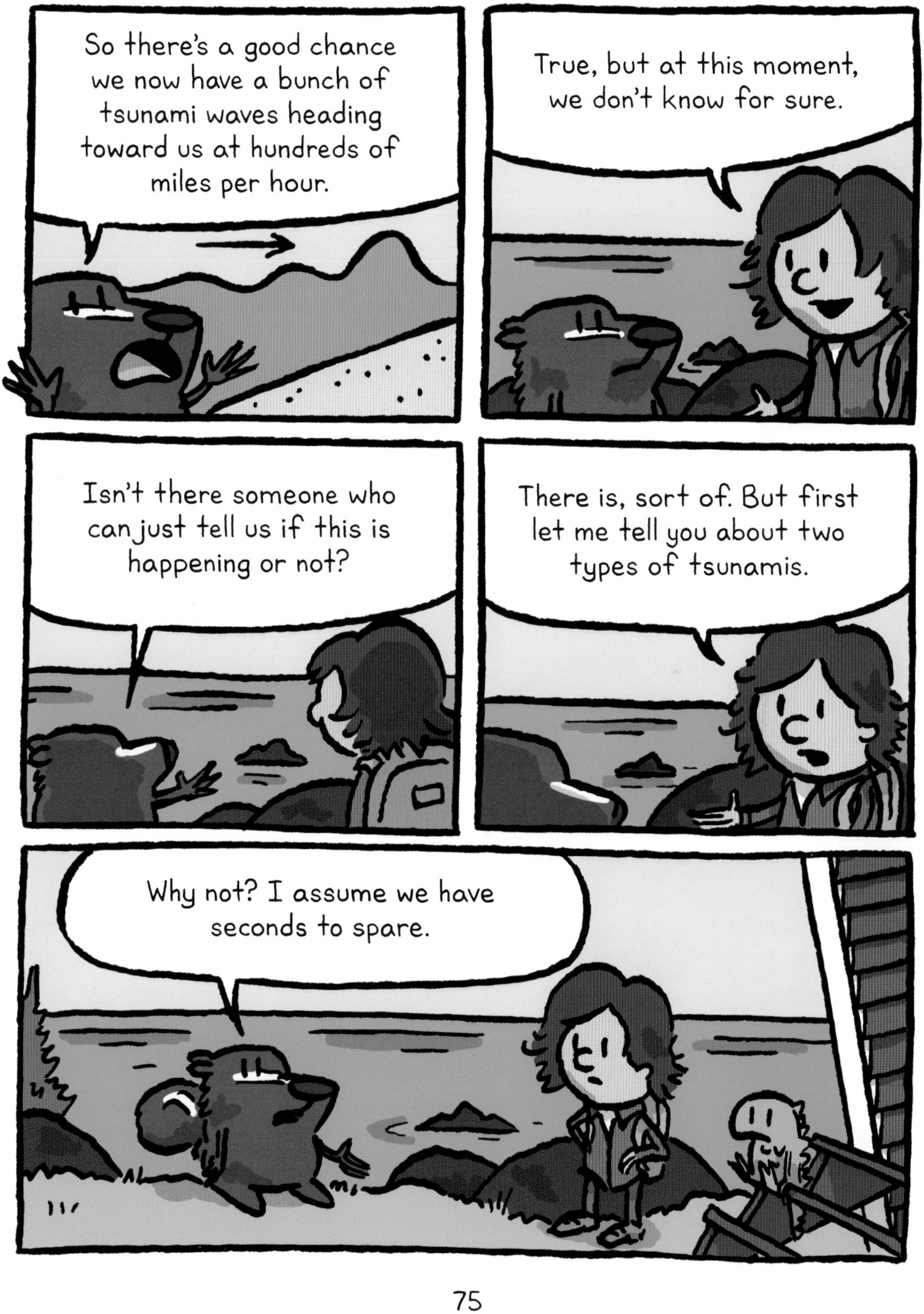
So there's a good chance we now have a bunch of tsunami waves heading toward us at hundreds of miles per hour.
True, but at this moment, we don't know for sure.
Isn't there someone who can just tell us if this is happening or not?
There is, sort of. But first let me tell you about two types of tsunamis.
Why not? I assume we have seconds to spare.

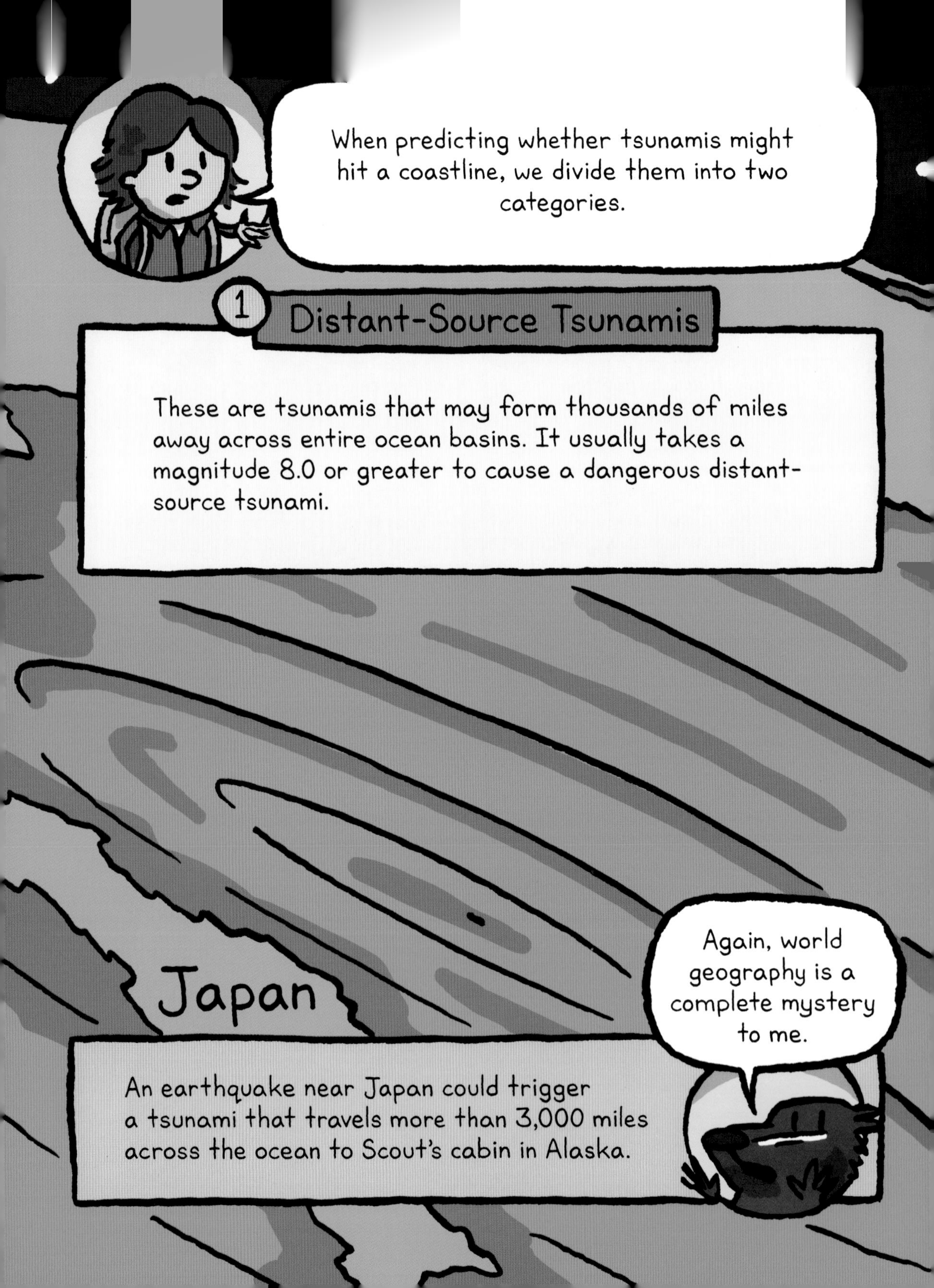
When predicting whether tsunamis might hit a coastline, we divide them into two categories.
1 Distant-Source Tsunamis
These are tsunamis that may form thousands of miles away across entire ocean basins. It usually takes a magnitude 8.0 or greater to cause a dangerous distant-source tsunami.
Japan
Again, world geography is a complete mystery to me.
An earthquake near Japan could trigger a tsunami that travels more than 3,000 miles across the ocean to Scout's cabin in Alaska.

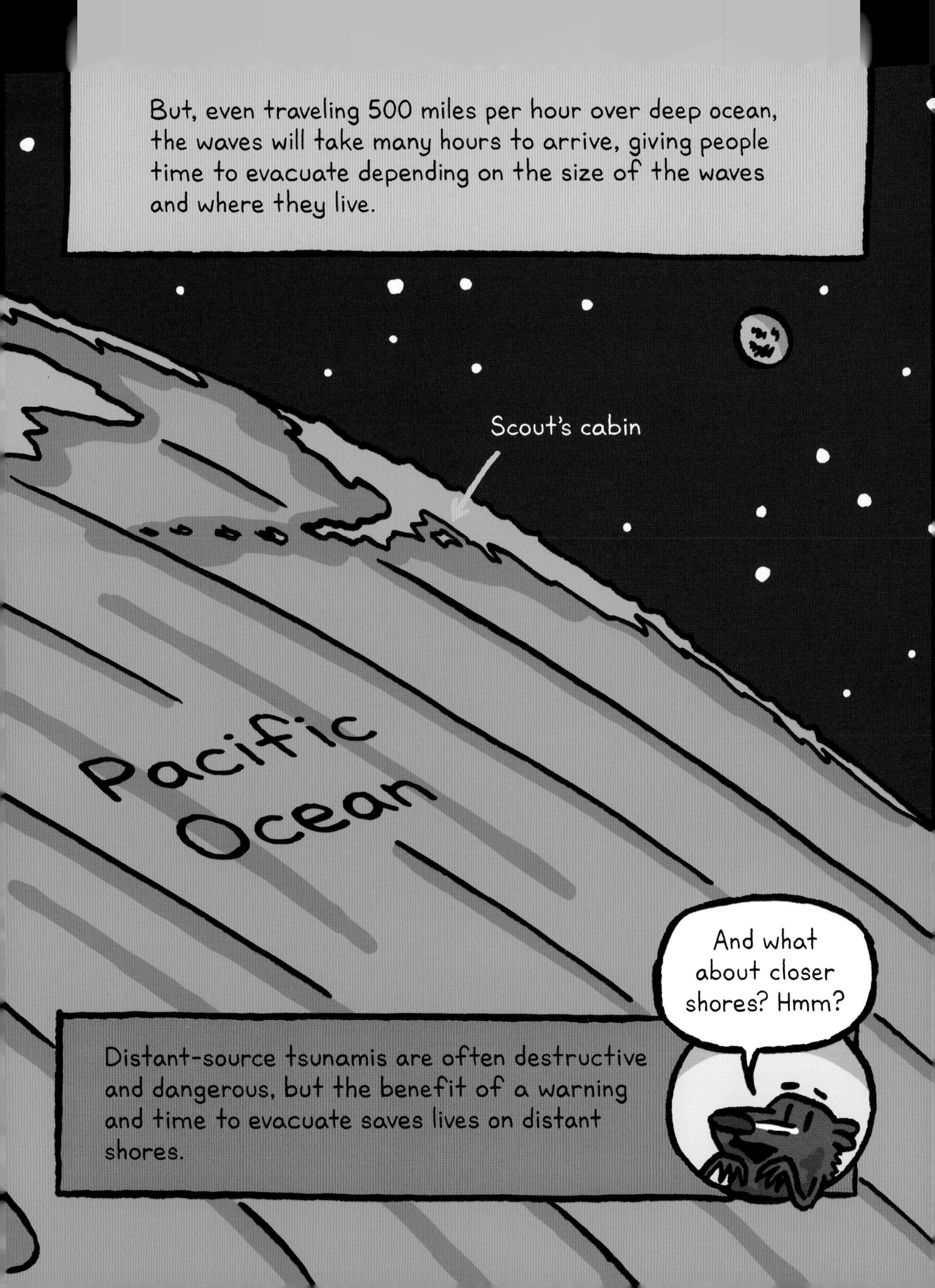
But, even traveling 500 miles per hour over deep ocean, the waves will take many hours to arrive, giving people time to evacuate depending on the size of the waves and where they live.
Scout's cabin
Pacific Ocean
Distant-source tsunamis are often destructive and dangerous, but the benefit of a warning and time to evacuate saves lives on distant shores.
And what about closer shores? Hmm?

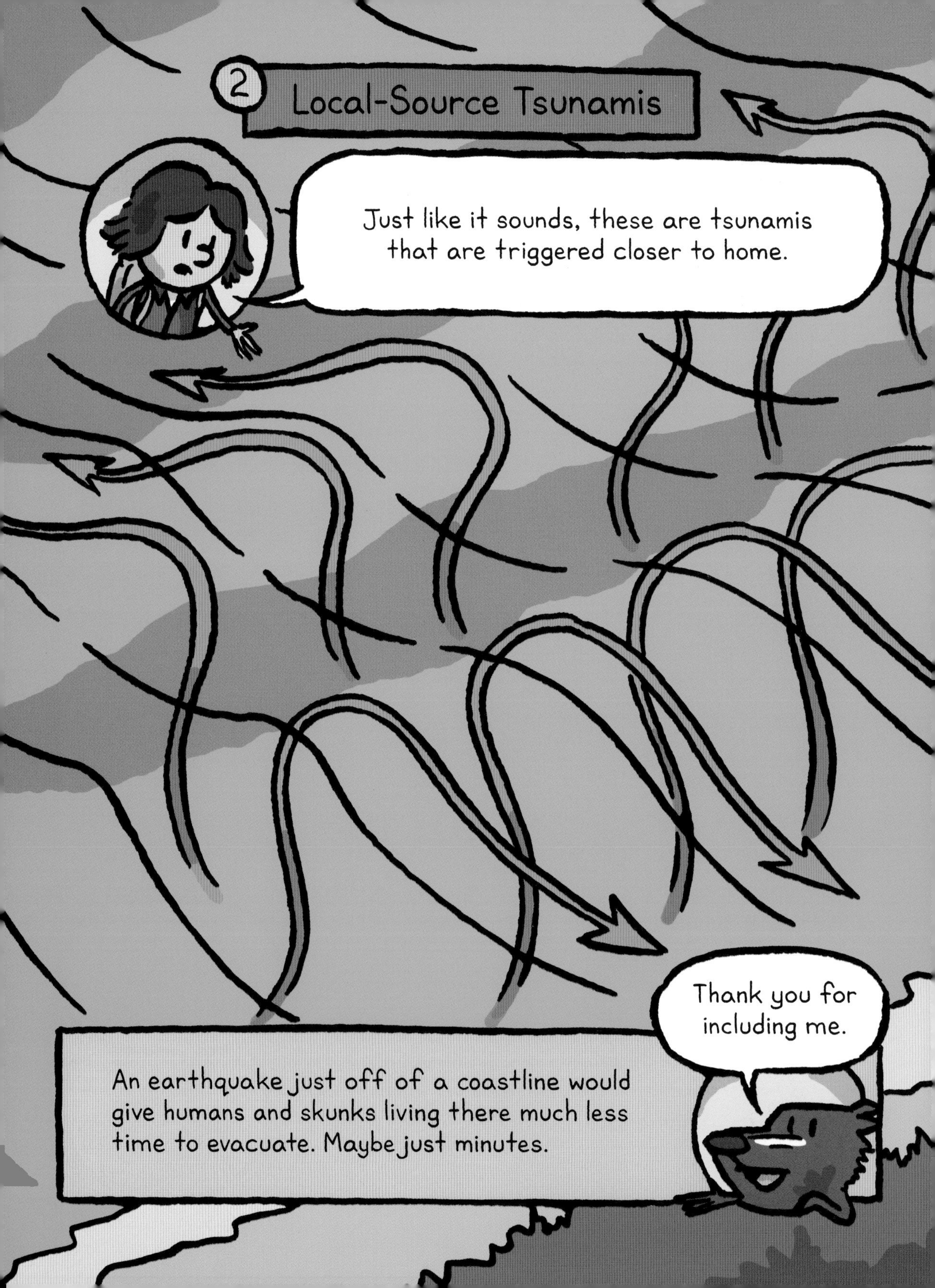
2
Local-Source Tsunamis
Just like it sounds, these are tsunamis that are triggered closer to home.
Thank you for including me.
An earthquake just off of a coastline would give humans and skunks living there much less time to evacuate. Maybe just minutes.

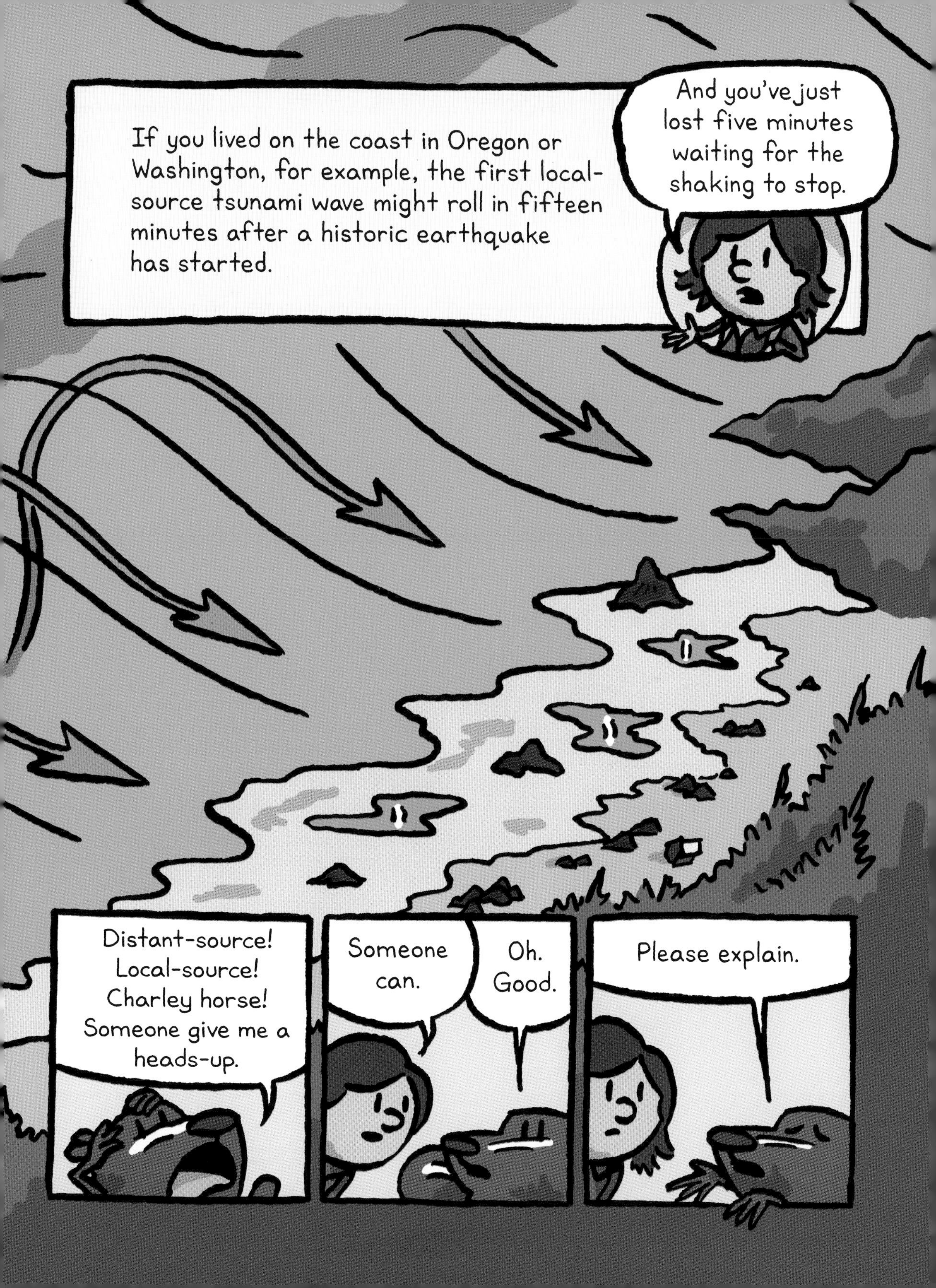
If you lived on the coast in Oregon or Washington, for example, the first local-source tsunami wave might roll in fifteen minutes after a historic earthquake has started.
And you've just lost five minutes waiting for the shaking to stop.
Distant-source! Local-source! Charley horse! Someone give me a heads-up.
Someone can.
Oh. Good.
Please explain.

Tsunami Forecasting

In some places and cases, your best bet will be government-operated Tsunami Warning Centers. Two of these are monitoring twenty-four hours a day and are able to detect earthquakes anywhere in the world using seismic networks that provide information about an earthquake's location, depth, and size.

Pacific Tsunami Warning Center Honolulu, Hawaii

National Tsunami Warning Center Palmer, Alaska

When an earthquake occurs, they can quickly use its strength and location to determine whether a tsunami is possible, along with . . .

- Wave height
- Where it could strike
- When it could strike
- How long it could last
- How much flooding is likely

That screen never works.

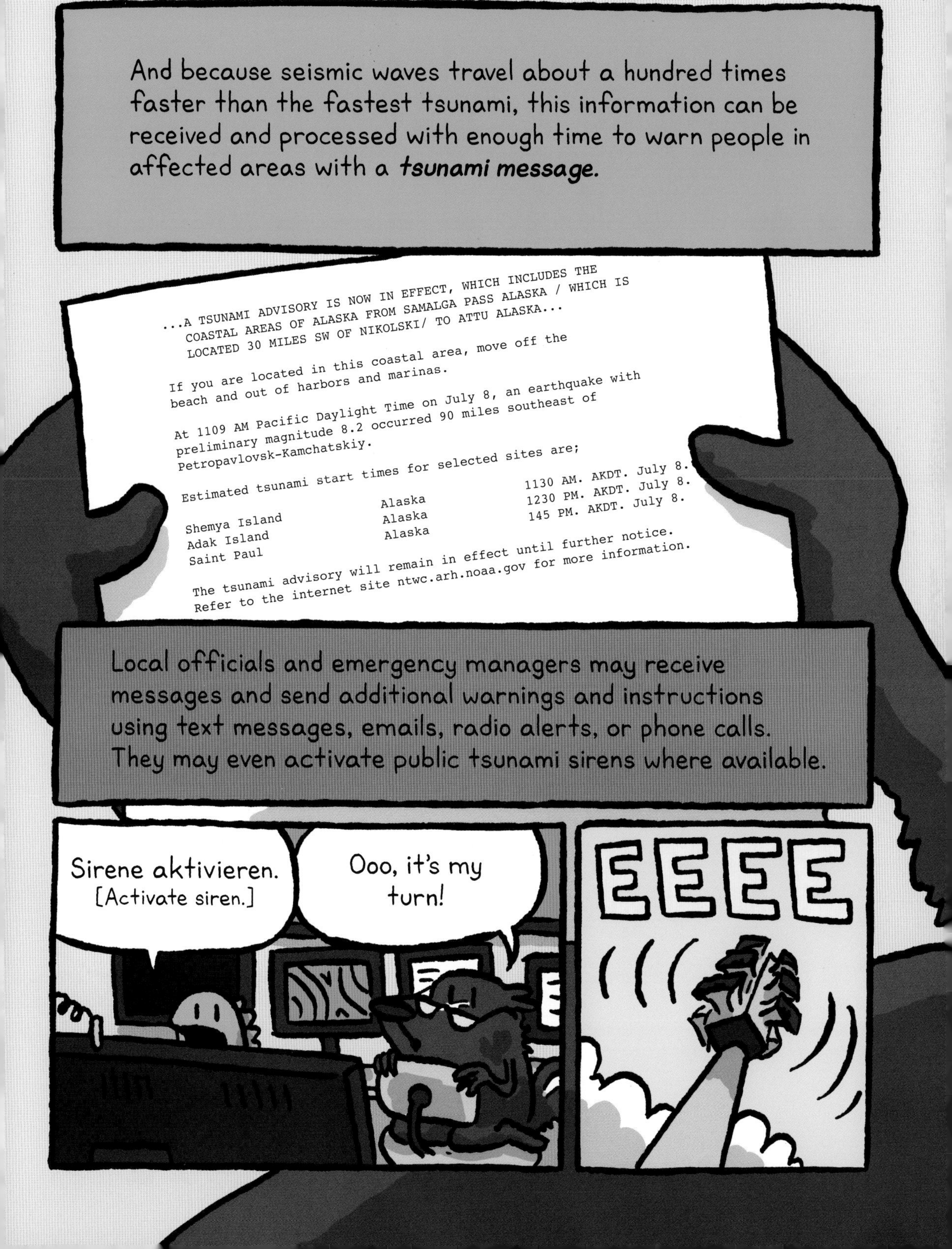
And because seismic waves travel about a hundred times faster than the fastest tsunami, this information can be received and processed with enough time to warn people in affected areas with a ***tsunami message.***
...A TSUNAMI ADVISORY IS NOW IN EFFECT, WHICH INCLUDES THE COASTAL AREAS OF ALASKA FROM SAMALGA PASS ALASKA / WHICH IS LOCATED 30 MILES SW OF NIKOLSKI/ TO ATTU ALASKA...
If you are located in this coastal area, move off the beach and out of harbors and marinas.
At 1109 AM Pacific Daylight Time on July 8, an earthquake with preliminary magnitude 8.2 occurred 90 miles southeast of Petropavlovsk-Kamchatskiy.
Estimated tsunami start times for selected sites are;
Shemya Island Alaska 1130 AM. AKDT. July 8.
Adak Island Alaska 1230 PM. AKDT. July 8.
Saint Paul Alaska 145 PM. AKDT. July 8.
The tsunami advisory will remain in effect until further notice.
Refer to the internet site ntwc.arh.noaa.gov for more information.
Local officials and emergency managers may receive messages and send additional warnings and instructions using text messages, emails, radio alerts, or phone calls. They may even activate public tsunami sirens where available.
Sirene aktivieren. [Activate siren.]
Ooo, it's my turn!
EEEE

The message is sent. Now the Tsunami Warning Centers start looking at water-level networks for changes that indicate tsunami waves. This information can then be used to refine, update, or cancel tsunami bulletins and warnings. There are two main water-level network components:

1 DART Systems — *Deep-ocean Assessment and Reporting of Tsunamis*

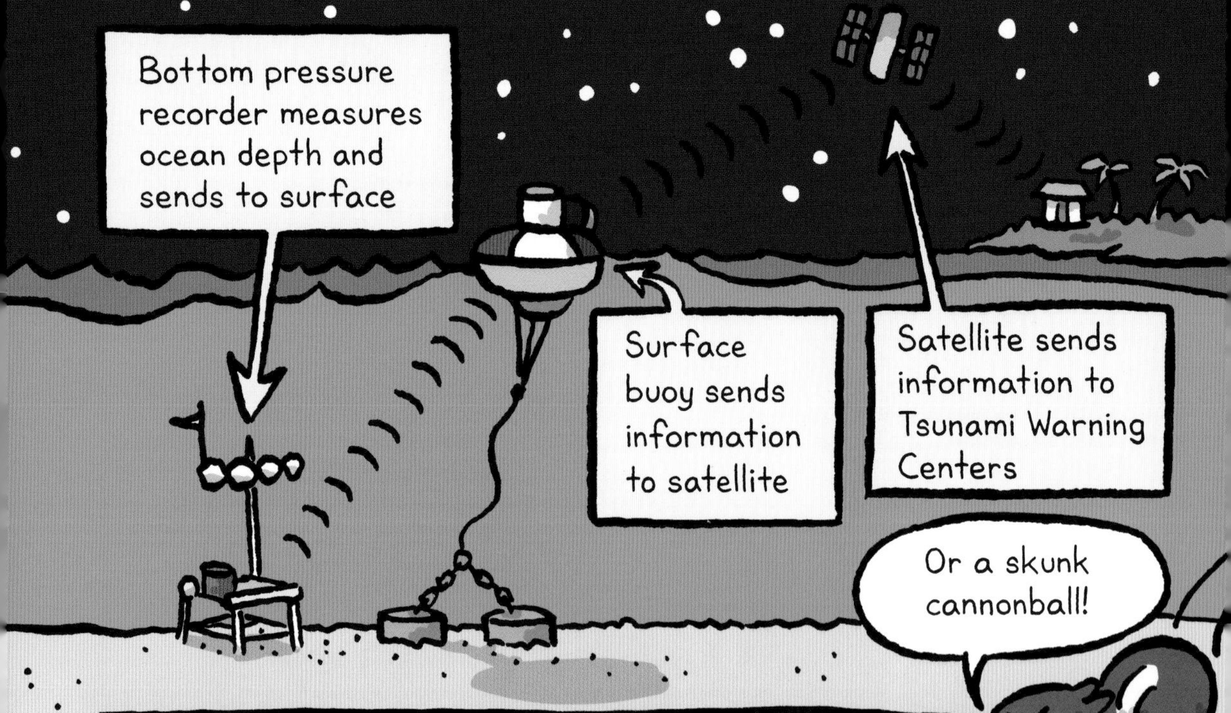

Bottom pressure recorder measures ocean depth and sends to surface
Surface buoy sends information to satellite
Satellite sends information to Tsunami Warning Centers
Or a skunk cannonball!

DART systems also allow warning centers to detect tsunamis with causes that may have been missed like volcanos or landslides.

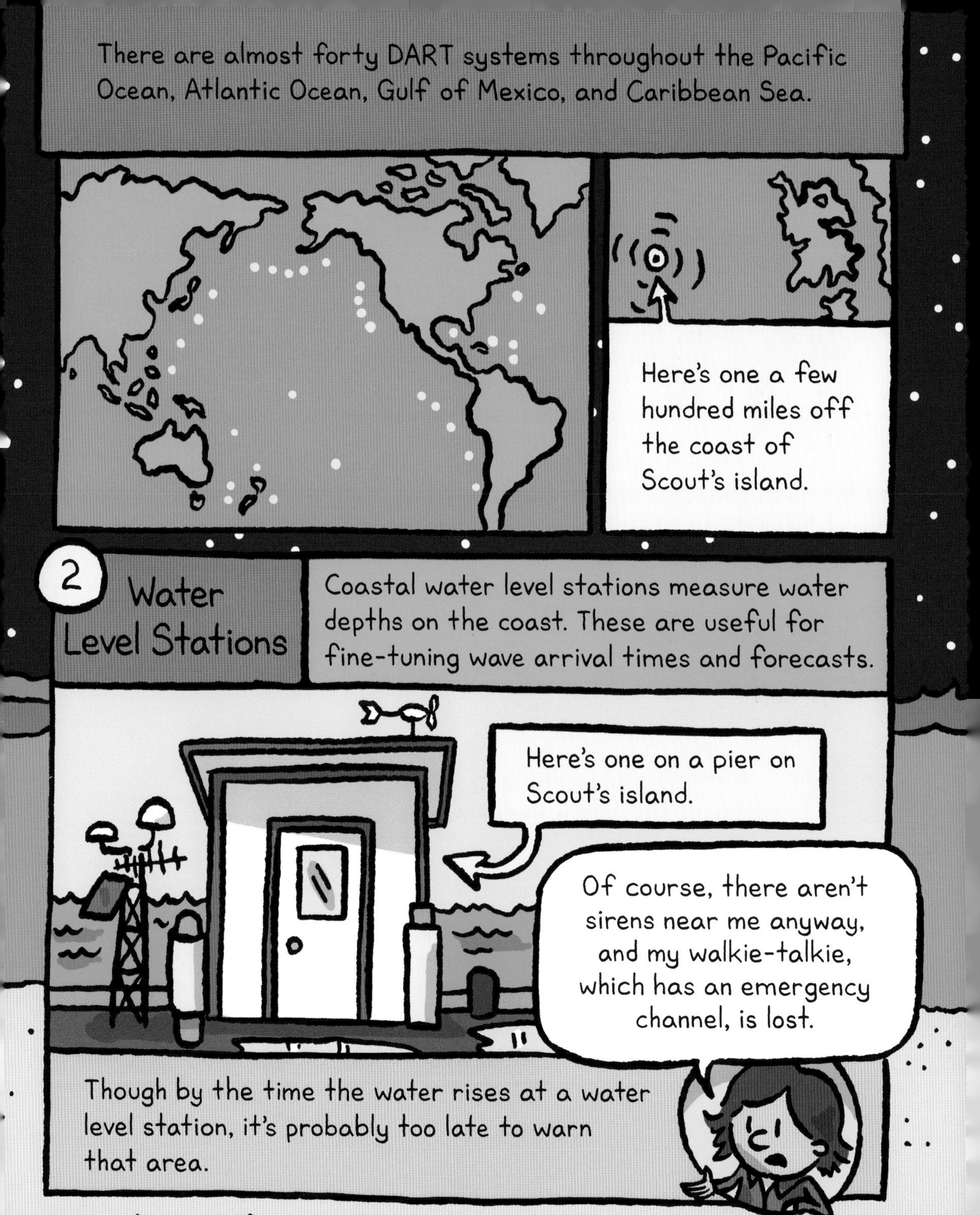
There are almost forty DART systems throughout the Pacific Ocean, Atlantic Ocean, Gulf of Mexico, and Caribbean Sea.
Here's one a few hundred miles off the coast of Scout's island.
2
Water Level Stations
Coastal water level stations measure water depths on the coast. These are useful for fine-tuning wave arrival times and forecasts.
Here's one on a pier on Scout's island.
Of course, there aren't sirens near me anyway, and my walkie-talkie, which has an emergency channel, is lost.
Though by the time the water rises at a water level station, it's probably too late to warn that area.

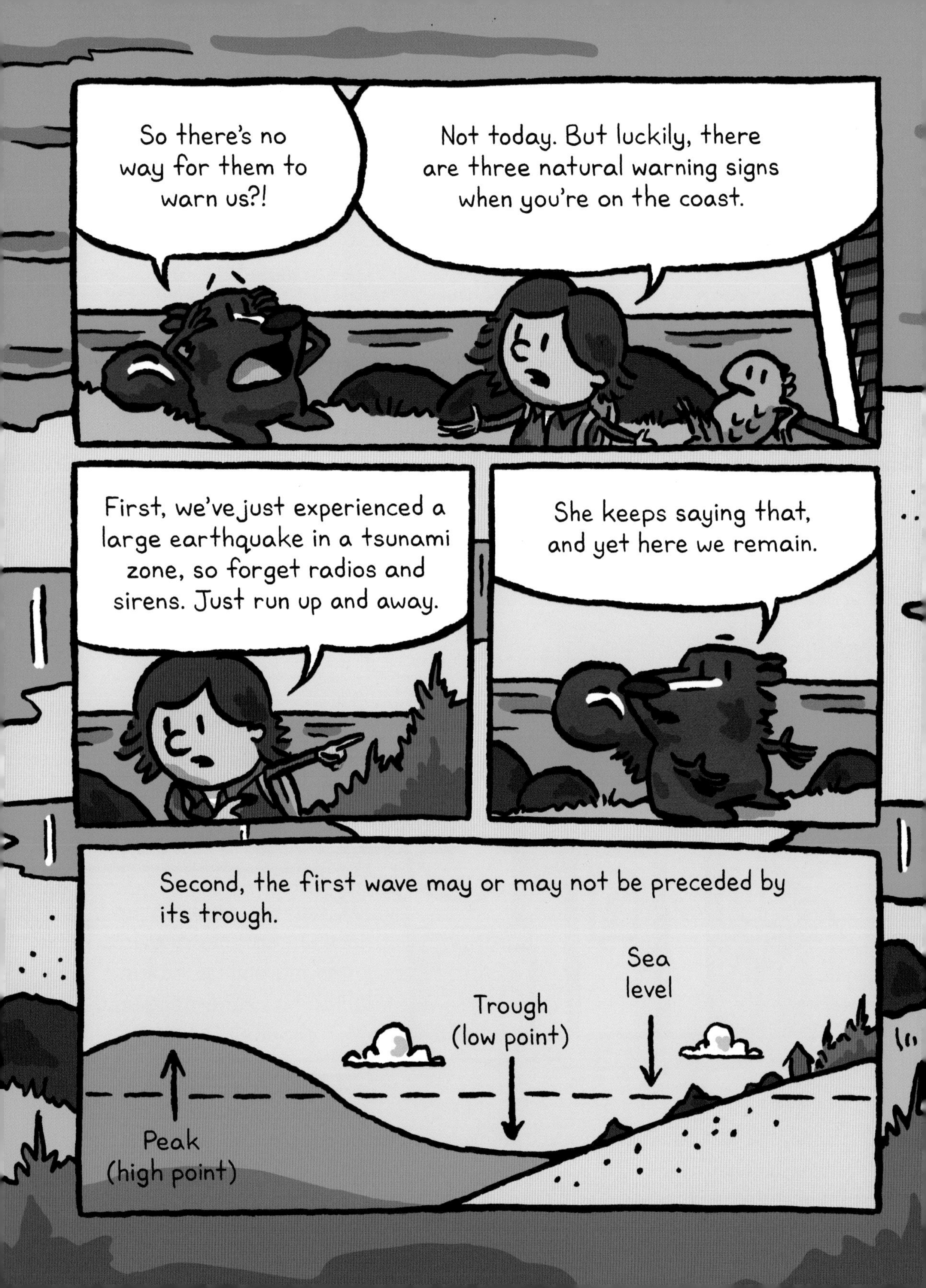
So there's no way for them to warn us?!
Not today. But luckily, there are three natural warning signs when you're on the coast.
First, we've just experienced a large earthquake in a tsunami zone, so forget radios and sirens. Just run up and away.
She keeps saying that, and yet here we remain.
Second, the first wave may or may not be preceded by its trough.
Sea level
Trough (low point)
Peak (high point)

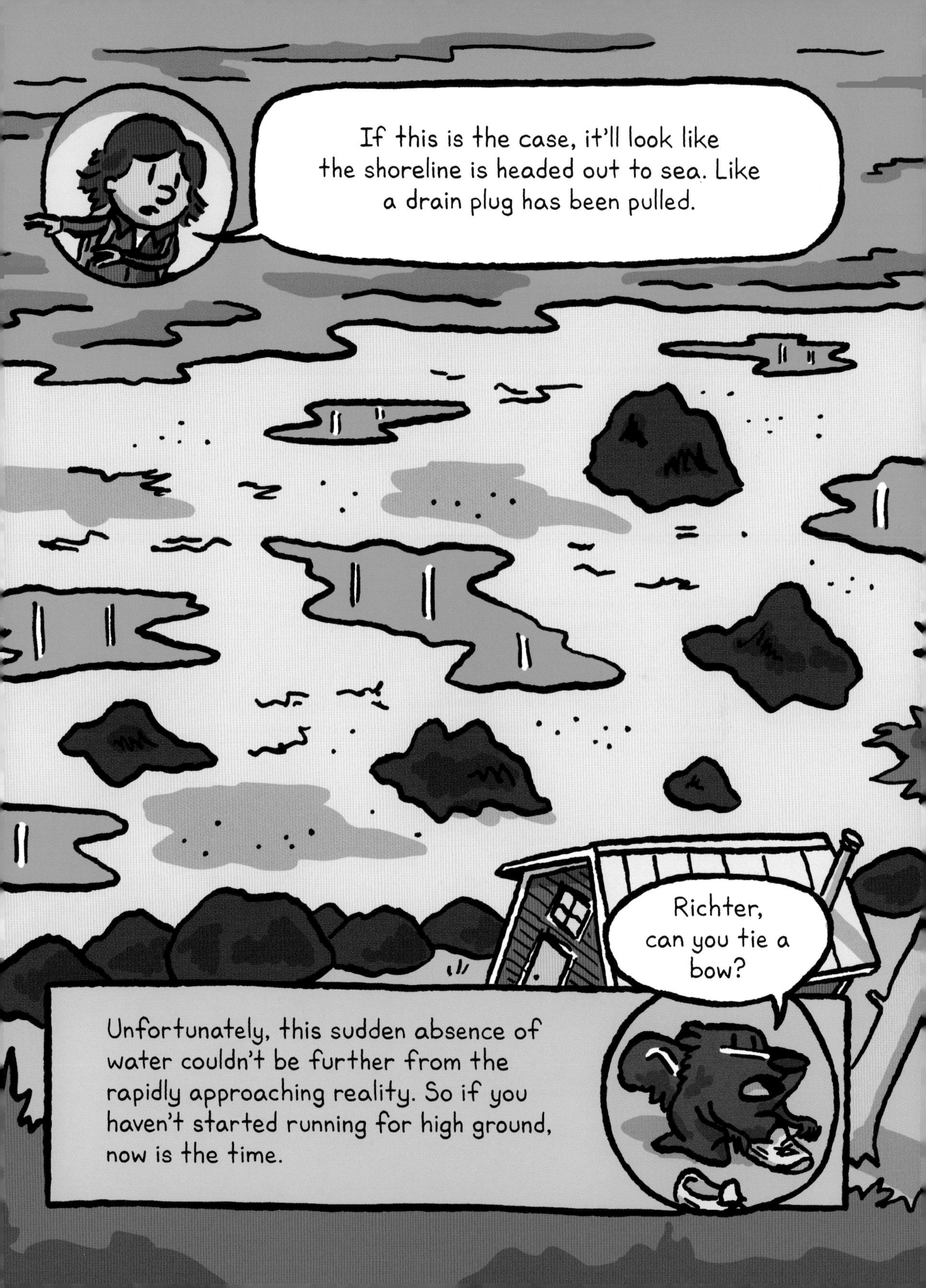
If this is the case, it'll look like the shoreline is headed out to sea. Like a drain plug has been pulled.
Richter, can you tie a bow?
Unfortunately, this sudden absence of water couldn't be further from the rapidly approaching reality. So if you haven't started running for high ground, now is the time.

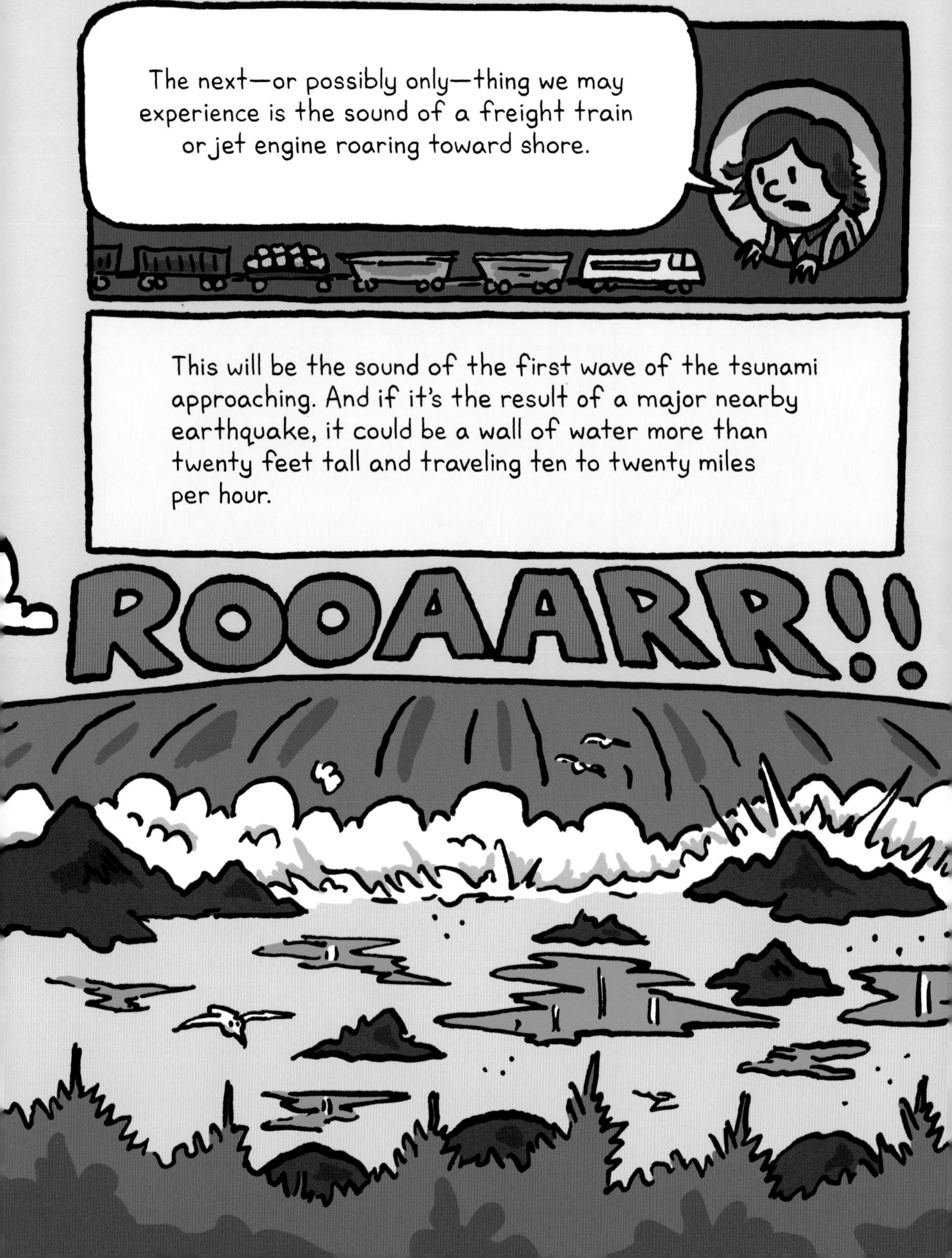
The next—or possibly only—thing we may experience is the sound of a freight train or jet engine roaring toward shore.
This will be the sound of the first wave of the tsunami approaching. And if it's the result of a major nearby earthquake, it could be a wall of water more than twenty feet tall and traveling ten to twenty miles per hour.
ROOAARR!!

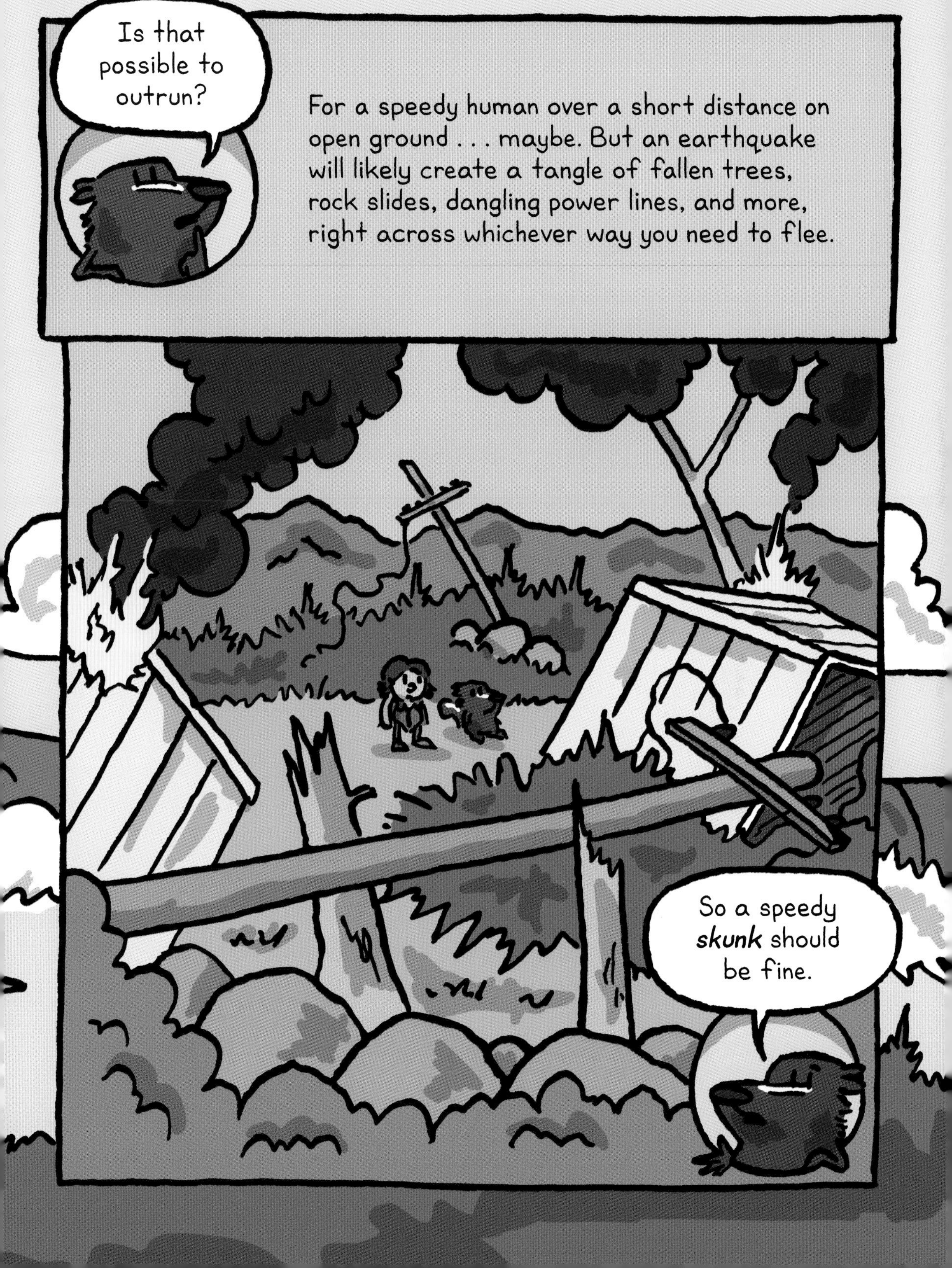
Is that possible to outrun?
For a speedy human over a short distance on open ground . . . maybe. But an earthquake will likely create a tangle of fallen trees, rock slides, dangling power lines, and more, right across whichever way you need to flee.
So a speedy *skunk* should be fine.

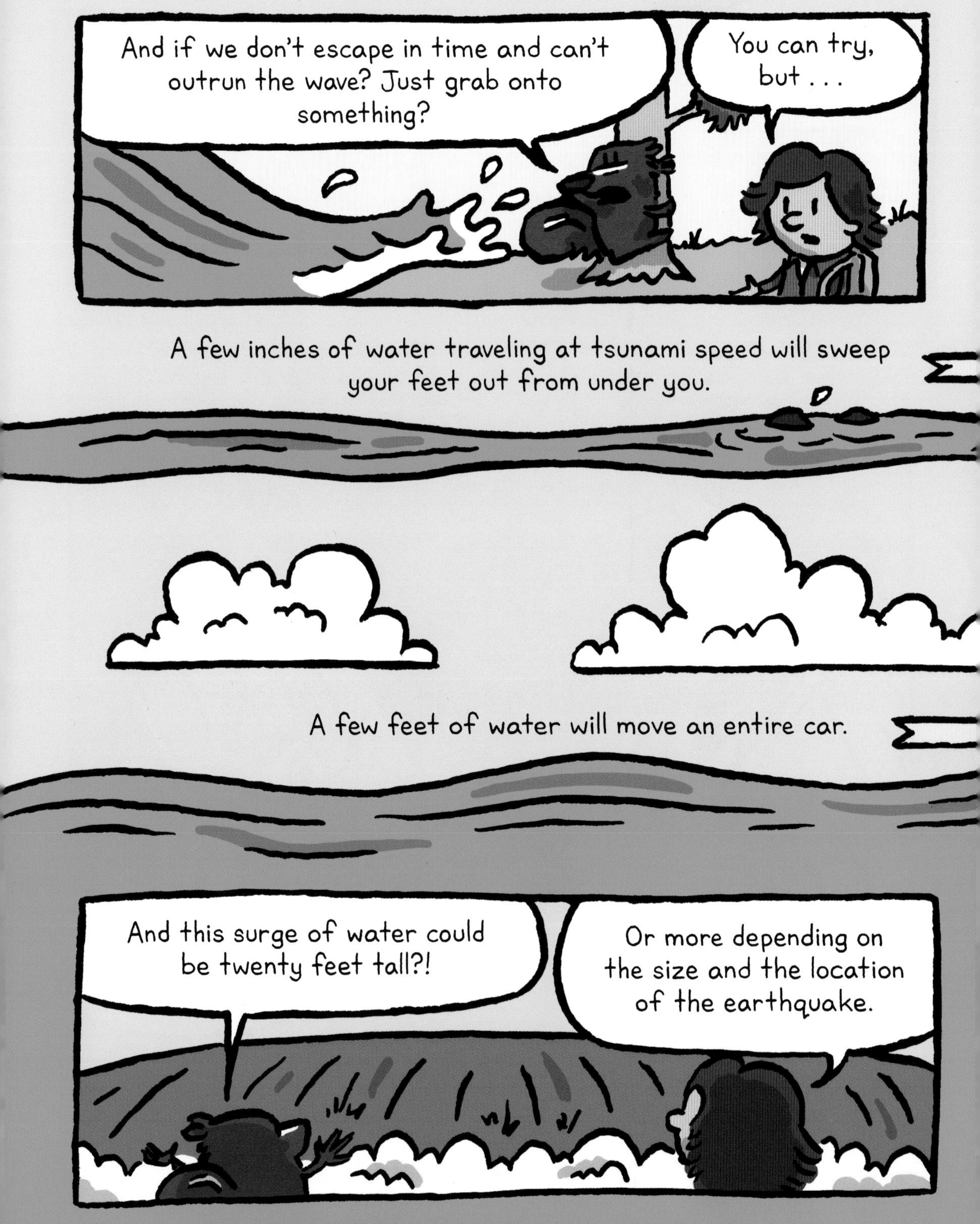
And if we don't escape in time and can't outrun the wave? Just grab onto something?
You can try, but . . .
A few inches of water traveling at tsunami speed will sweep your feet out from under you.
A few feet of water will move an entire car.
And this surge of water could be twenty feet tall?!
Or more depending on the size and the location of the earthquake.

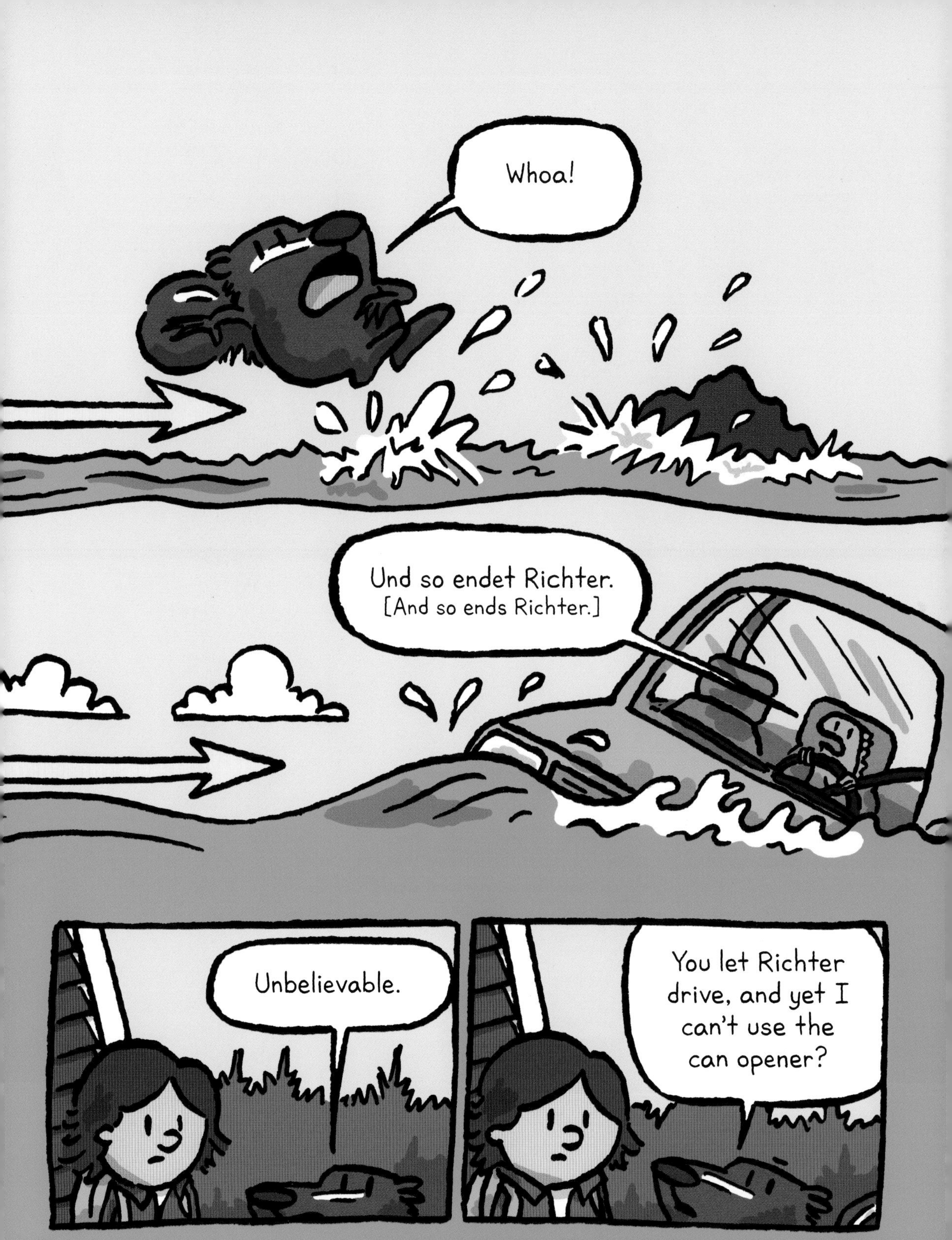
Whoa!
Und so endet Richter.
[And so ends Richter.]
Unbelievable.
You let Richter drive, and yet I can't use the can opener?

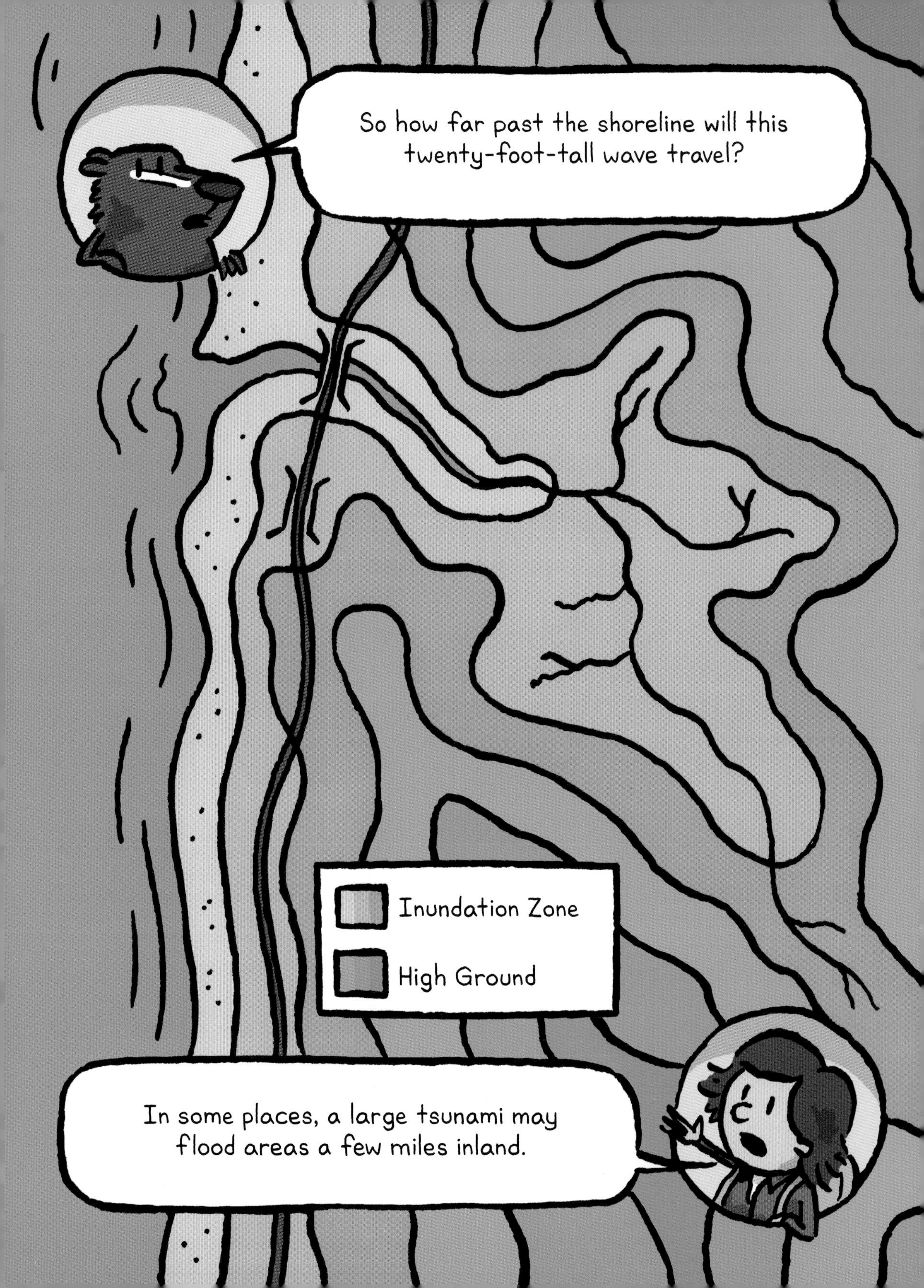
So how far past the shoreline will this twenty-foot-tall wave travel?
Inundation Zone
High Ground
In some places, a large tsunami may flood areas a few miles inland.

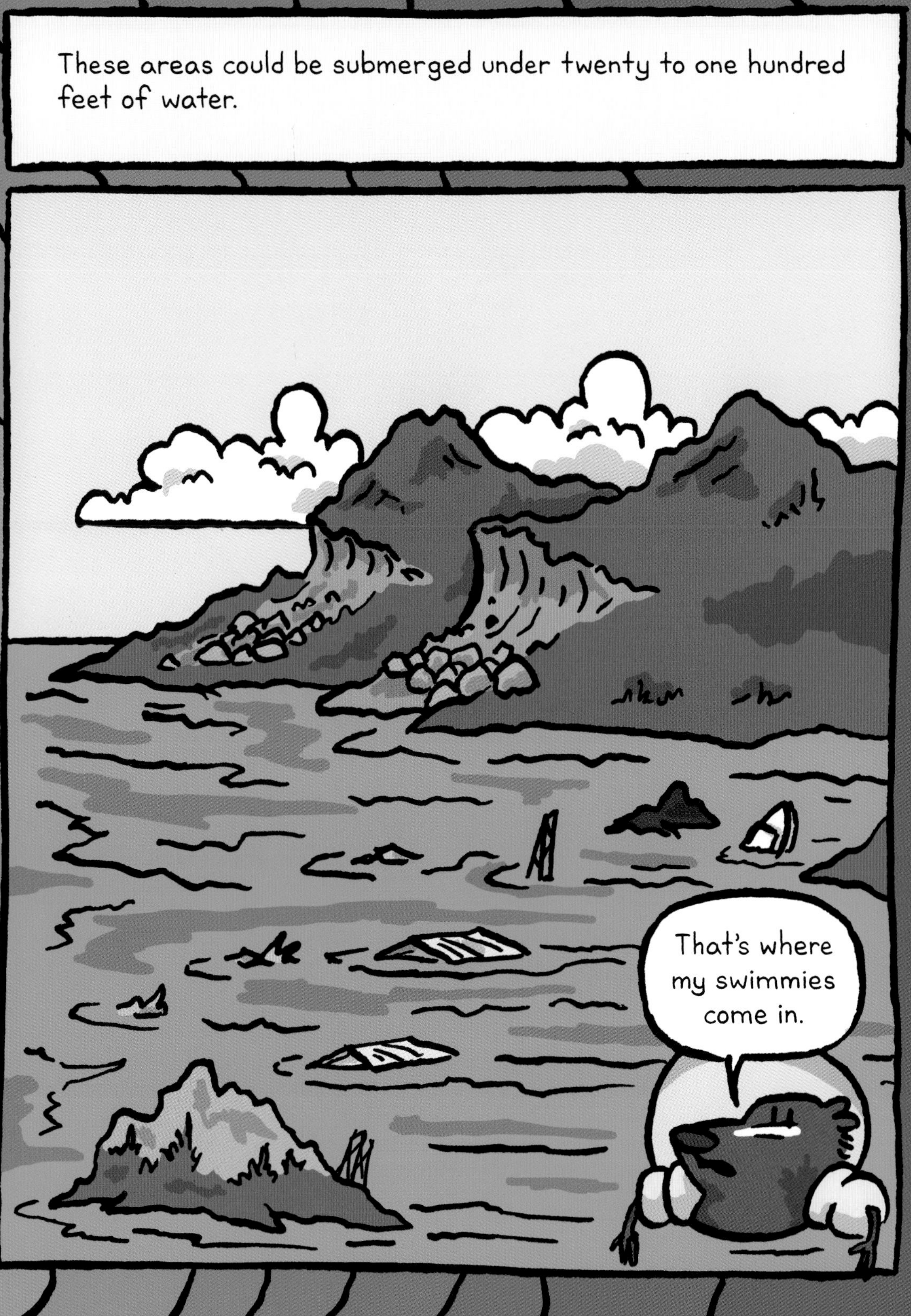
These areas could be submerged under twenty to one hundred feet of water.
That's where my swimmies come in.

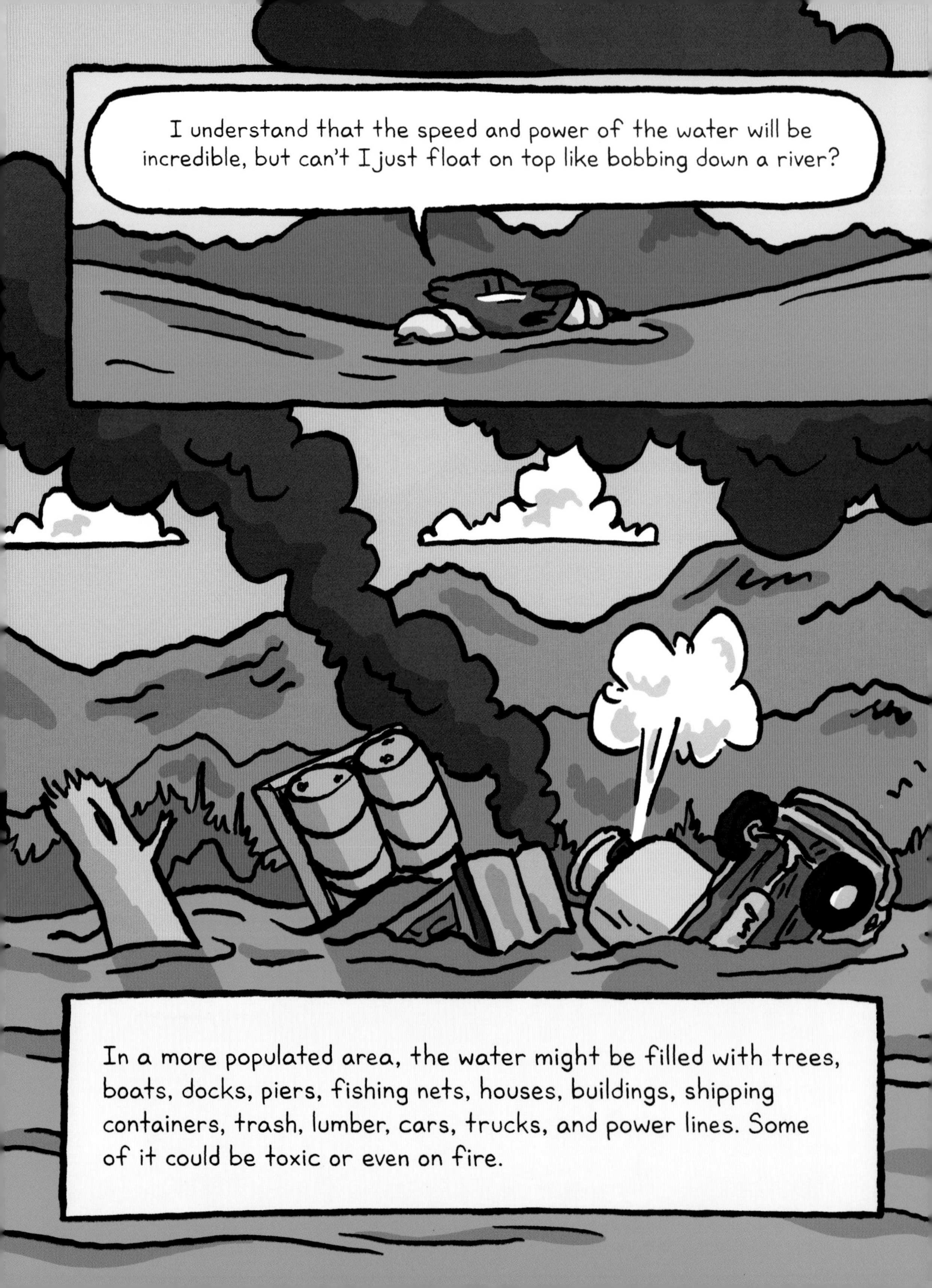
I understand that the speed and power of the water will be incredible, but can't I just float on top like bobbing down a river?
In a more populated area, the water might be filled with trees, boats, docks, piers, fishing nets, houses, buildings, shipping containers, trash, lumber, cars, trucks, and power lines. Some of it could be toxic or even on fire.

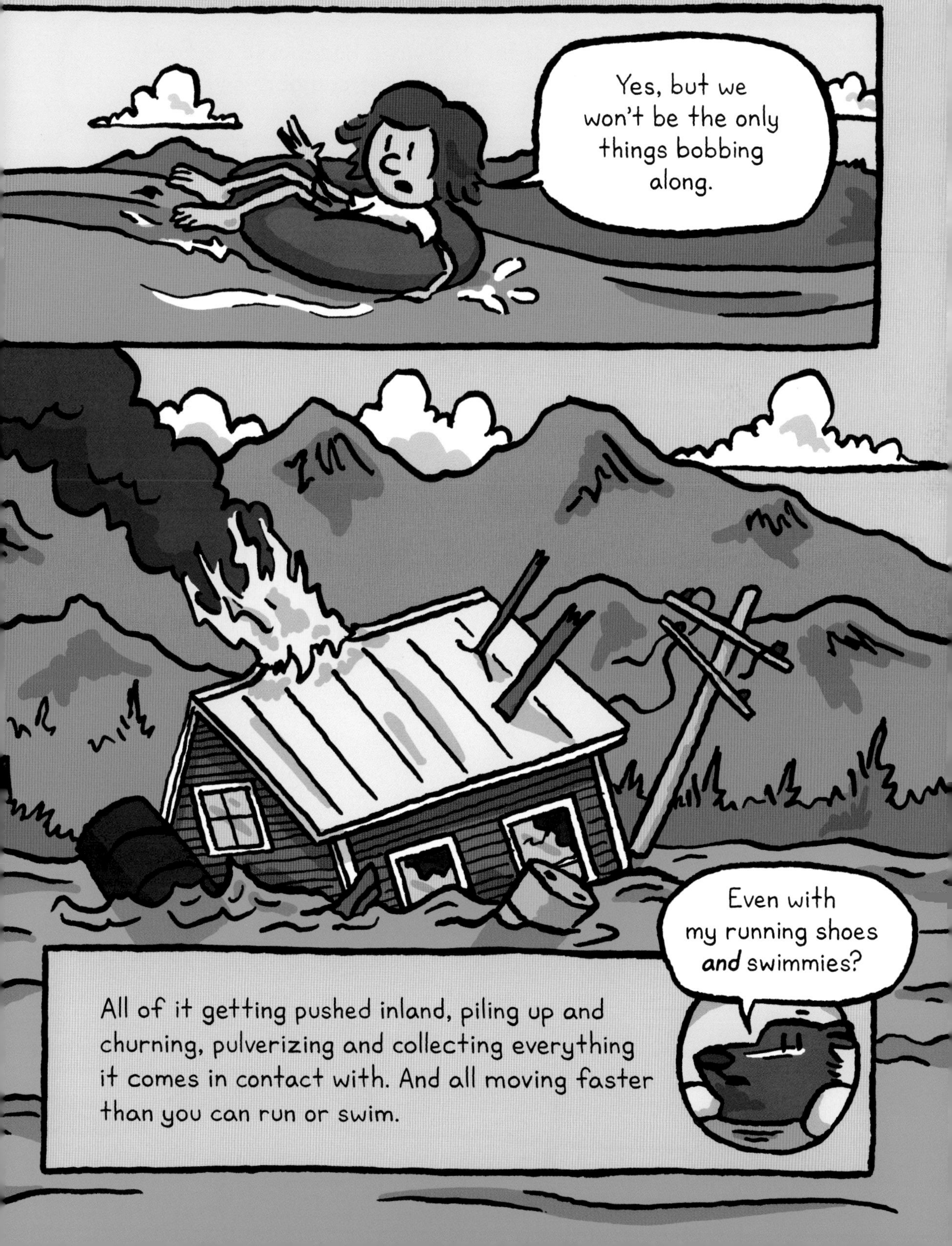
Yes, but we won't be the only things bobbing along.
All of it getting pushed inland, piling up and churning, pulverizing and collecting everything it comes in contact with. And all moving faster than you can run or swim.
Even with my running shoes *and* swimmies?

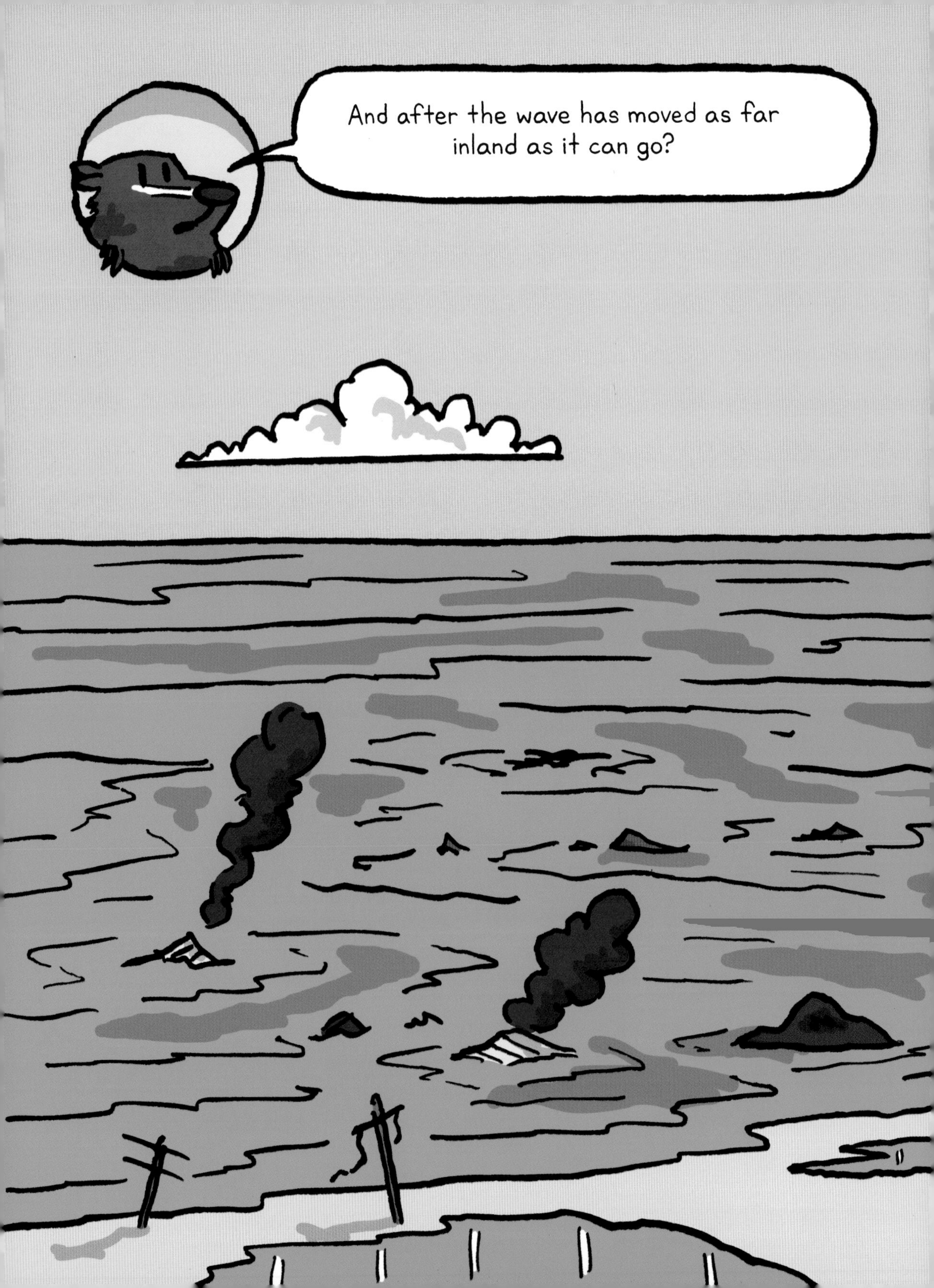
And after the wave has moved as far inland as it can go?

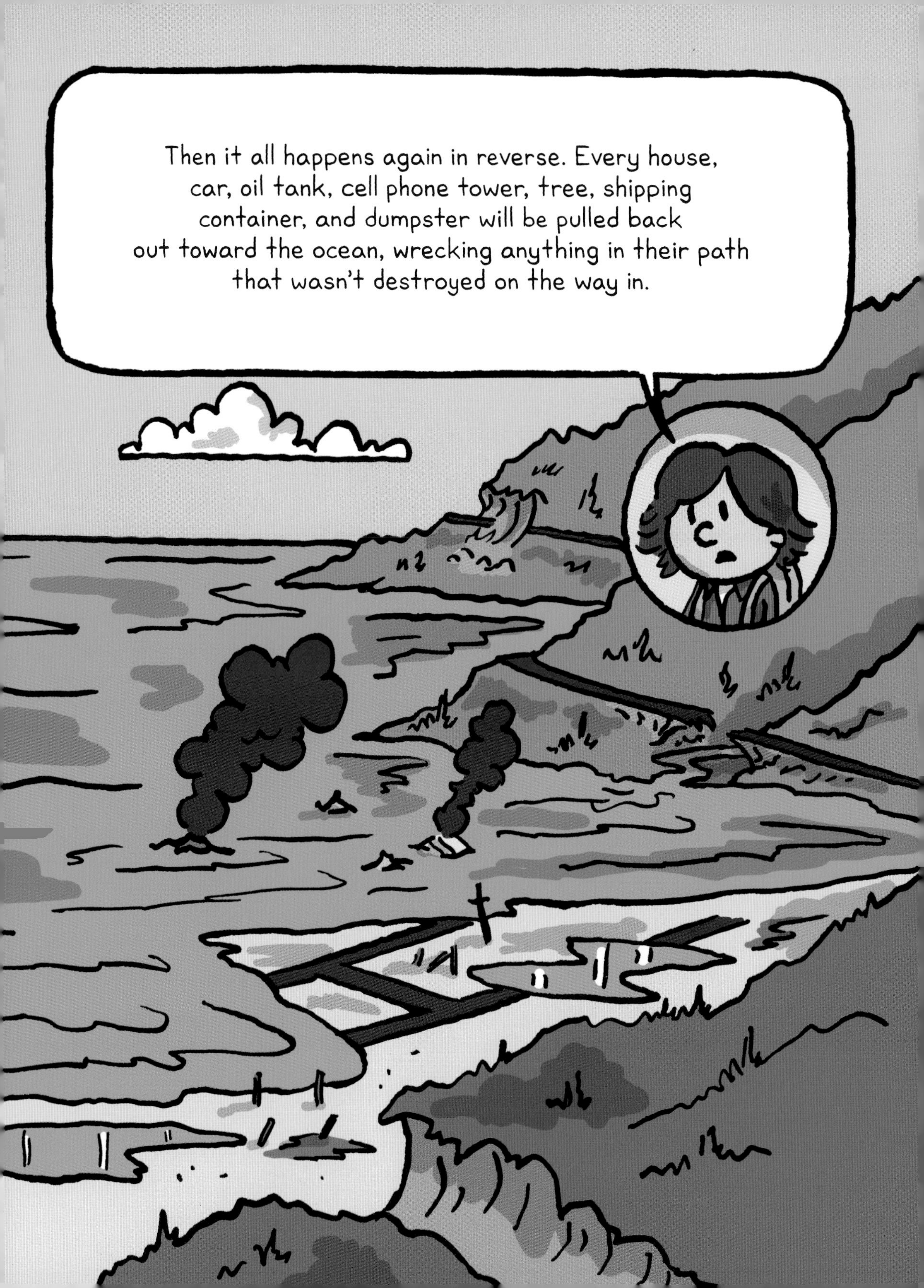
Then it all happens again in reverse. Every house, car, oil tank, cell phone tower, tree, shipping container, and dumpster will be pulled back out toward the ocean, wrecking anything in their path that wasn't destroyed on the way in.

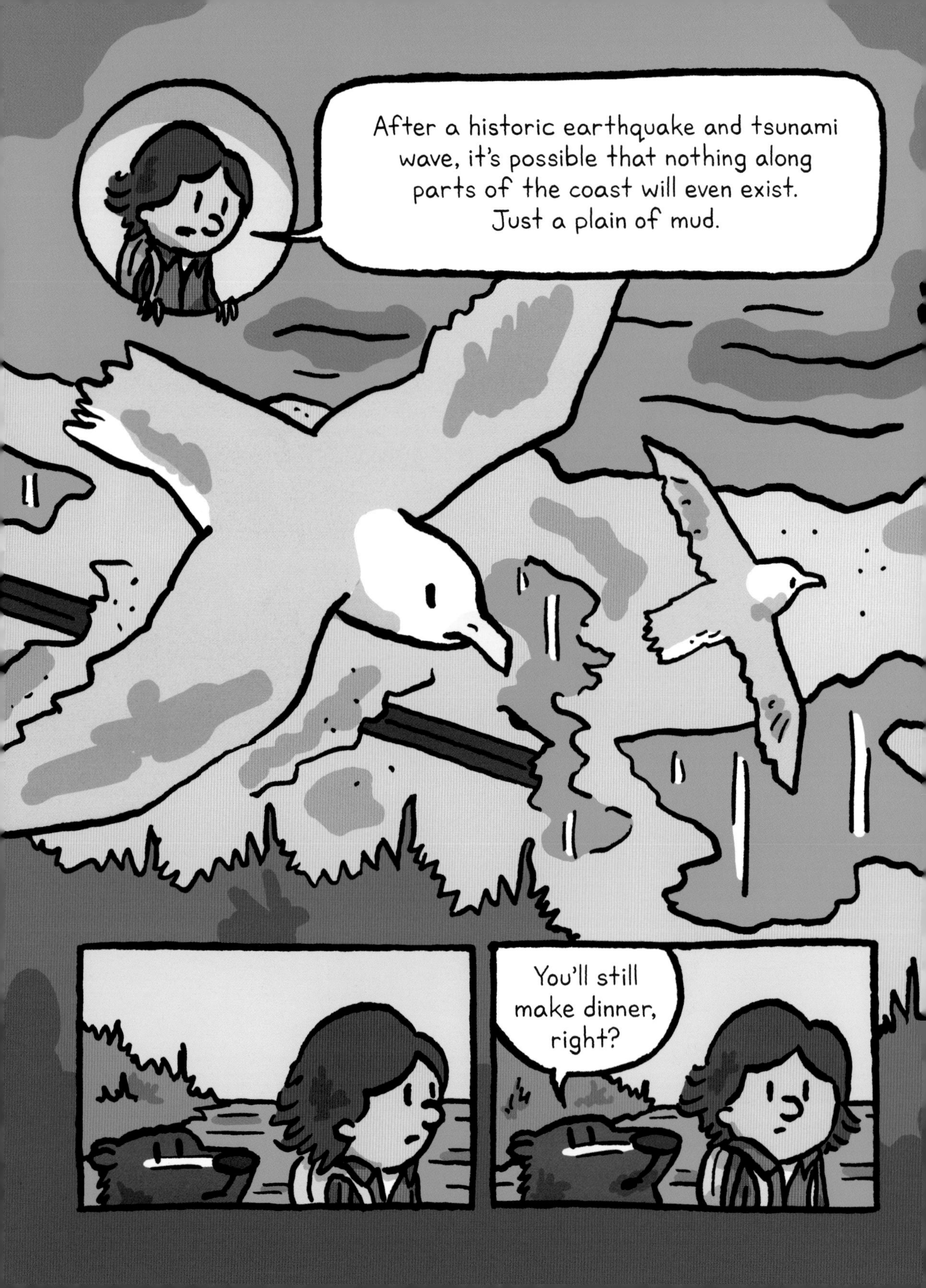
After a historic earthquake and tsunami wave, it's possible that nothing along parts of the coast will even exist. Just a plain of mud.
You'll still make dinner, right?

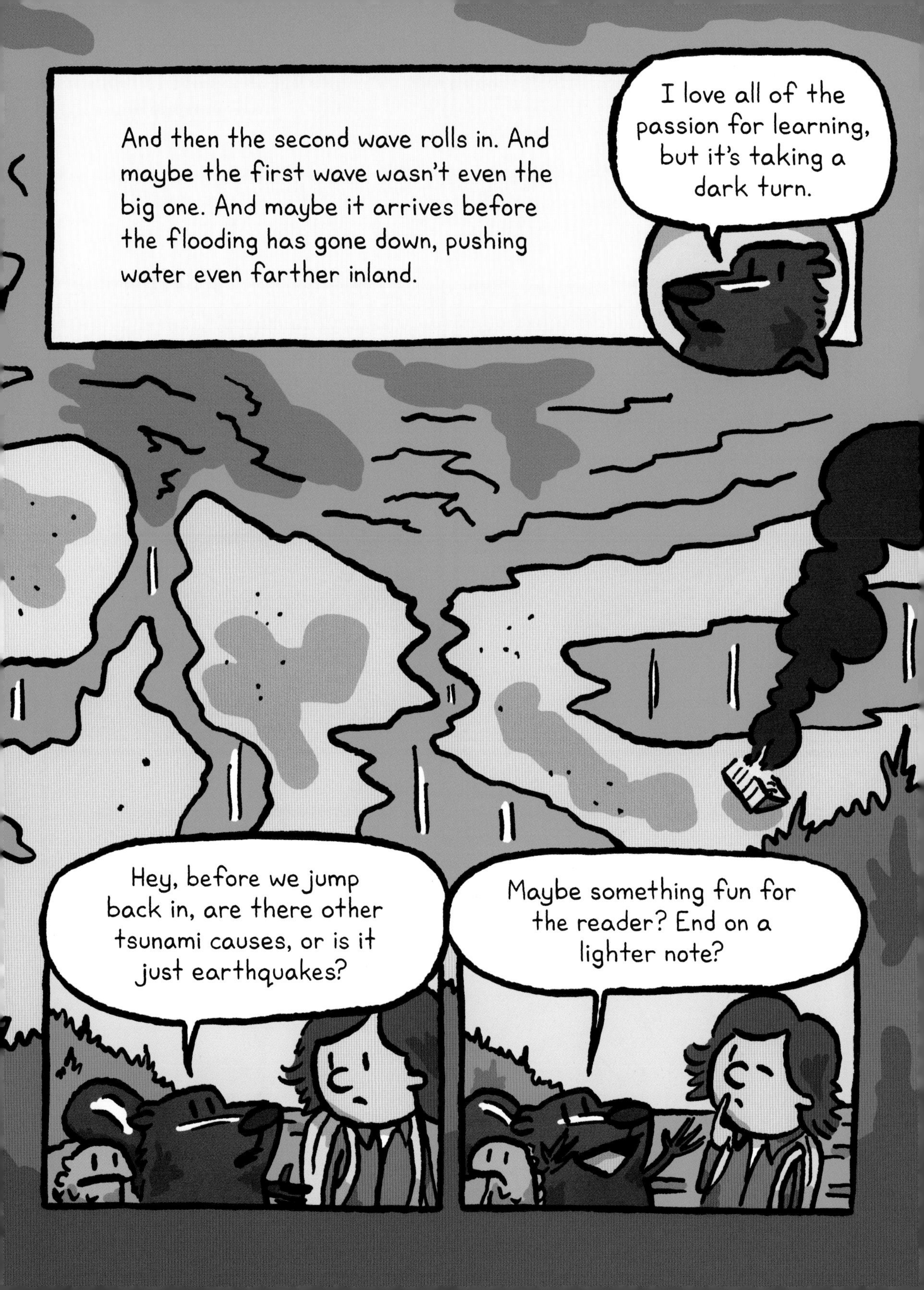
And then the second wave rolls in. And maybe the first wave wasn't even the big one. And maybe it arrives before the flooding has gone down, pushing water even farther inland.
I love all of the passion for learning, but it's taking a dark turn.
Hey, before we jump back in, are there other tsunami causes, or is it just earthquakes?
Maybe something fun for the reader? End on a lighter note?

Landslides

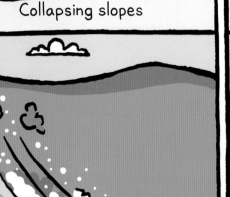

Above or below the water surface, landslides can push a lot of water. Often triggered by earthquakes, these can take a few forms.

Collapsing slopes

Falling boulders

Chunks of glaciers crashing into the sea

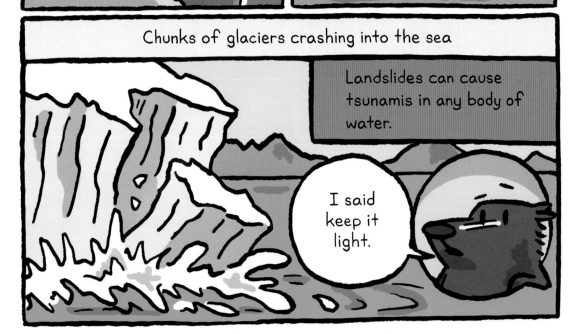

Landslides can cause tsunamis in any body of water.

I said keep it light.

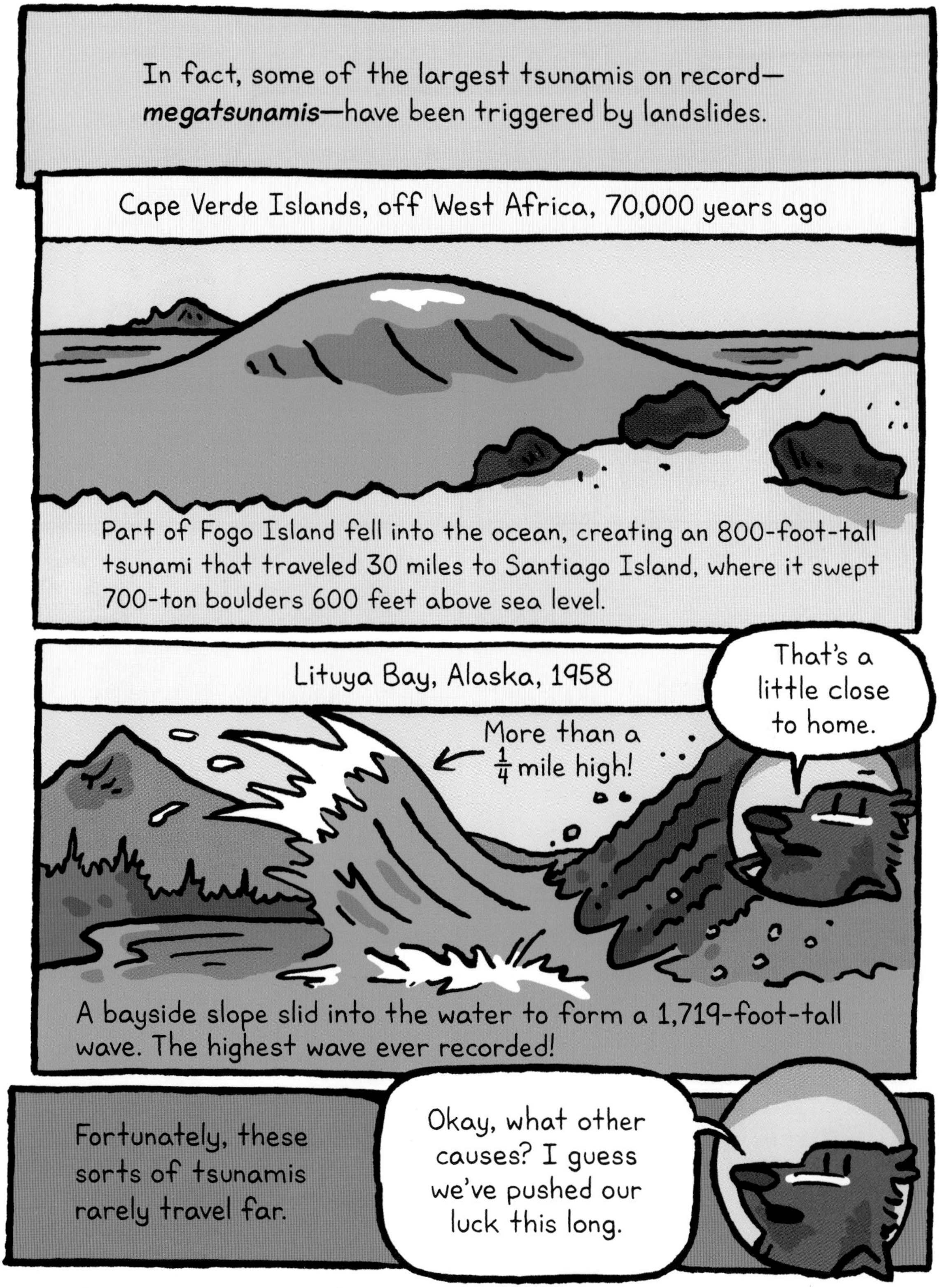
In fact, some of the largest tsunamis on record—***megatsunamis***—have been triggered by landslides.
Cape Verde Islands, off West Africa, 70,000 years ago
Part of Fogo Island fell into the ocean, creating an 800-foot-tall tsunami that traveled 30 miles to Santiago Island, where it swept 700-ton boulders 600 feet above sea level.
Lituya Bay, Alaska, 1958
More than a 1/4 mile high!
That's a little close to home.
A bayside slope slid into the water to form a 1,719-foot-tall wave. The highest wave ever recorded!
Fortunately, these sorts of tsunamis rarely travel far.
Okay, what other causes? I guess we've pushed our luck this long.

Volcanic Eruptions

Volcanos above and below water may cause tsunamis. When gas, ash, and rock suddenly explode or crators collapse, tsunamis are possible.

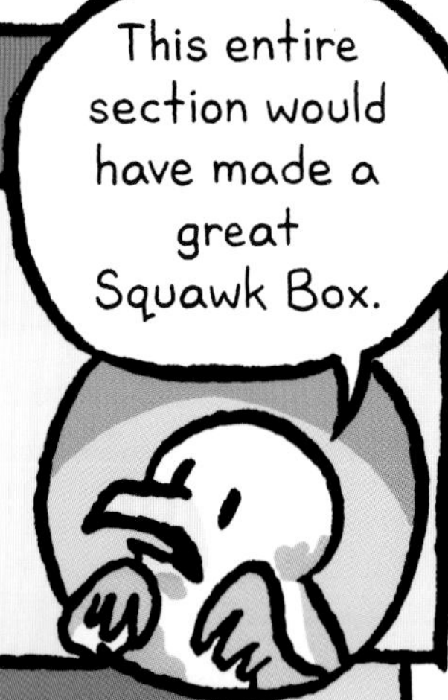
This entire section would have made a great Squawk Box.

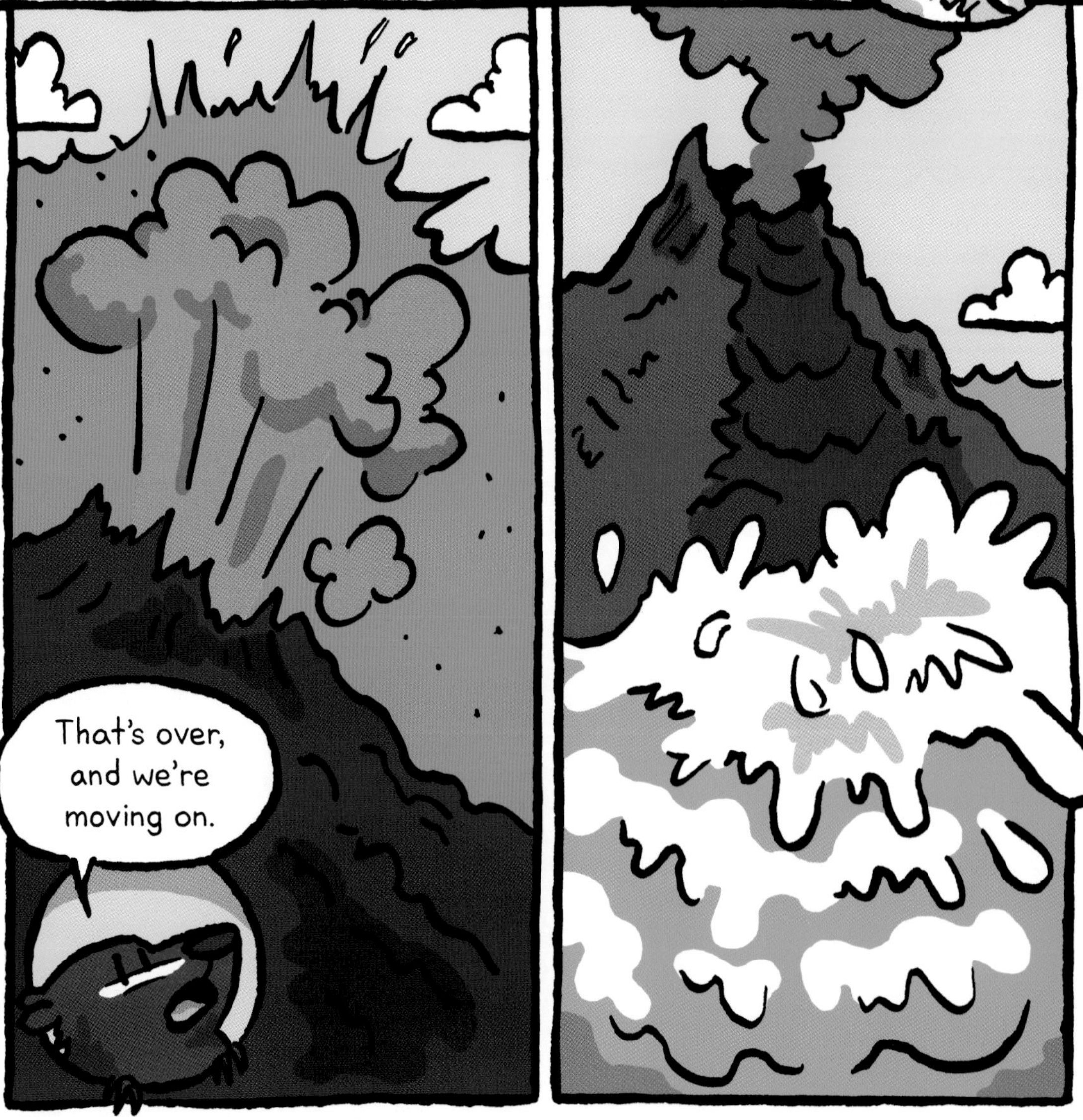
That's over, and we're moving on.

Meteotsunamis

Tsunamis caused by the weather. Fast-moving, high-pressure storms may push enough water to cause surges of waves.

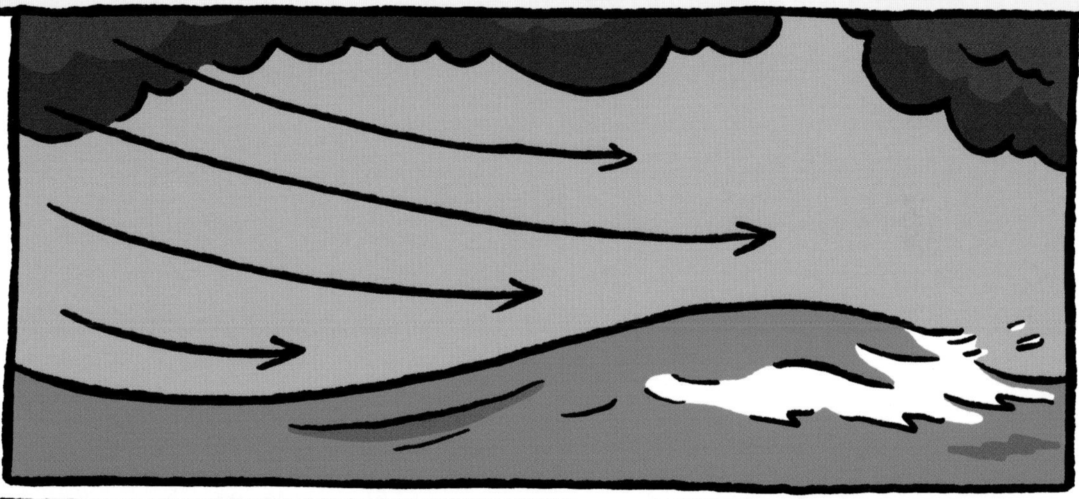

Called a *seiche* (sounds like saysh) when in lakes, ponds, and reservoirs, this rare event can cause a standing set of waves.

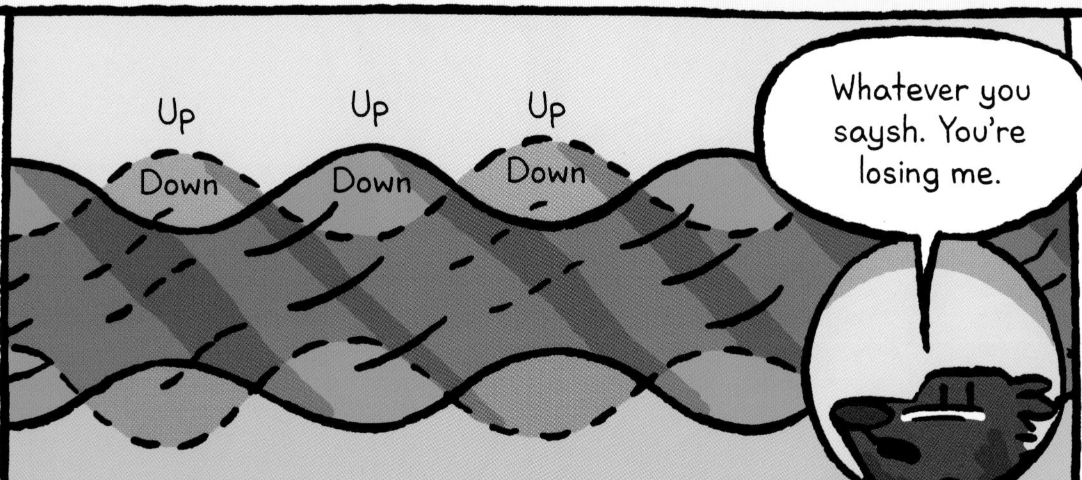
Up
Down
Up
Down
Up
Down
Whatever you saysh. You're losing me.

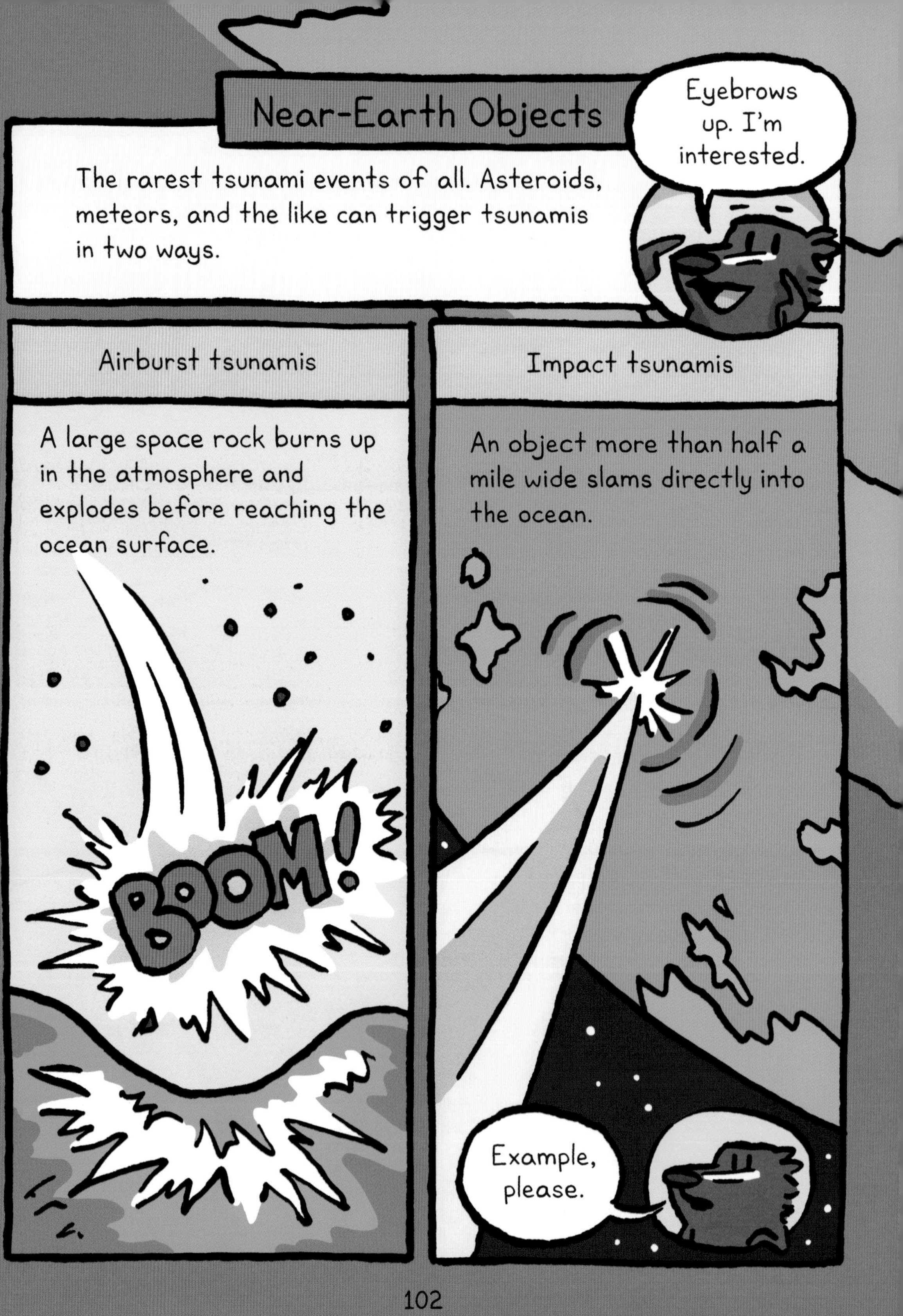
Near-Earth Objects
The rarest tsunami events of all. Asteroids, meteors, and the like can trigger tsunamis in two ways.
Eyebrows up. I'm interested.
Airburst tsunamis
A large space rock burns up in the atmosphere and explodes before reaching the ocean surface.
BOOM!
Impact tsunamis
An object more than half a mile wide slams directly into the ocean.
Example, please.

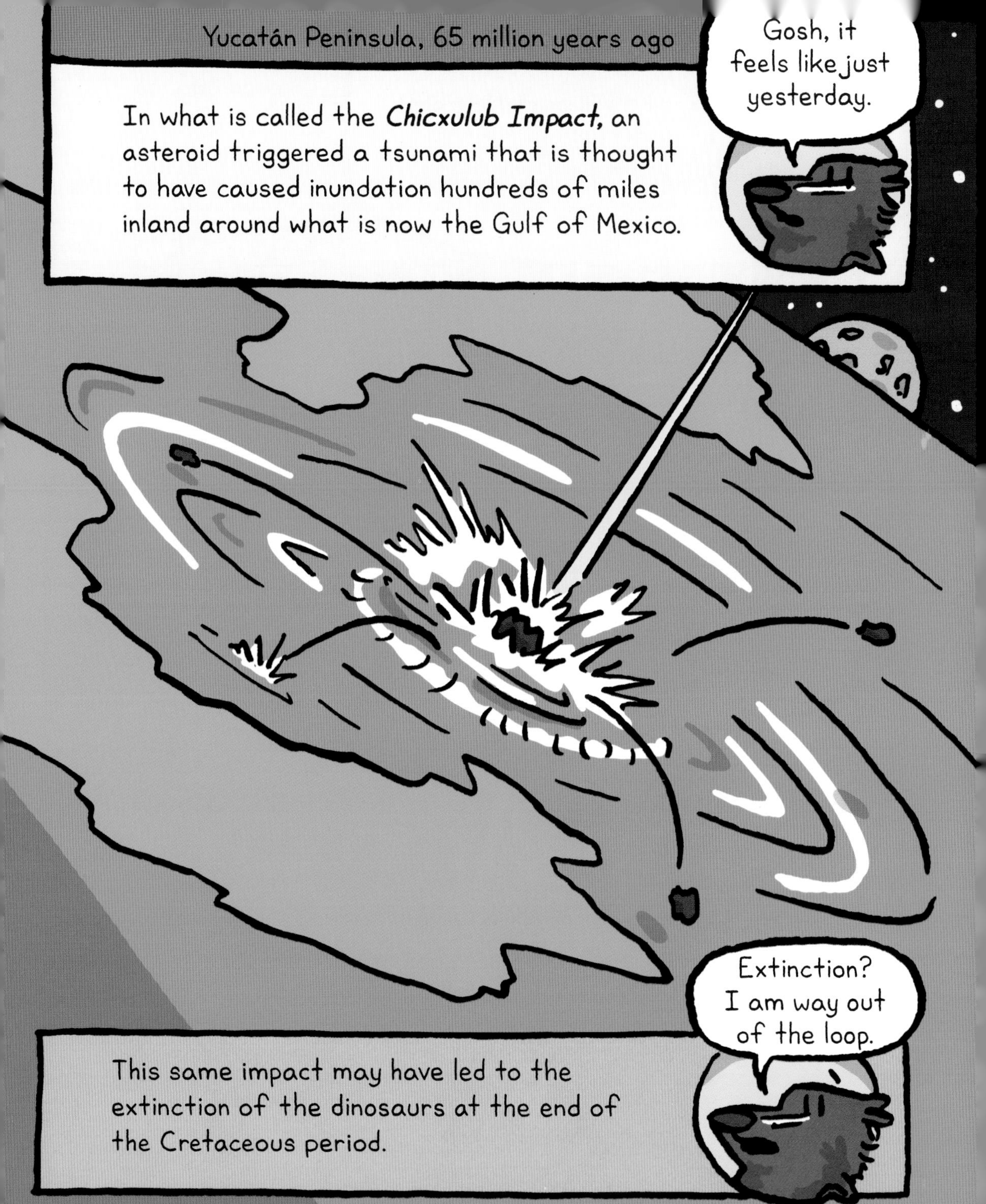
Yucatán Peninsula, 65 million years ago
In what is called the ***Chicxulub Impact,*** an asteroid triggered a tsunami that is thought to have caused inundation hundreds of miles inland around what is now the Gulf of Mexico.
Gosh, it feels like just yesterday.
This same impact may have led to the extinction of the dinosaurs at the end of the Cretaceous period.
Extinction? I am way out of the loop.

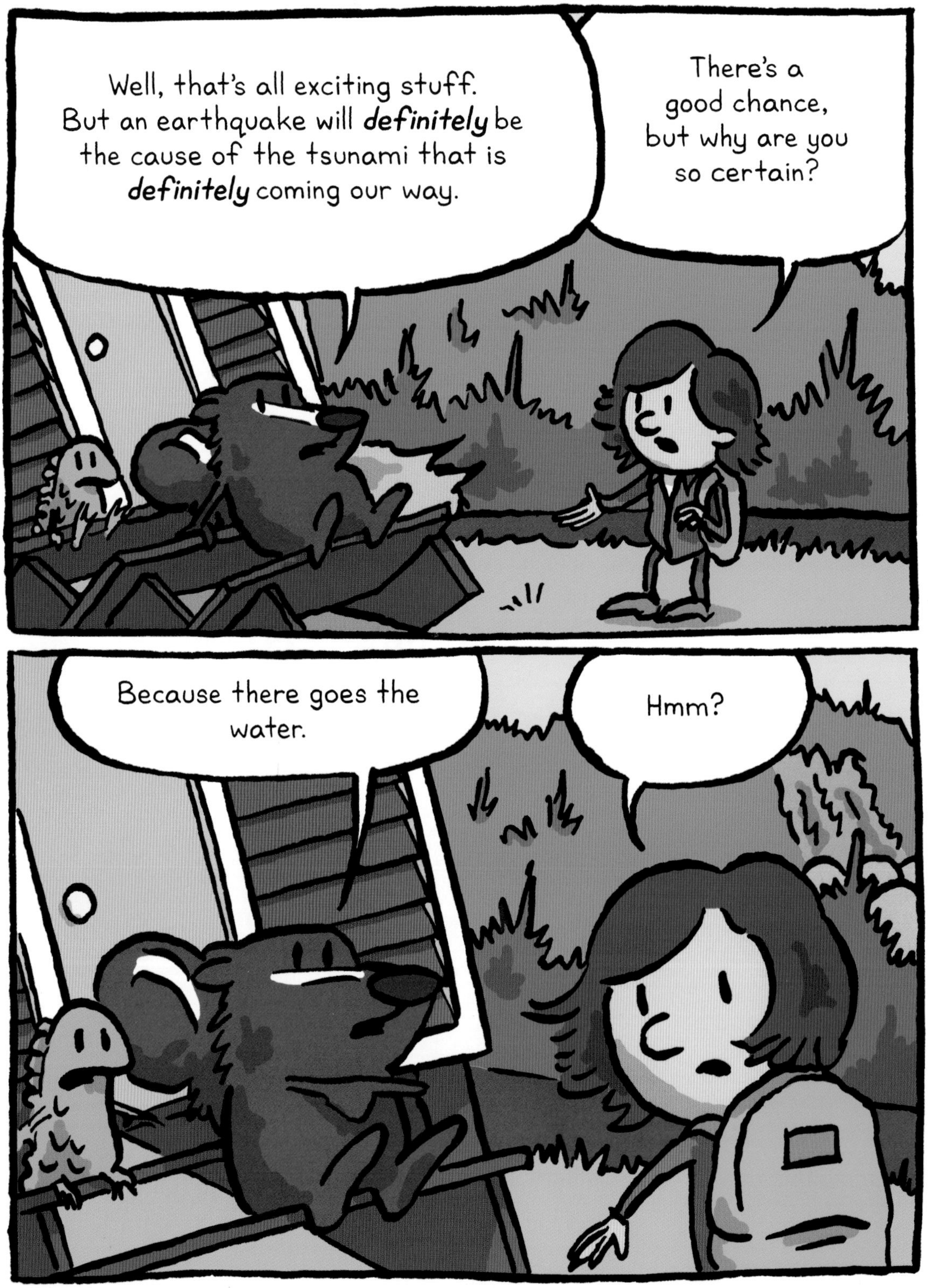
Well, that's all exciting stuff. But an earthquake will **definitely** be the cause of the tsunami that is **definitely** coming our way.
There's a good chance, but why are you so certain?
Because there goes the water.
Hmm?

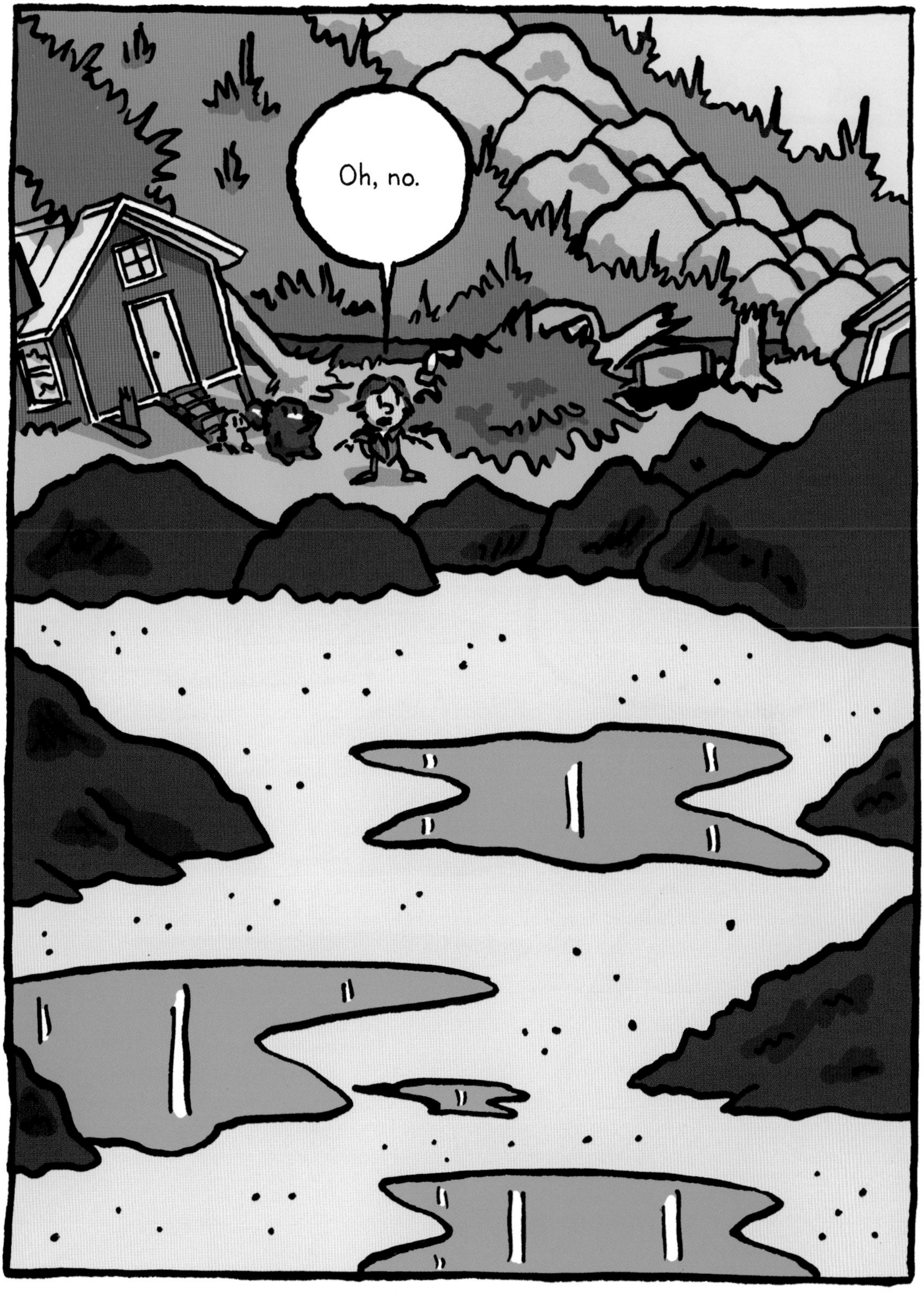
Oh, no.

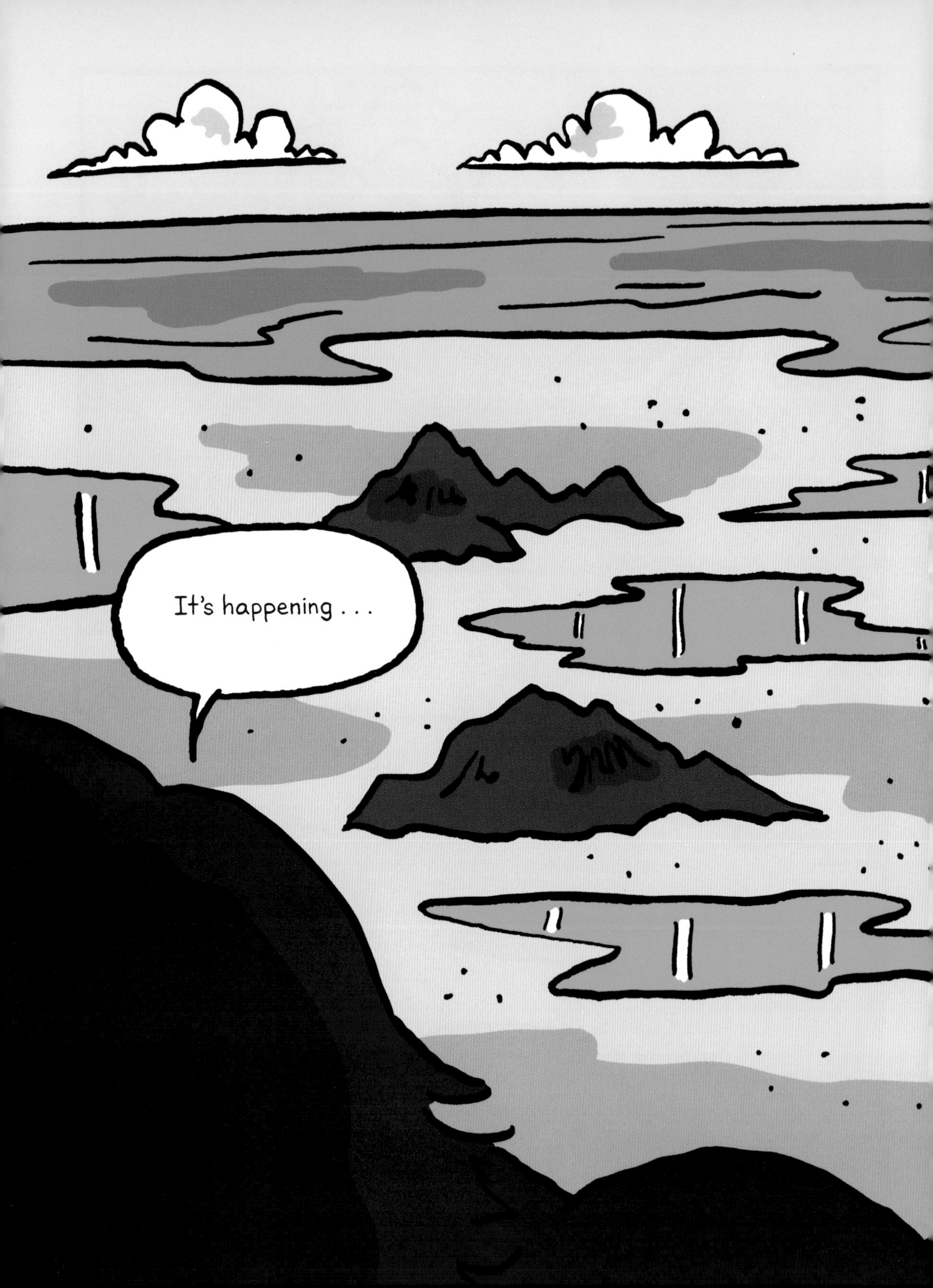
It's happening . . .

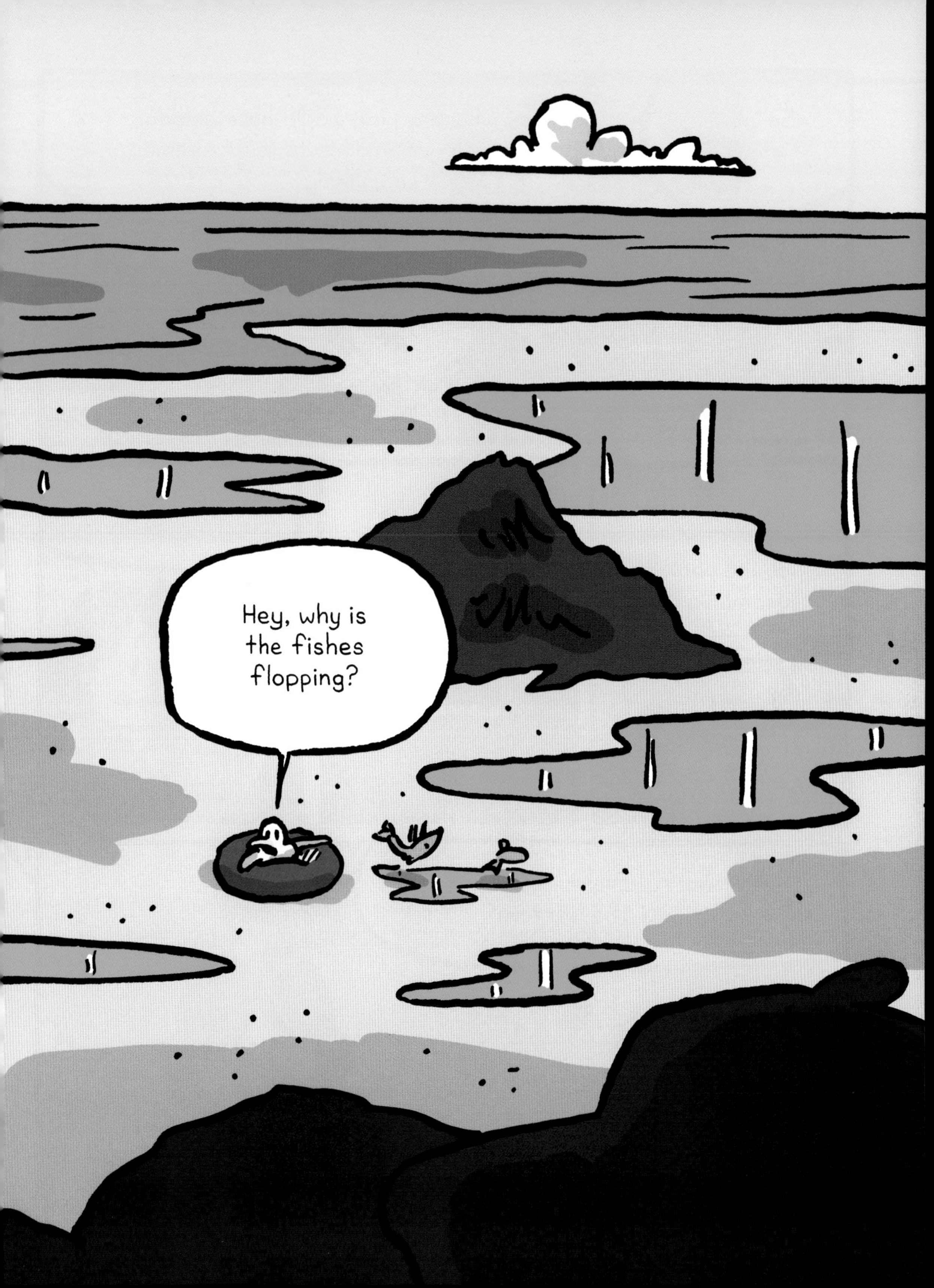
Hey, why is the fishes flopping?

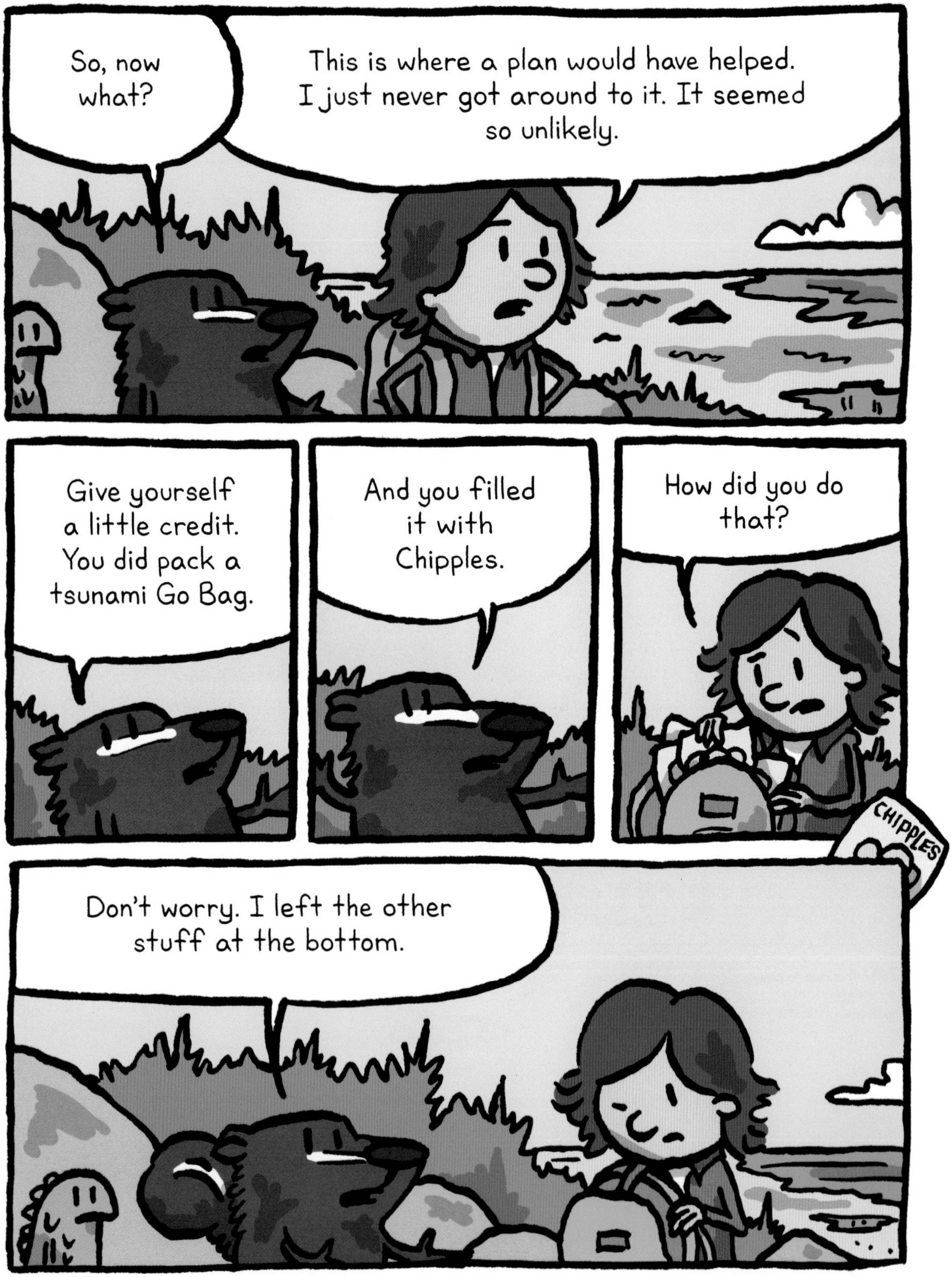
So, now what?
This is where a plan would have helped. I just never got around to it. It seemed so unlikely.
Give yourself a little credit. You did pack a tsunami Go Bag.
And you filled it with Chipples.
How did you do that?
CHIPPLES
Don't worry. I left the other stuff at the bottom.

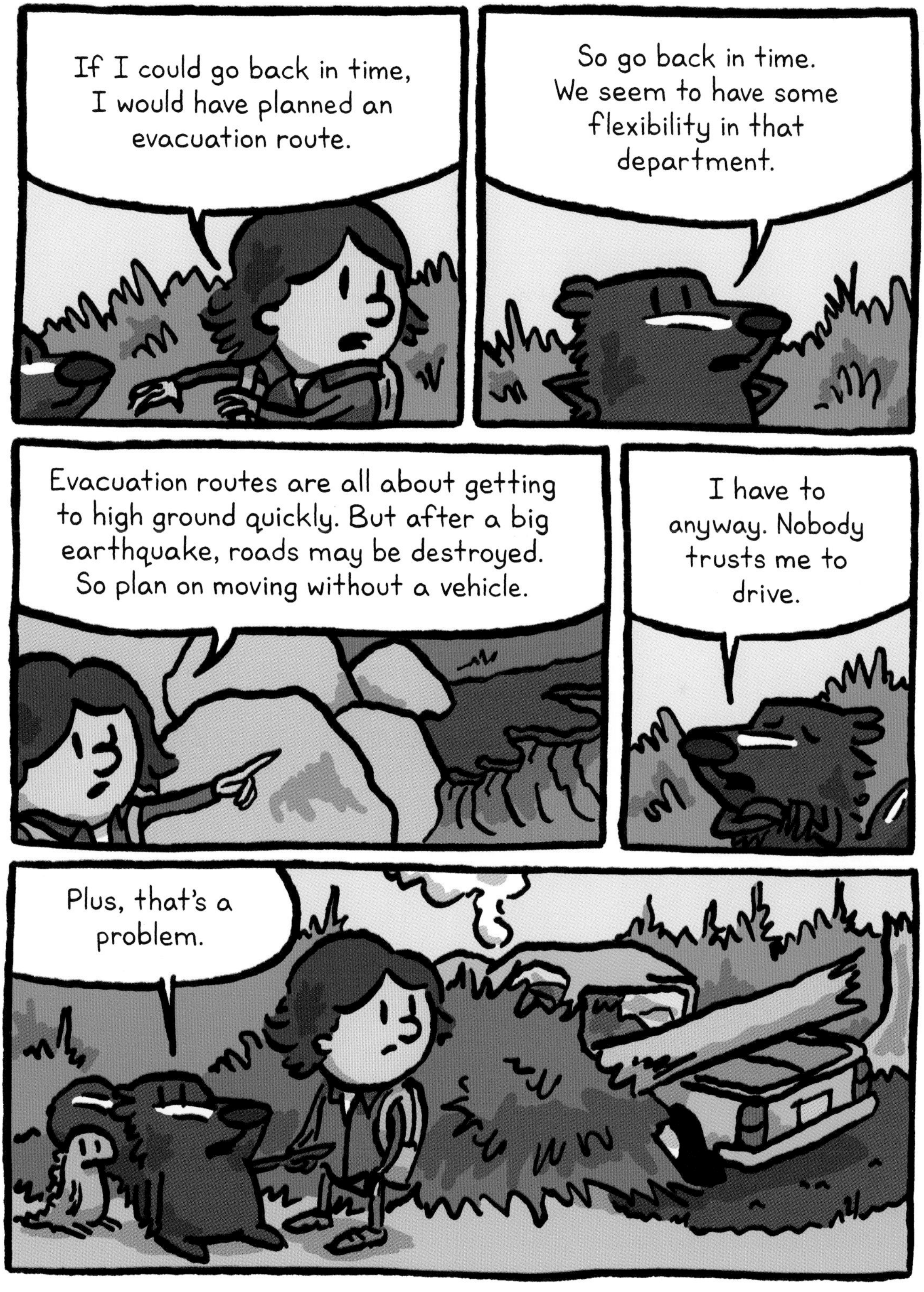
If I could go back in time, I would have planned an evacuation route.
So go back in time. We seem to have some flexibility in that department.
Evacuation routes are all about getting to high ground quickly. But after a big earthquake, roads may be destroyed. So plan on moving without a vehicle.
I have to anyway. Nobody trusts me to drive.
Plus, that's a problem.

Many communities within tsunami hazard zones have maps available to help plan your evacuation.*
Take the time to find your home or school as well as the fastest route to safety.

What about a nice place to get snacks?

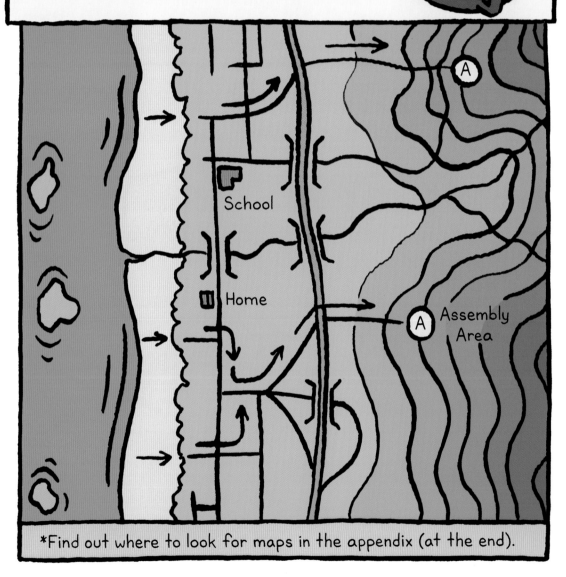

School

Home

A

A Assembly Area

*Find out where to look for maps in the appendix (at the end).

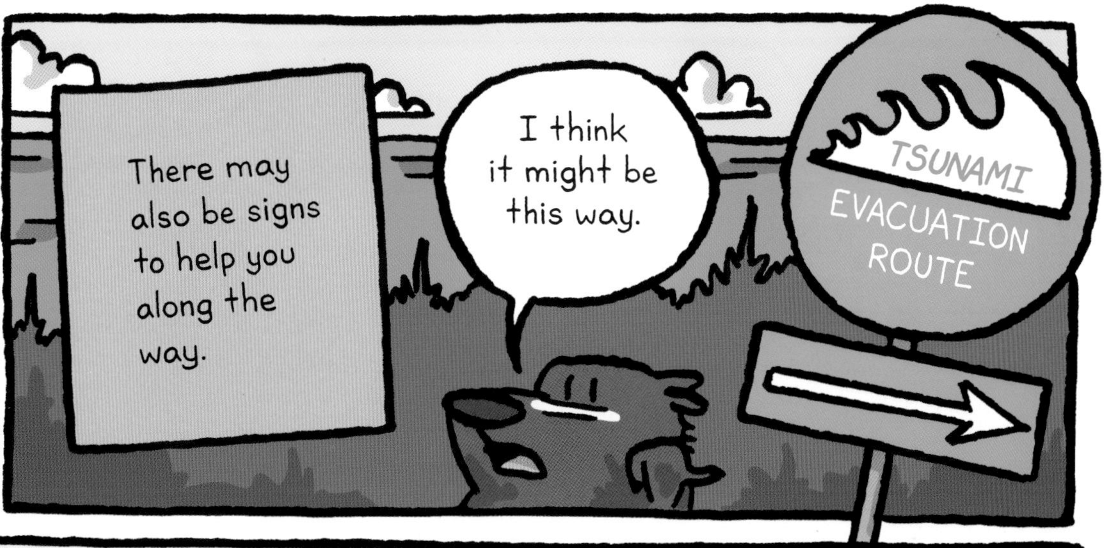
There may also be signs to help you along the way.
I think it might be this way.
TSUNAMI
EVACUATION ROUTE

Once you've figured out a route, it's helpful to practice walking it. Day and night. Rain or shine. Because earthquakes and tsunamis don't care about the time or the weather.

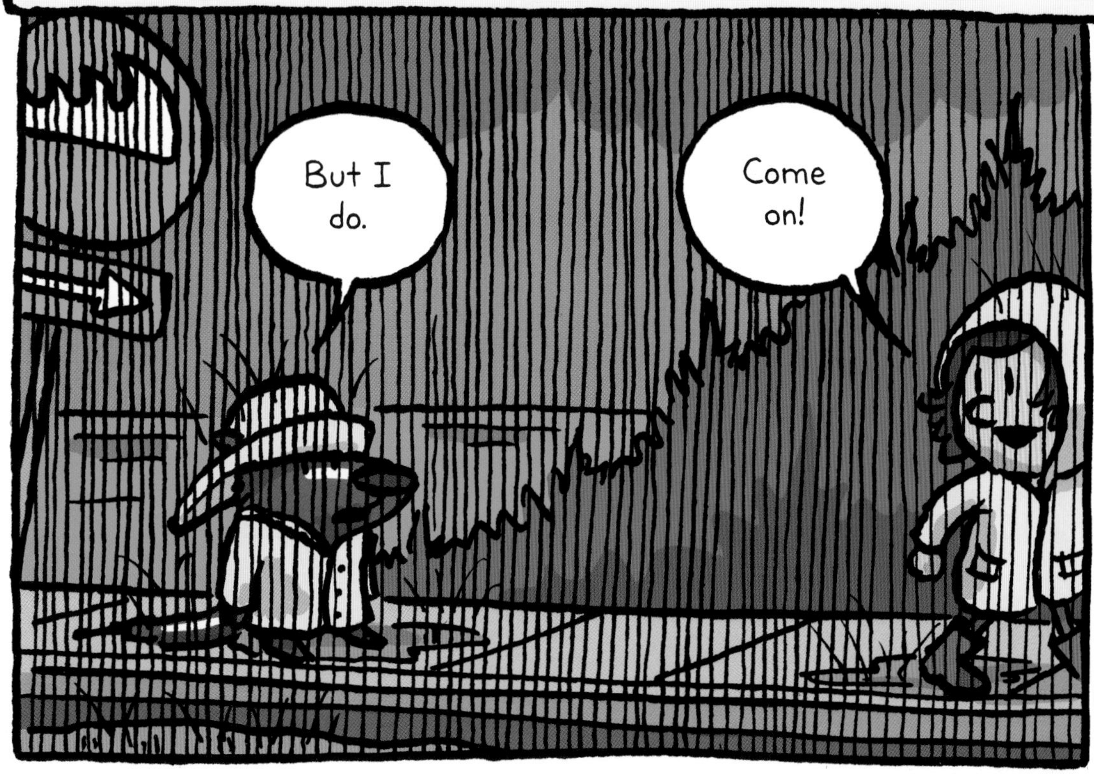
But I do.
Come on!

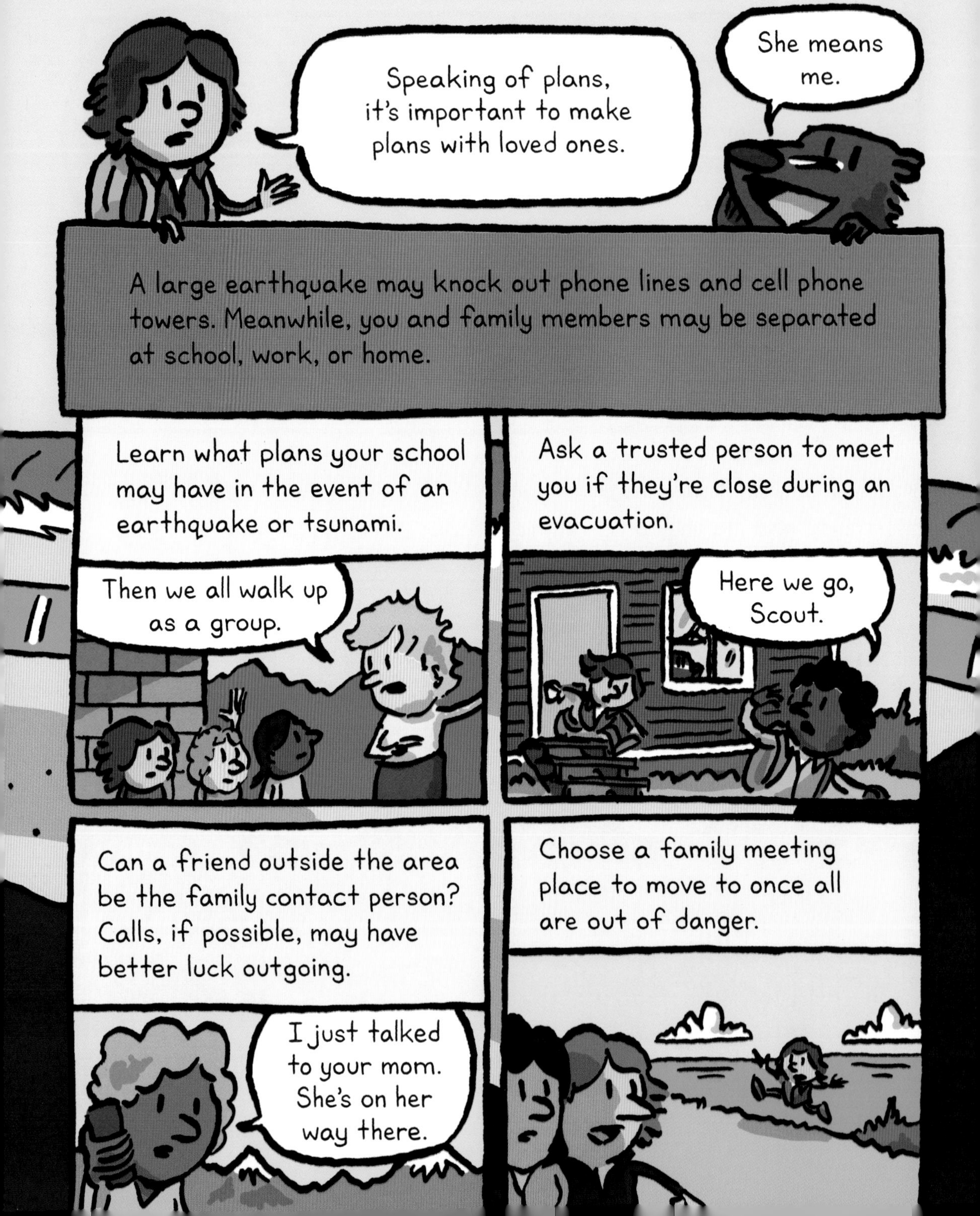
Speaking of plans, it's important to make plans with loved ones.
She means me.
A large earthquake may knock out phone lines and cell phone towers. Meanwhile, you and family members may be separated at school, work, or home.
Learn what plans your school may have in the event of an earthquake or tsunami.
Then we all walk up as a group.
Ask a trusted person to meet you if they're close during an evacuation.
Here we go, Scout.
Can a friend outside the area be the family contact person? Calls, if possible, may have better luck outgoing.
I just talked to your mom. She's on her way there.
Choose a family meeting place to move to once all are out of danger.

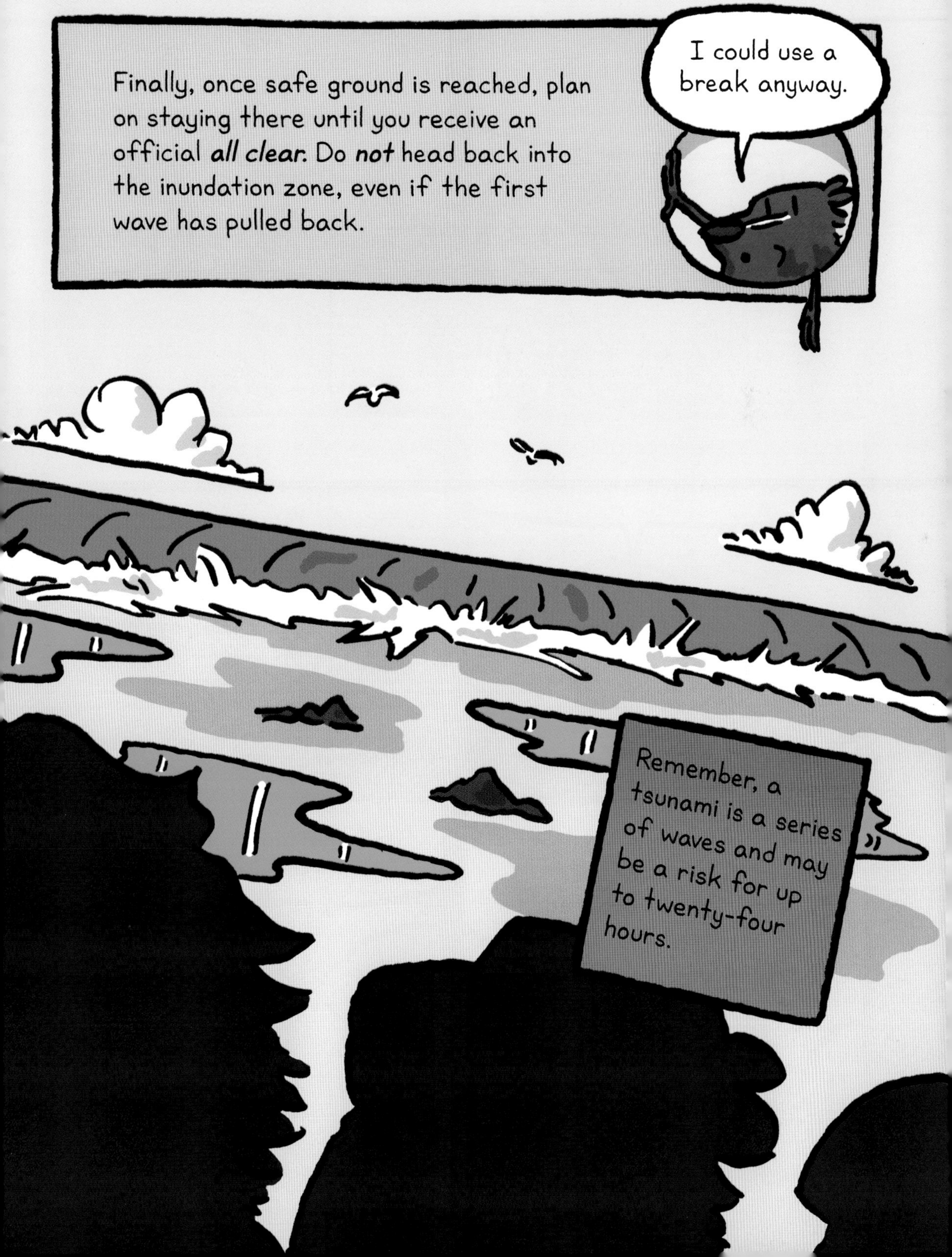
Finally, once safe ground is reached, plan on staying there until you receive an official ***all clear.*** Do ***not*** head back into the inundation zone, even if the first wave has pulled back.
I could use a break anyway.
Remember, a tsunami is a series of waves and may be a risk for up to twenty-four hours.

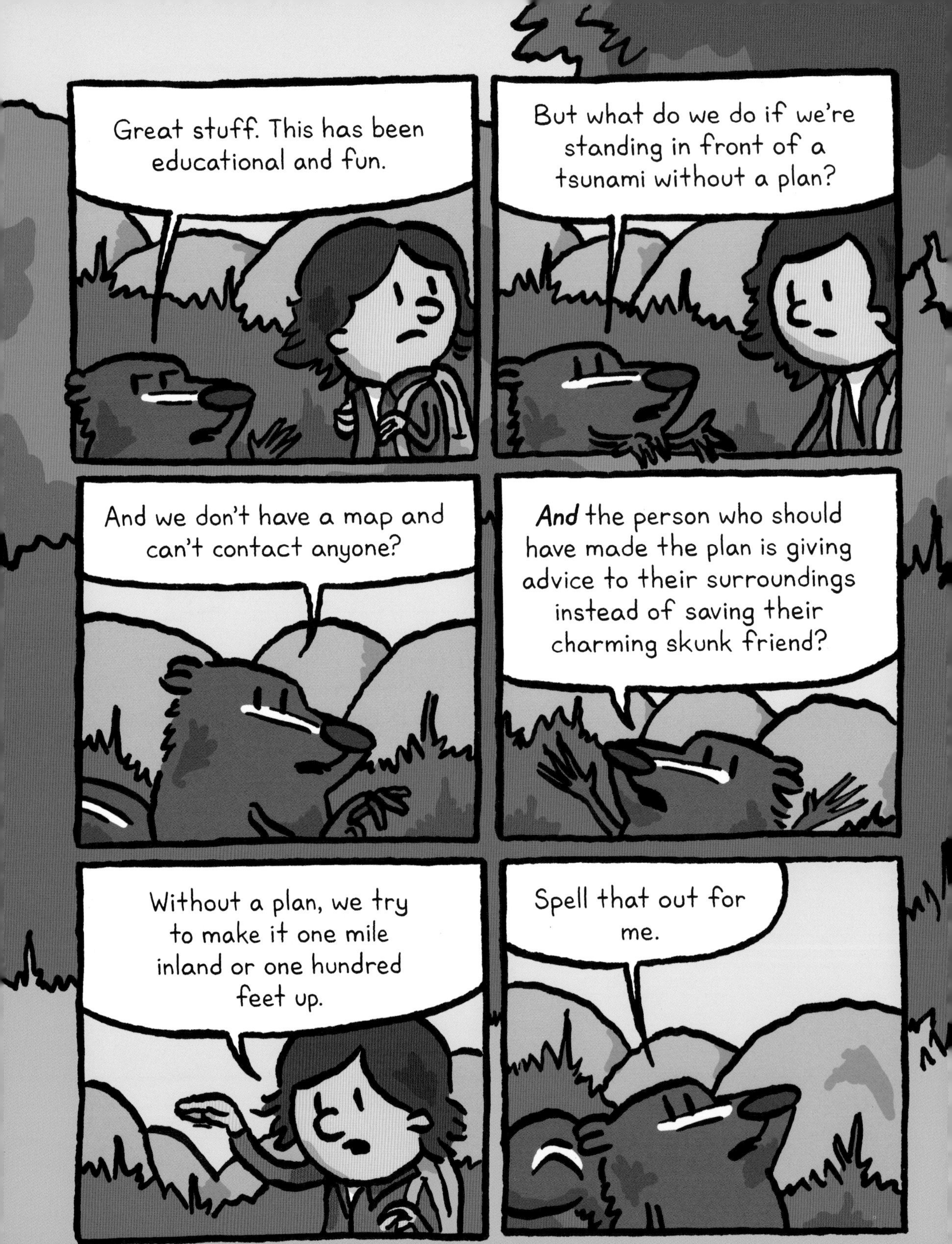
Great stuff. This has been educational and fun.
But what do we do if we're standing in front of a tsunami without a plan?
And we don't have a map and can't contact anyone?
And the person who should have made the plan is giving advice to their surroundings instead of saving their charming skunk friend?
Without a plan, we try to make it one mile inland or one hundred feet up.
Spell that out for me.

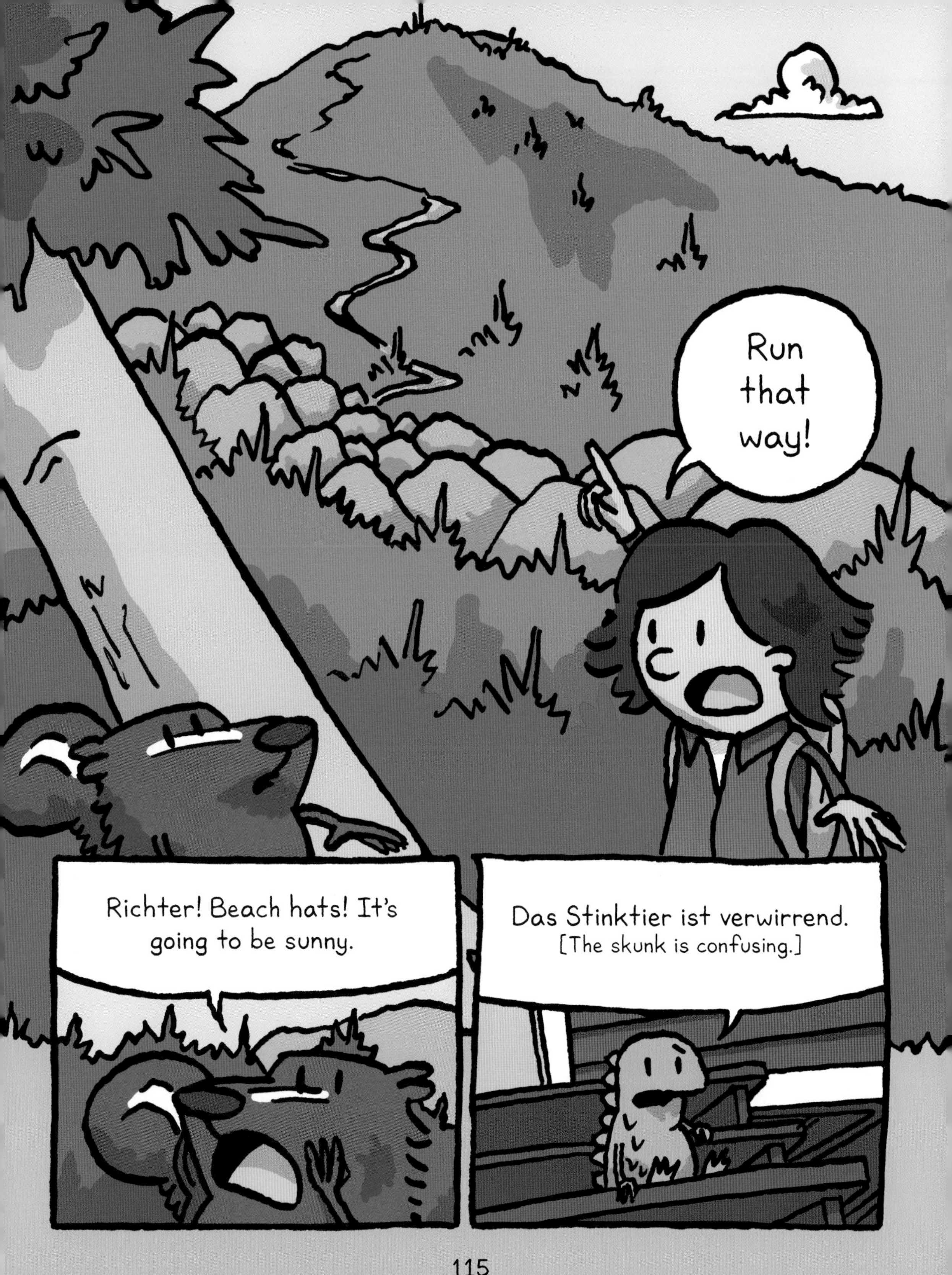
Run that way!
Richter! Beach hats! It's going to be sunny.
Das Stinktier ist verwirrend.
[The skunk is confusing.]

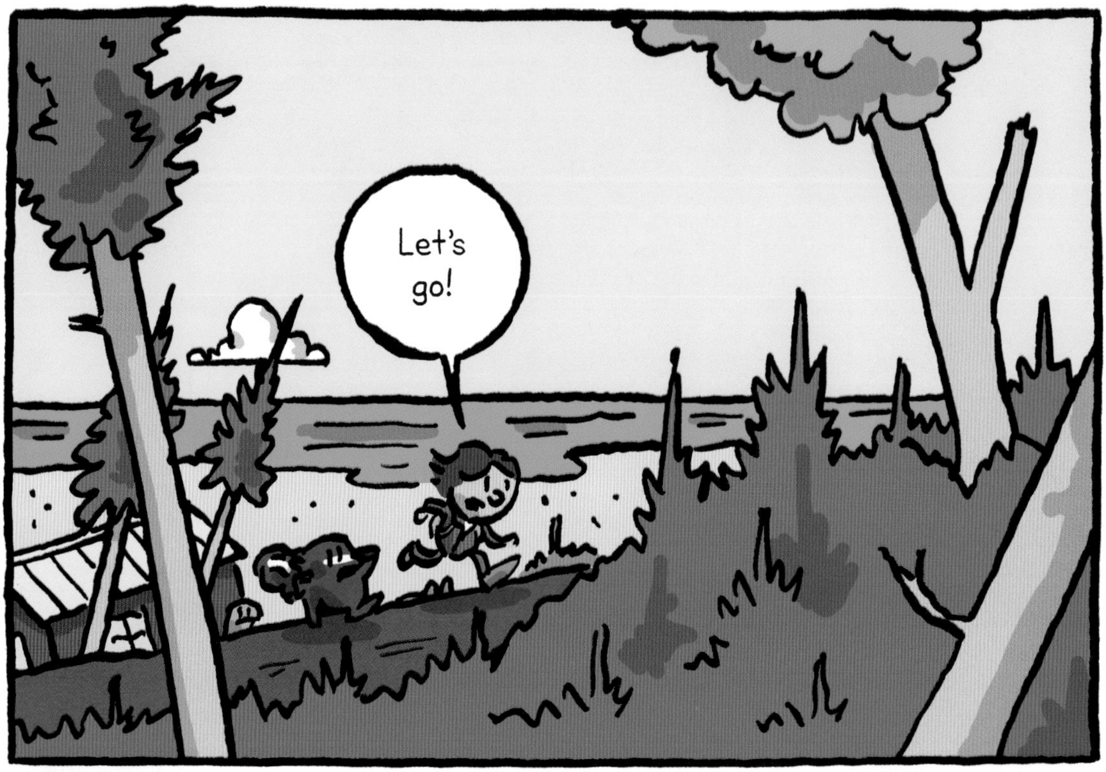
Let's go!

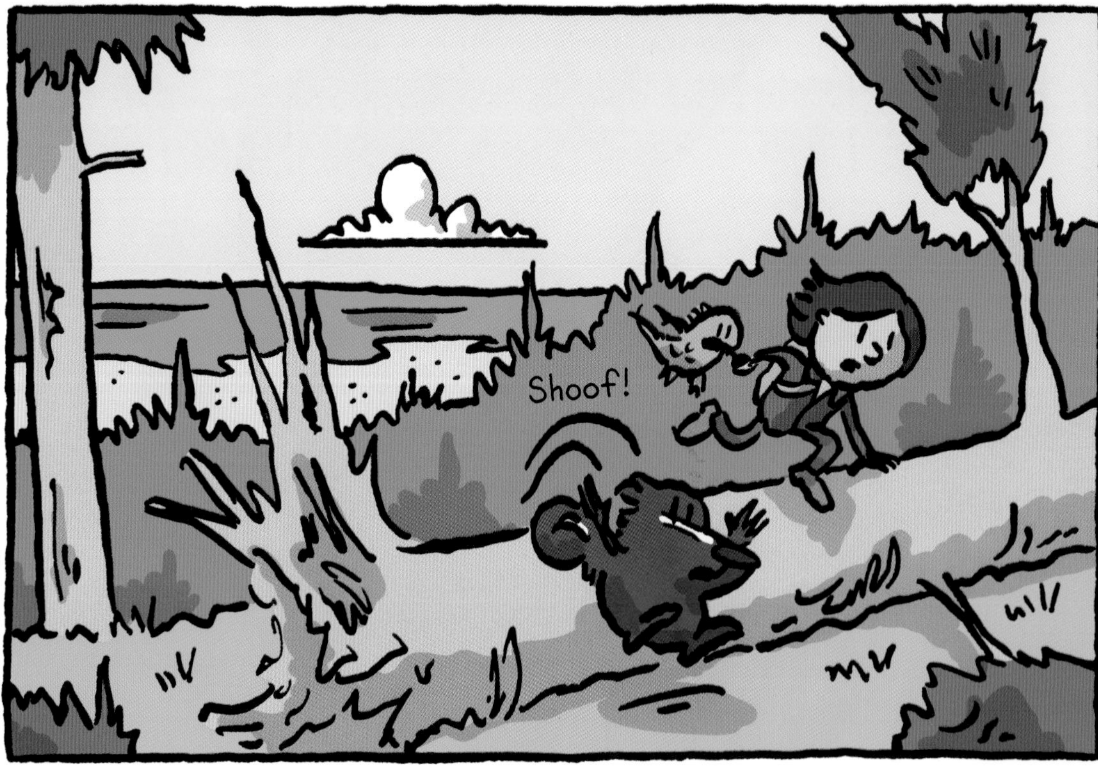
Shoof!

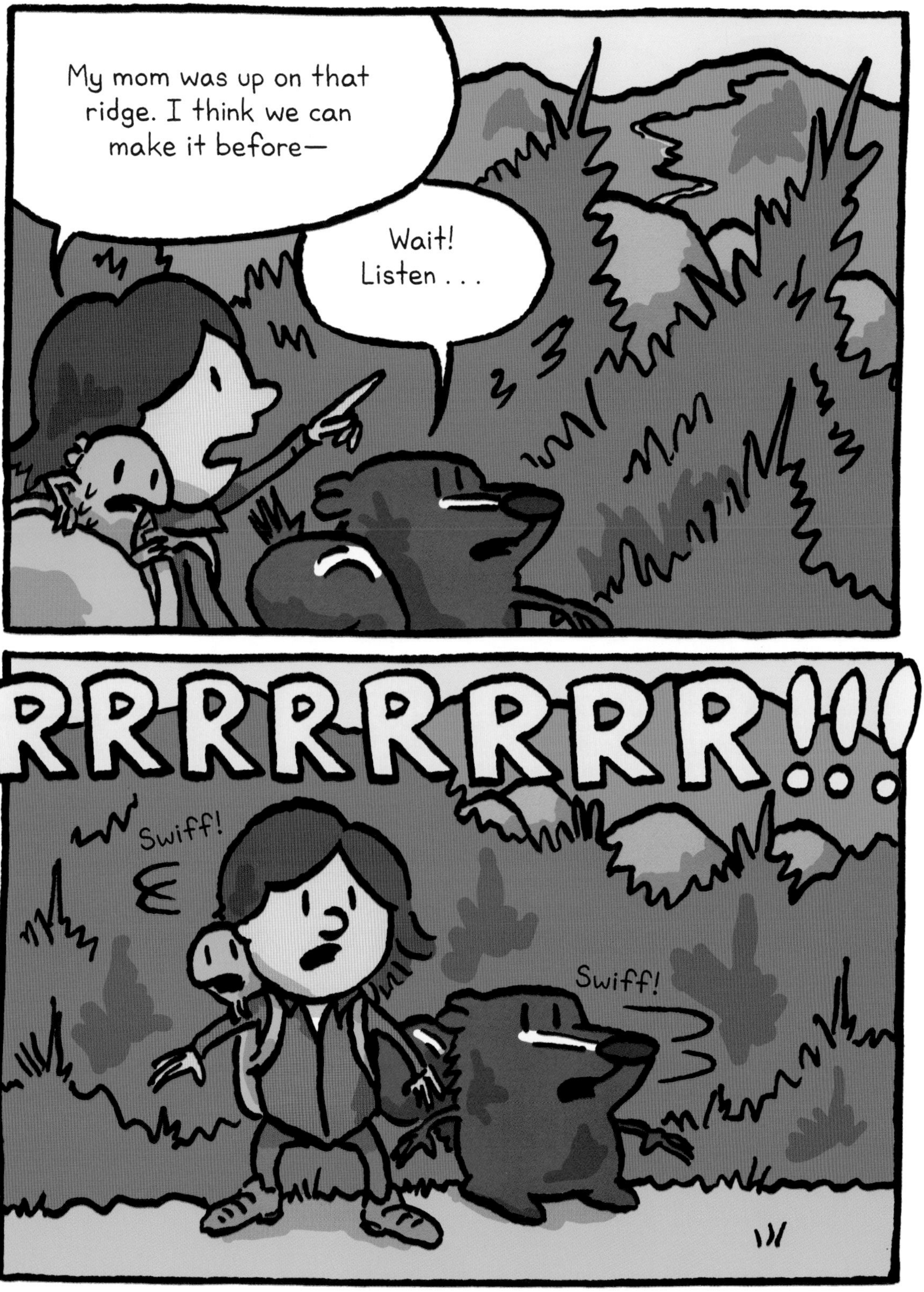
My mom was up on that ridge. I think we can make it before—
Wait! Listen . . .
RRRRRRRR!!!
Swiff!
Swiff!

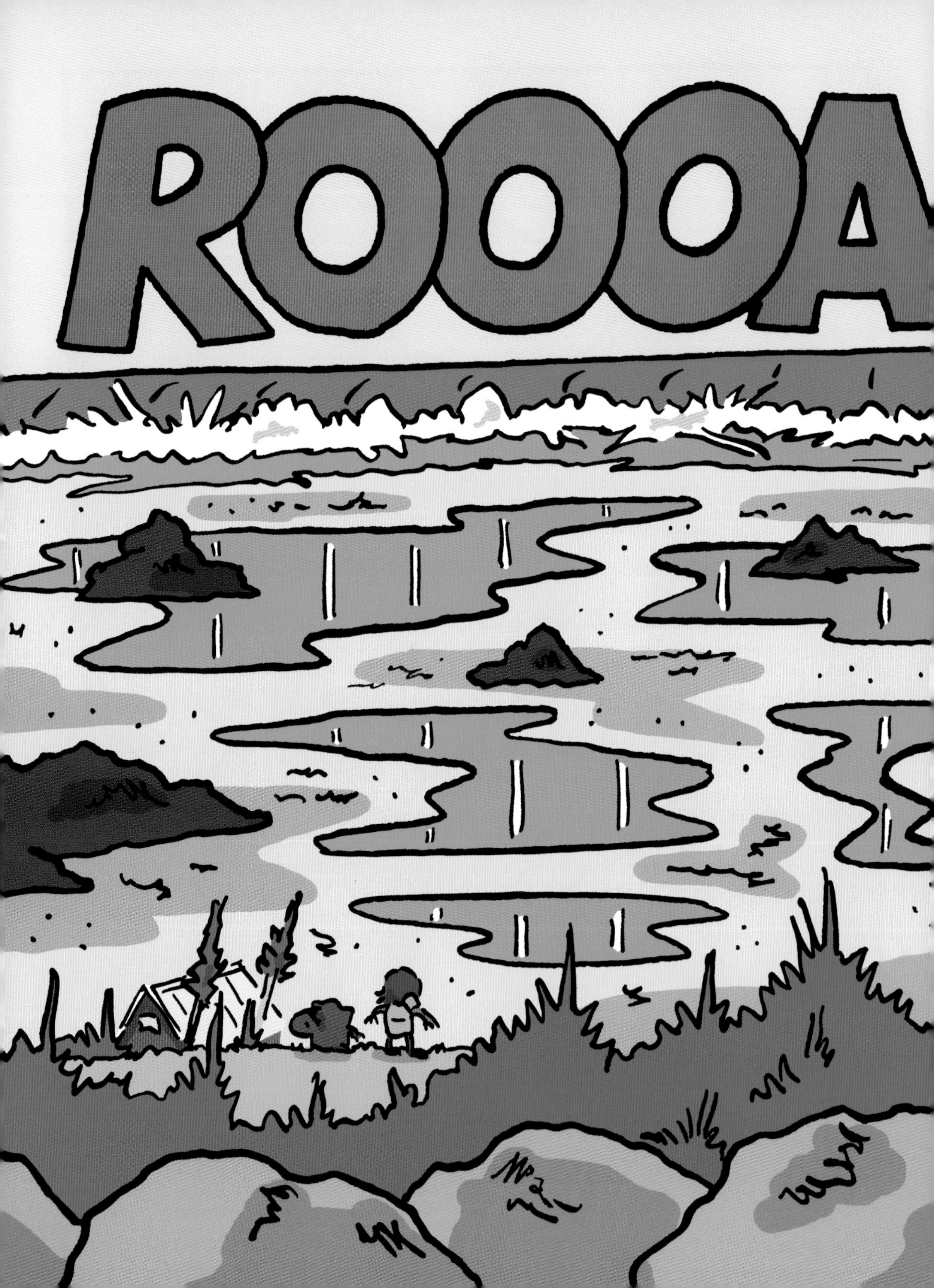
ROOOA

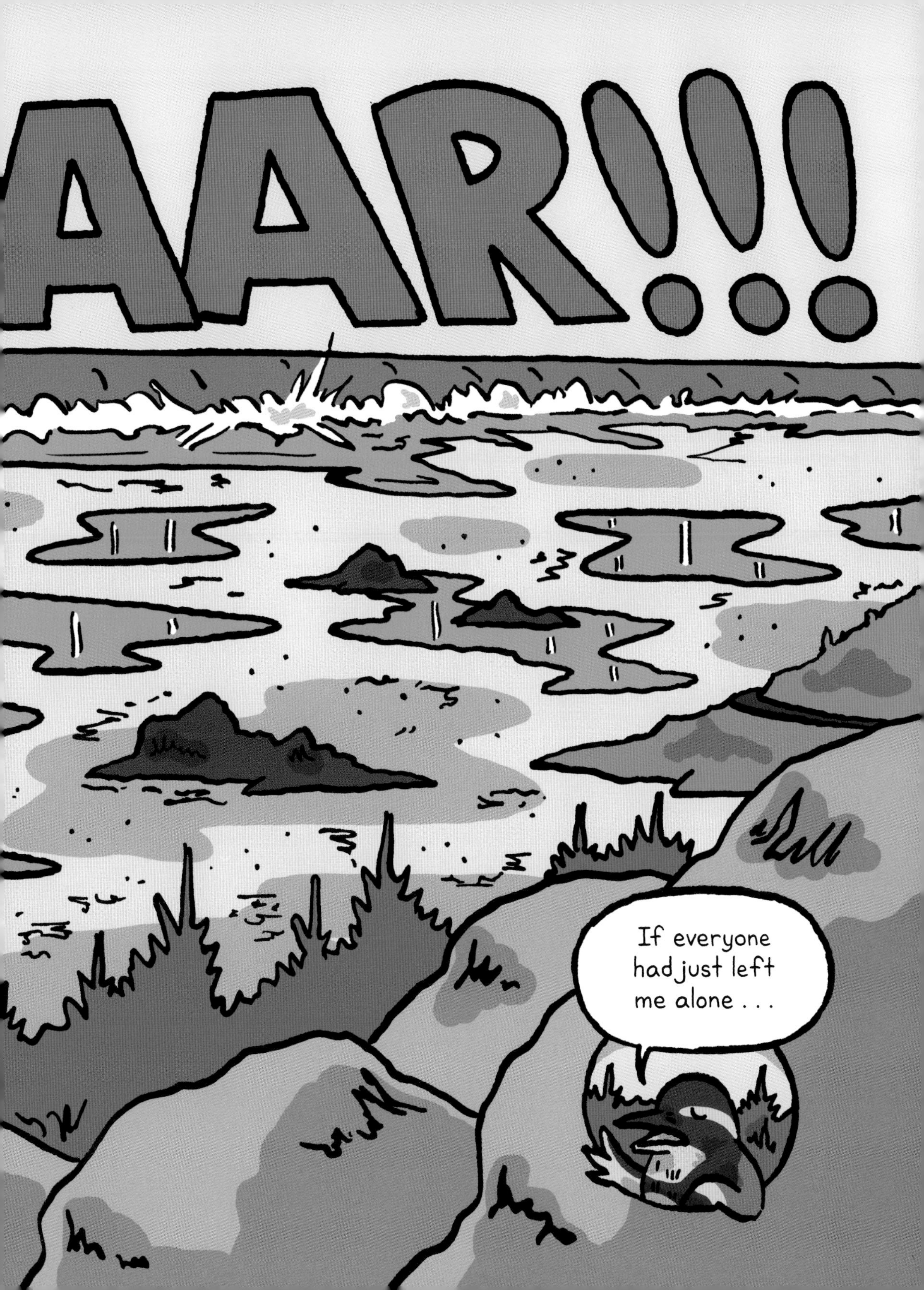
AAR!!!
If everyone had just left me alone . . .

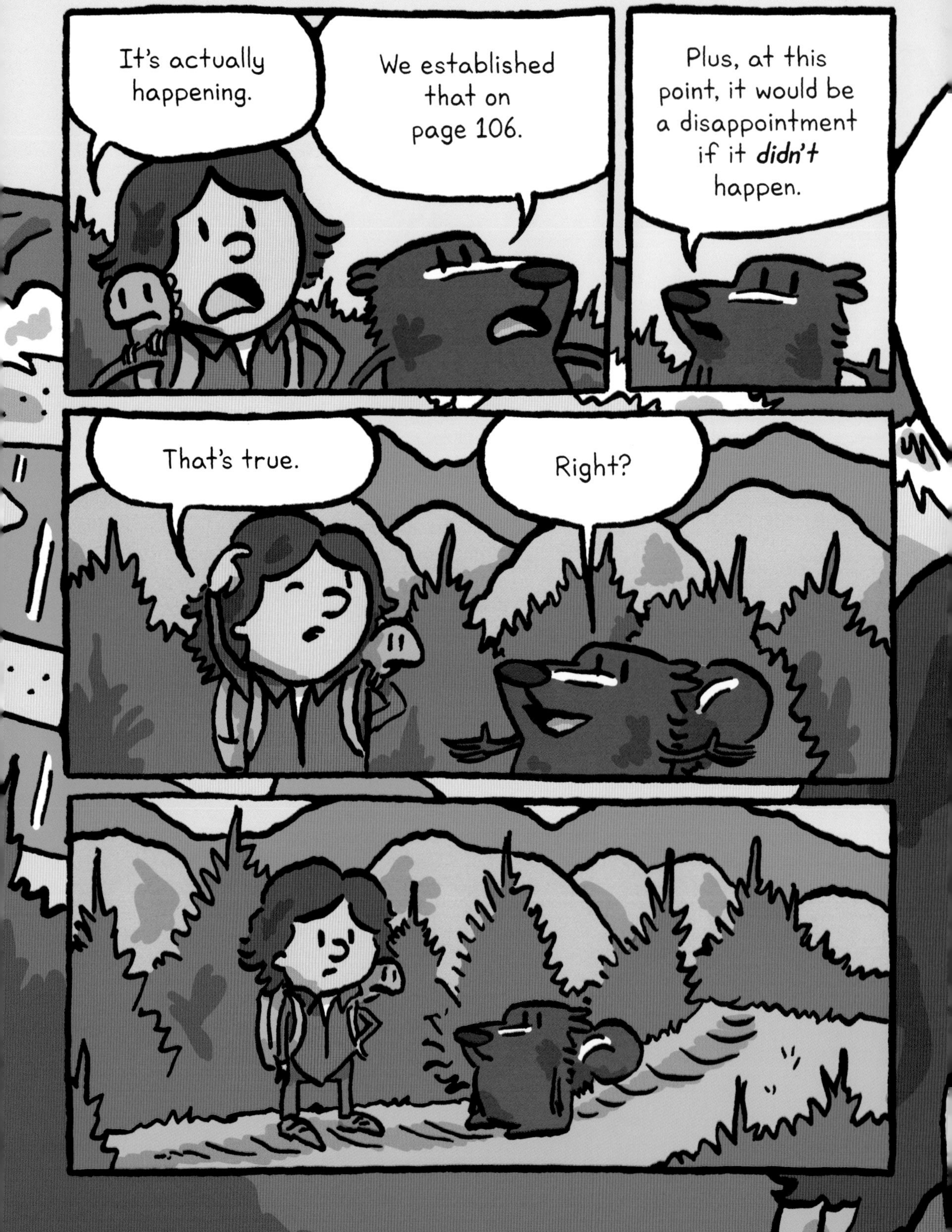

It's actually happening.
We established that on page 106.
Plus, at this point, it would be a disappointment if it ***didn't*** happen.
That's true.
Right?

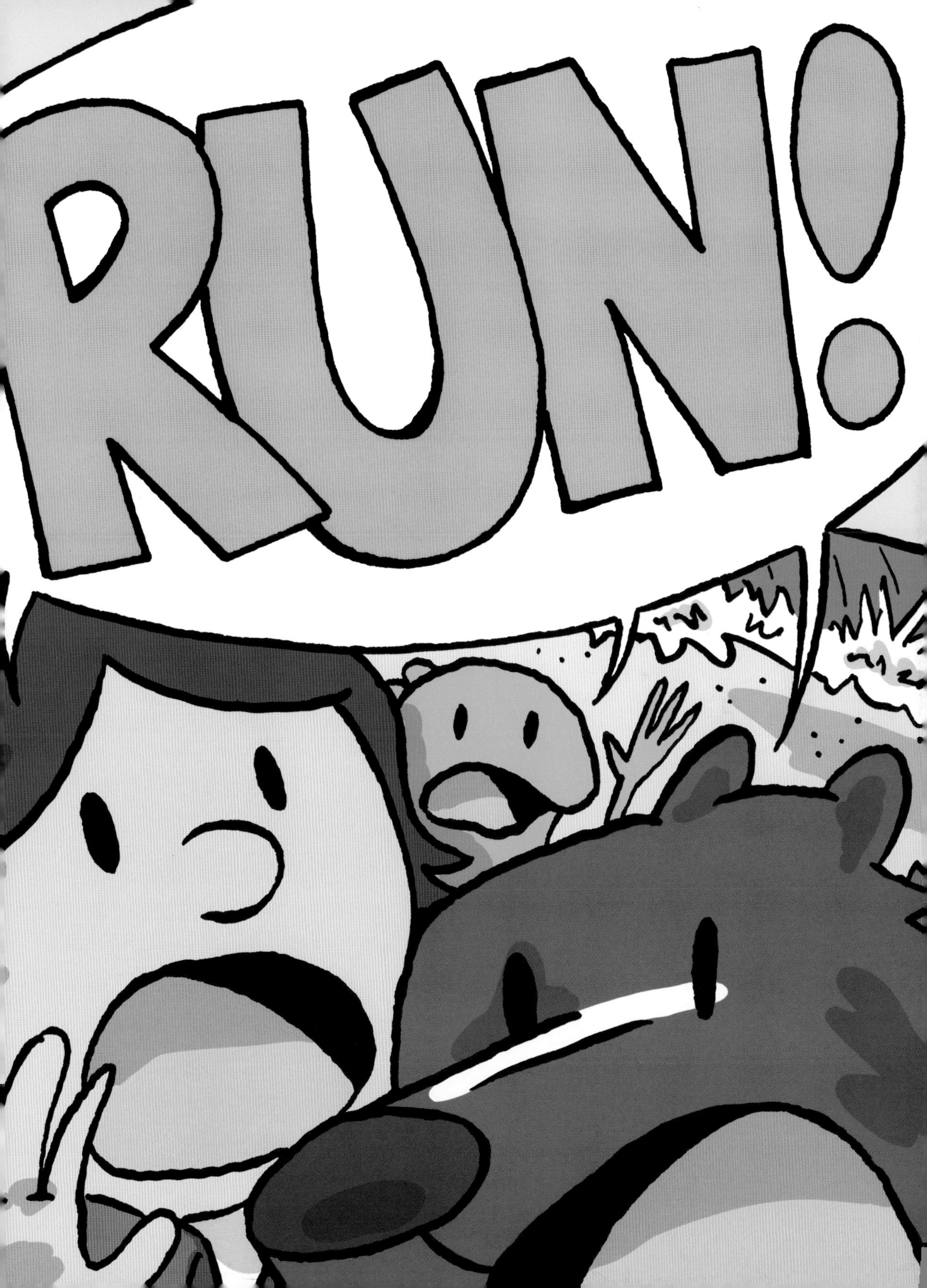
RUN!

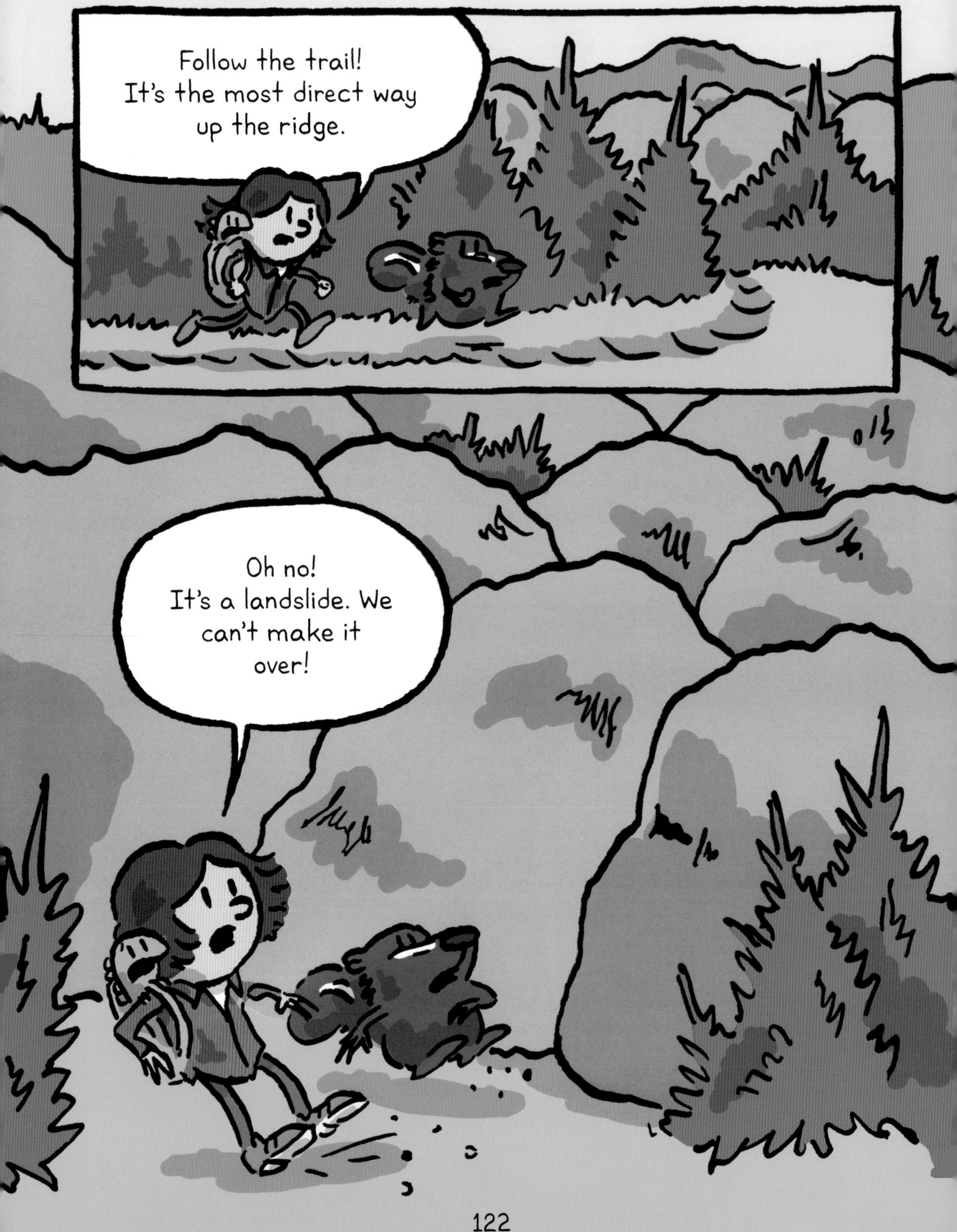
Follow the trail! It's the most direct way up the ridge.
Oh no! It's a landslide. We can't make it over!

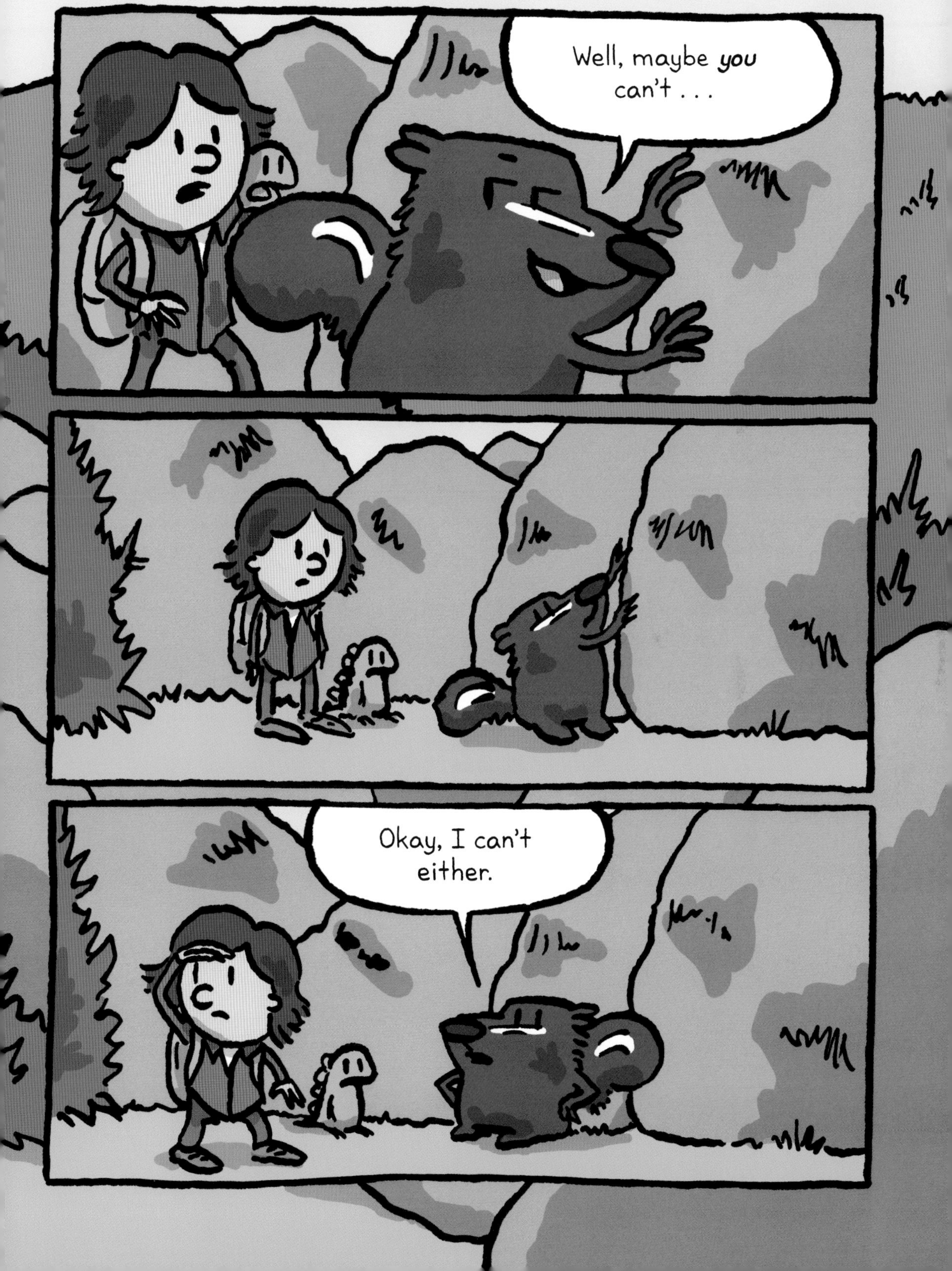
Well, maybe *you* can't . . .
Okay, I can't either.

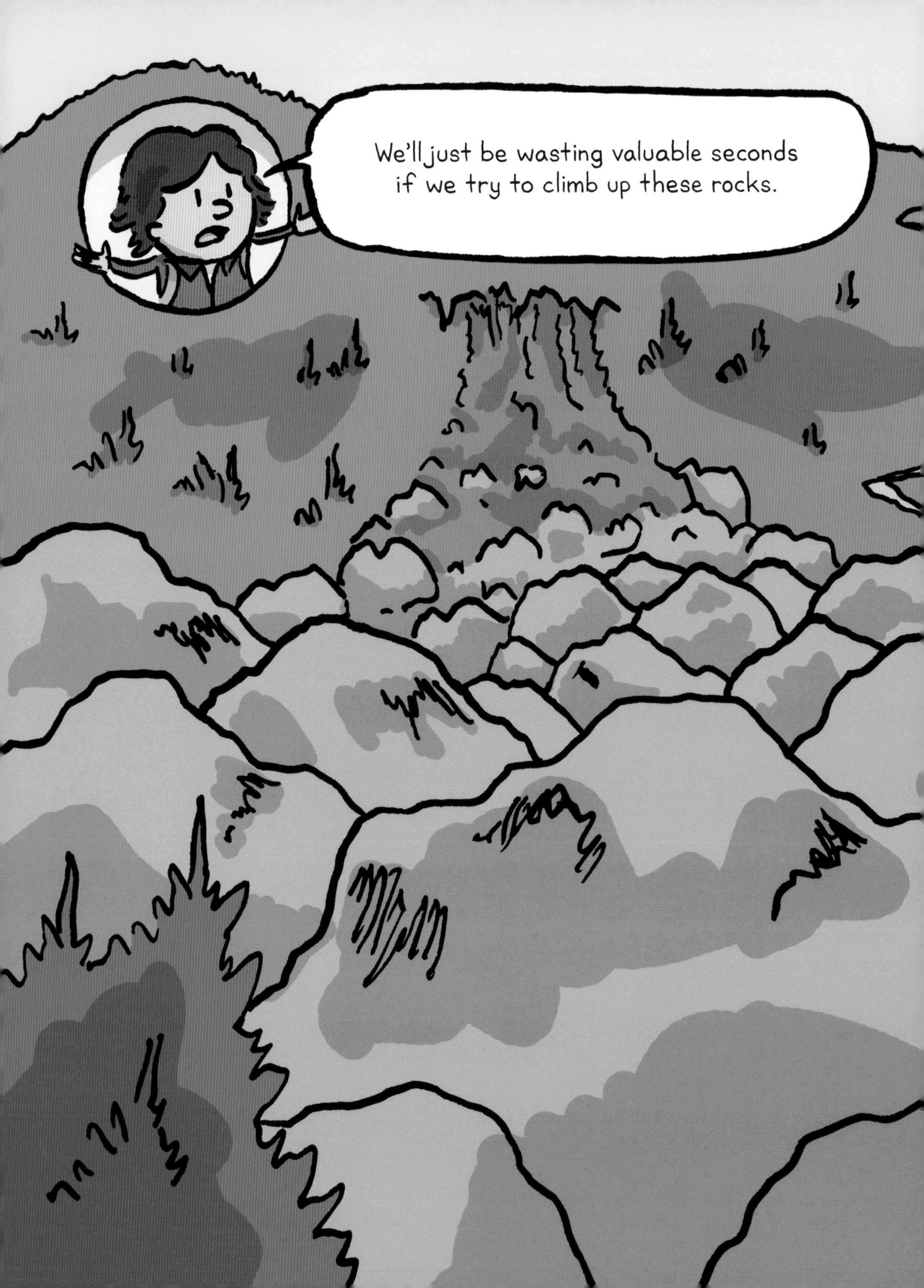
We'll just be wasting valuable seconds if we try to climb up these rocks.

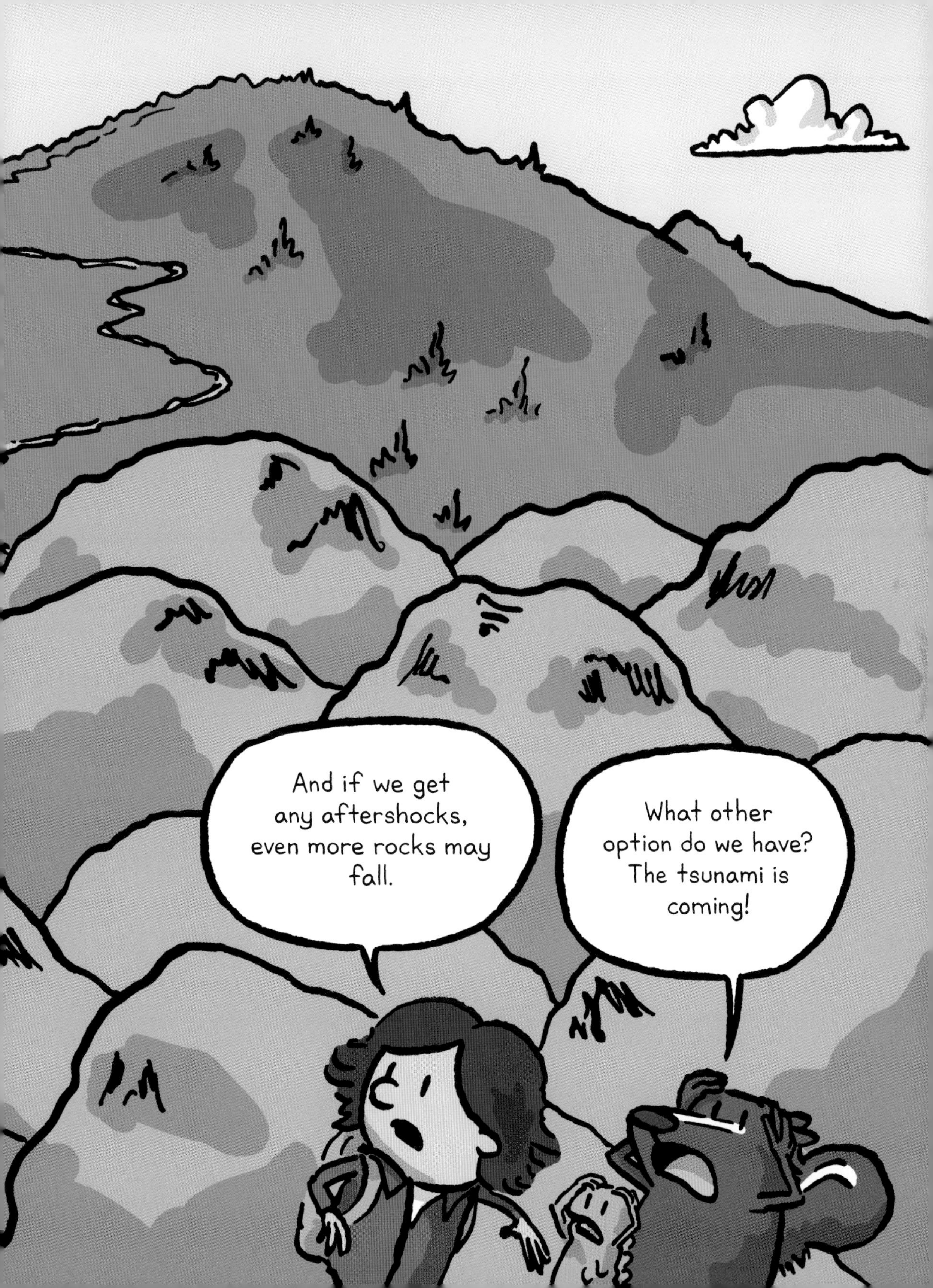
And if we get any aftershocks, even more rocks may fall.
What other option do we have? The tsunami is coming!

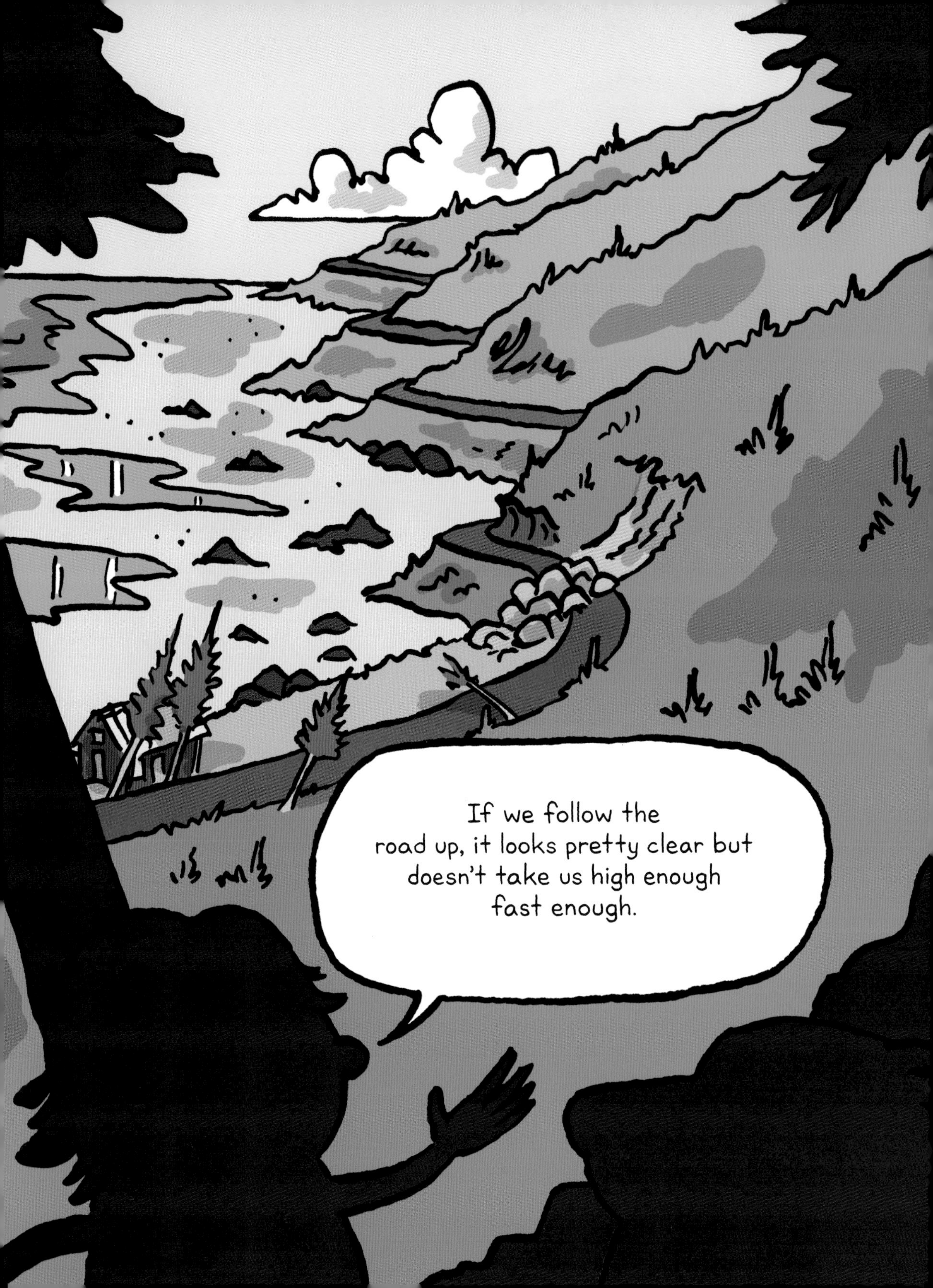
If we follow the road up, it looks pretty clear but doesn't take us high enough fast enough.

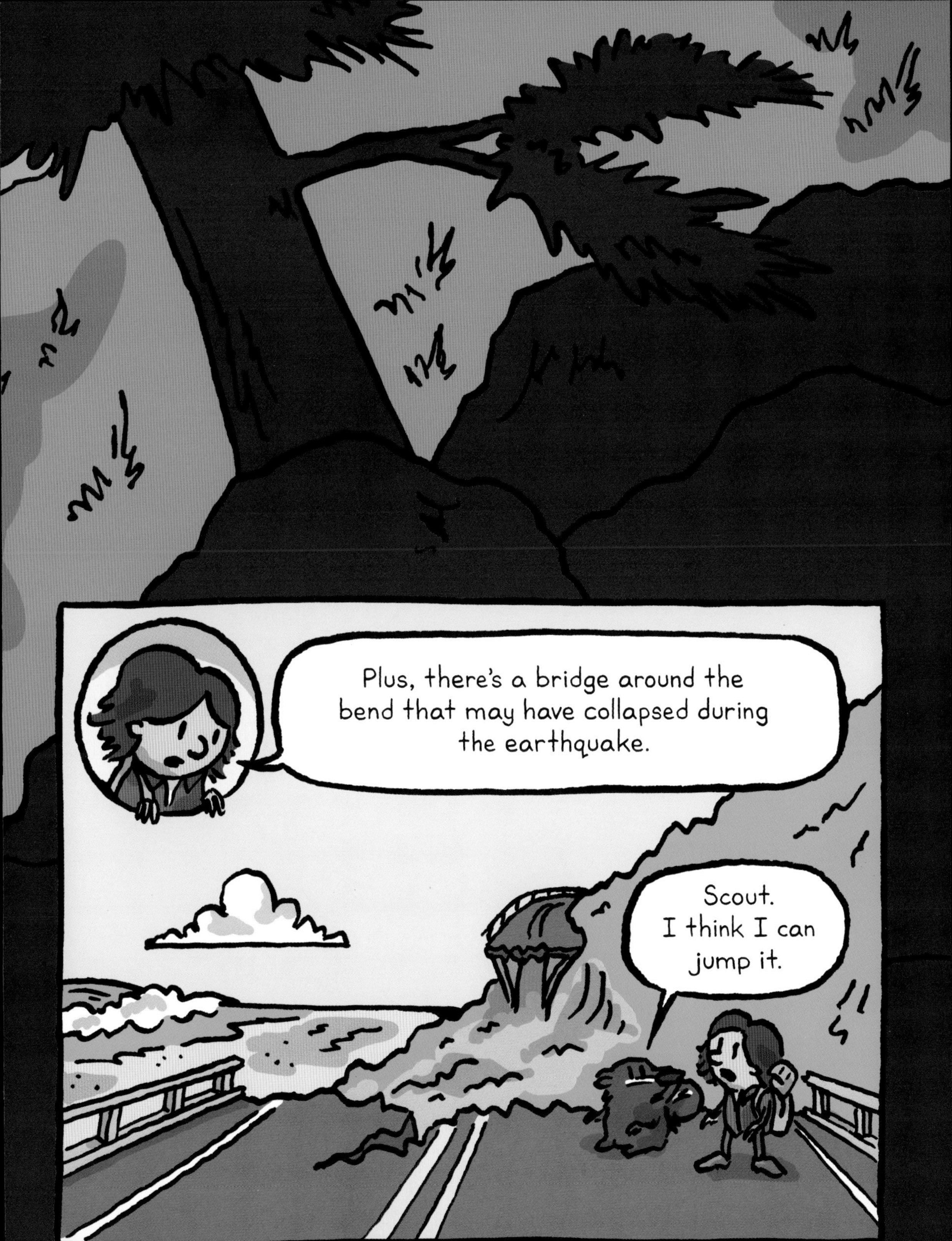
Plus, there's a bridge around the bend that may have collapsed during the earthquake.
Scout.
I think I can jump it.

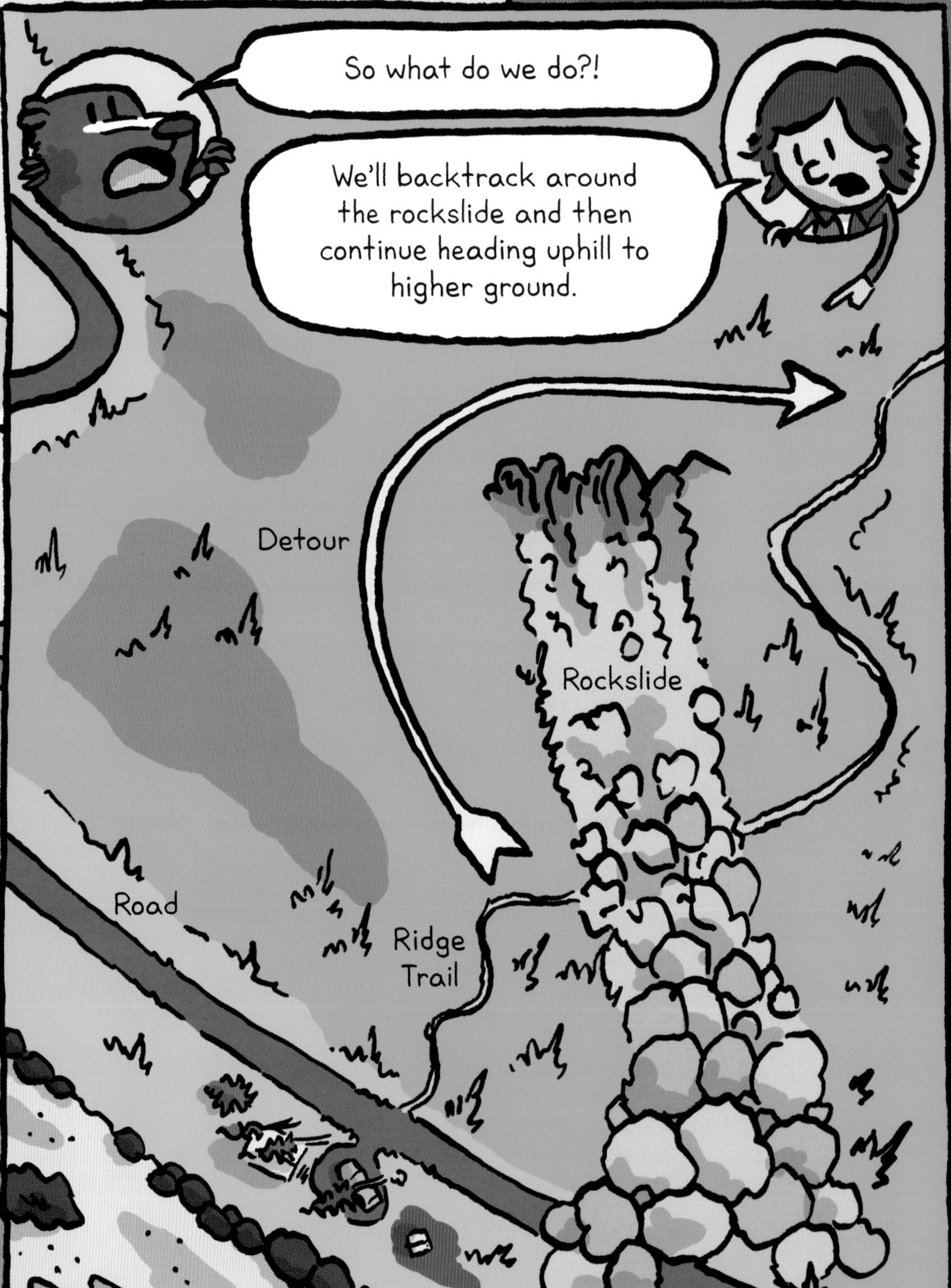
So what do we do?!
We'll backtrack around the rockslide and then continue heading uphill to higher ground.
Detour
Rockslide
Road
Ridge Trail

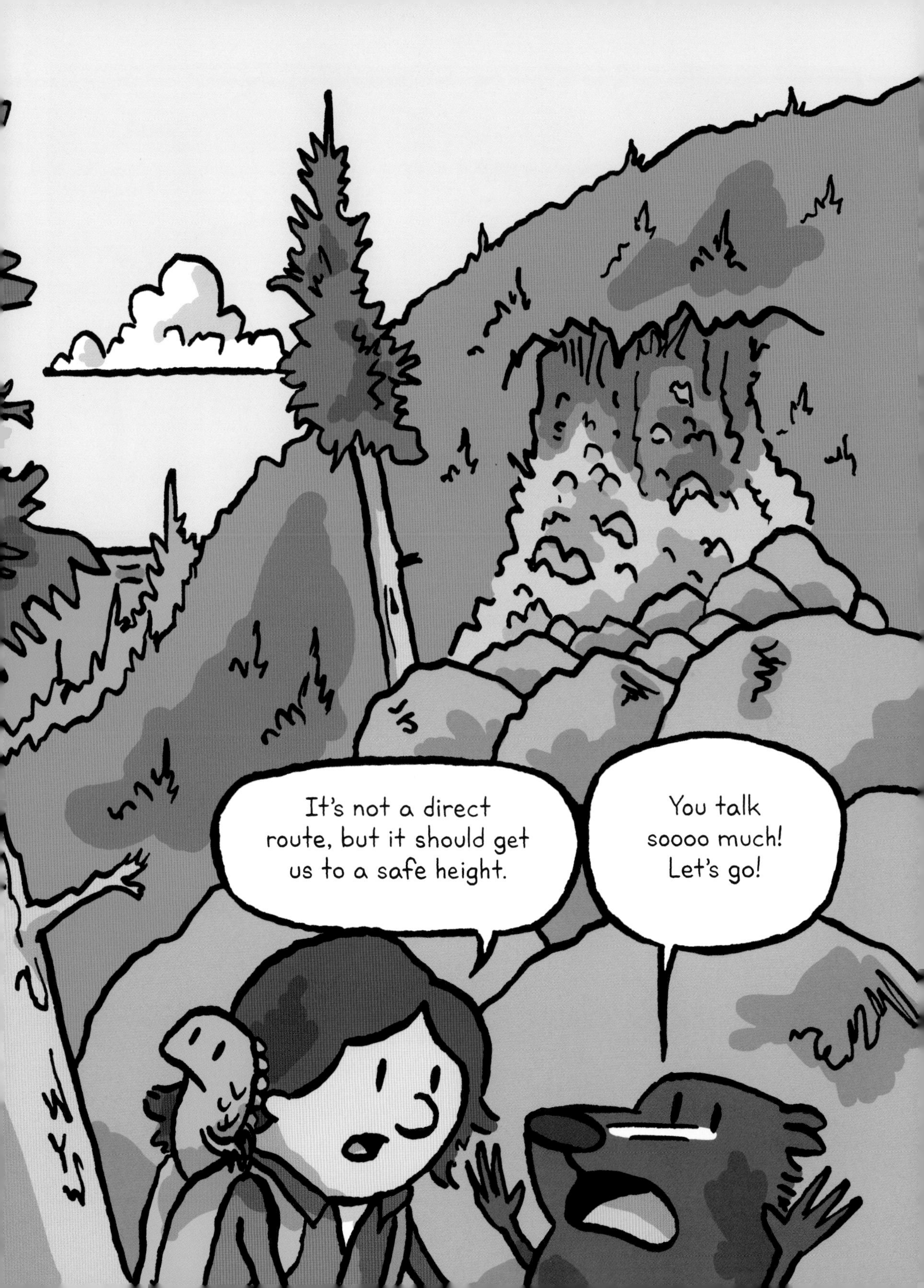
It's not a direct route, but it should get us to a safe height.
You talk soooo much! Let's go!

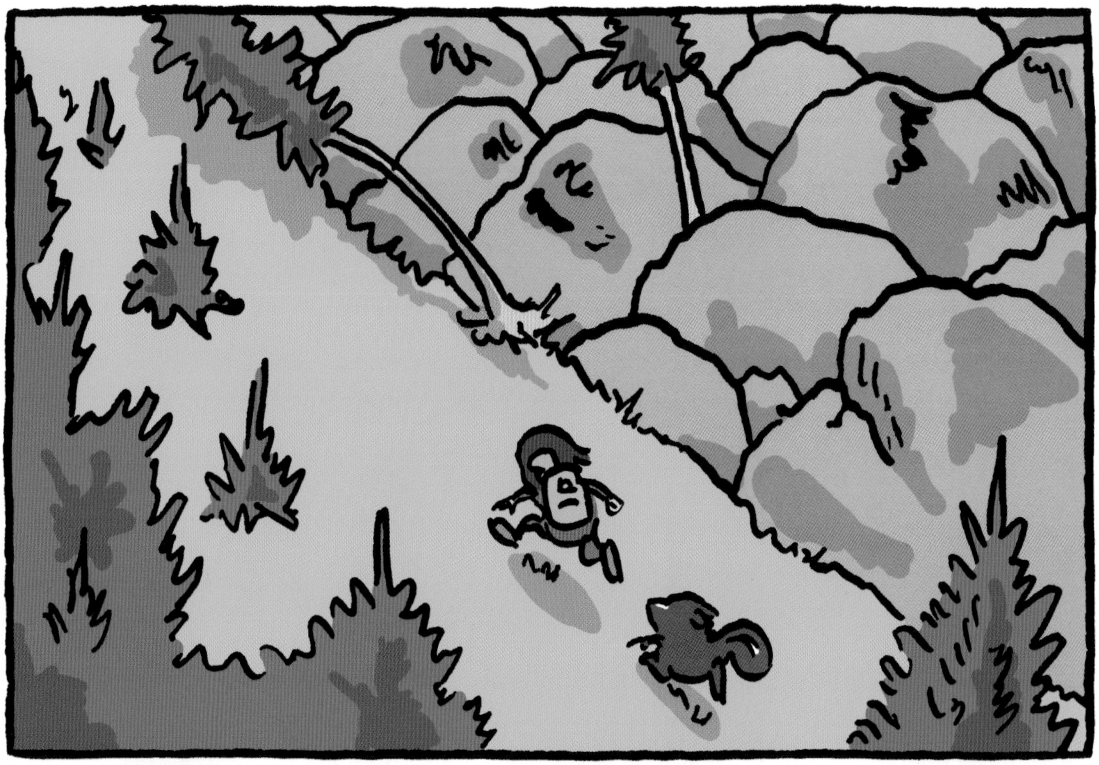

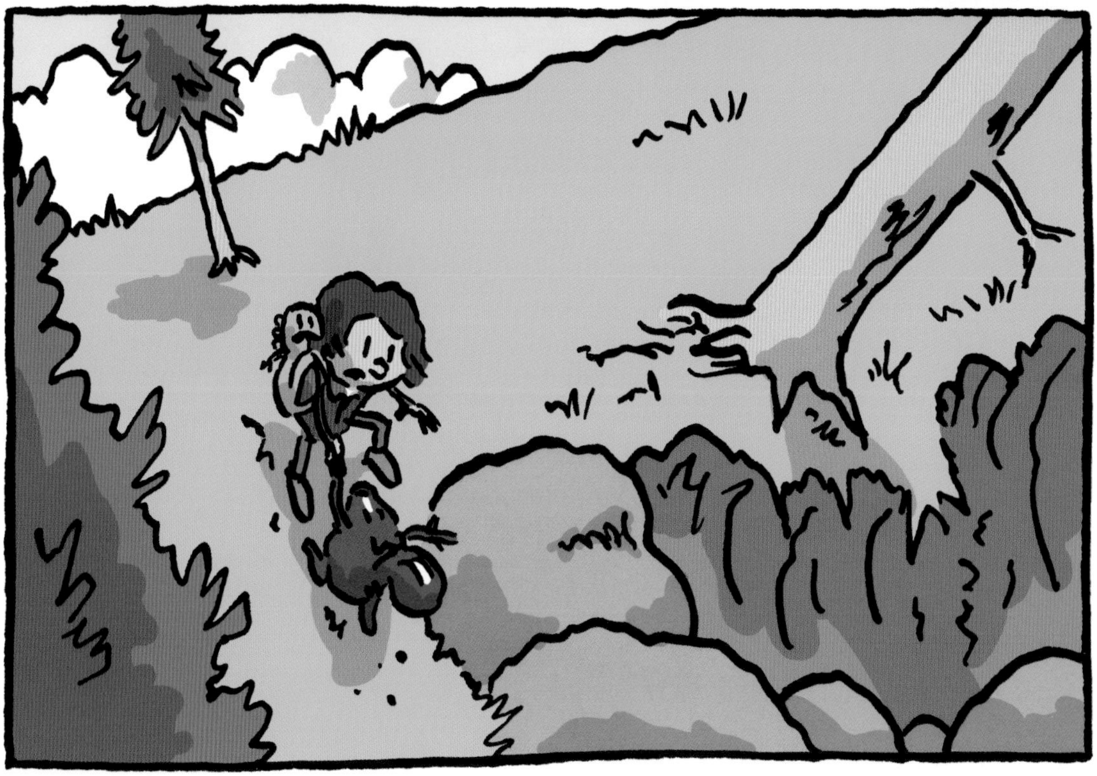

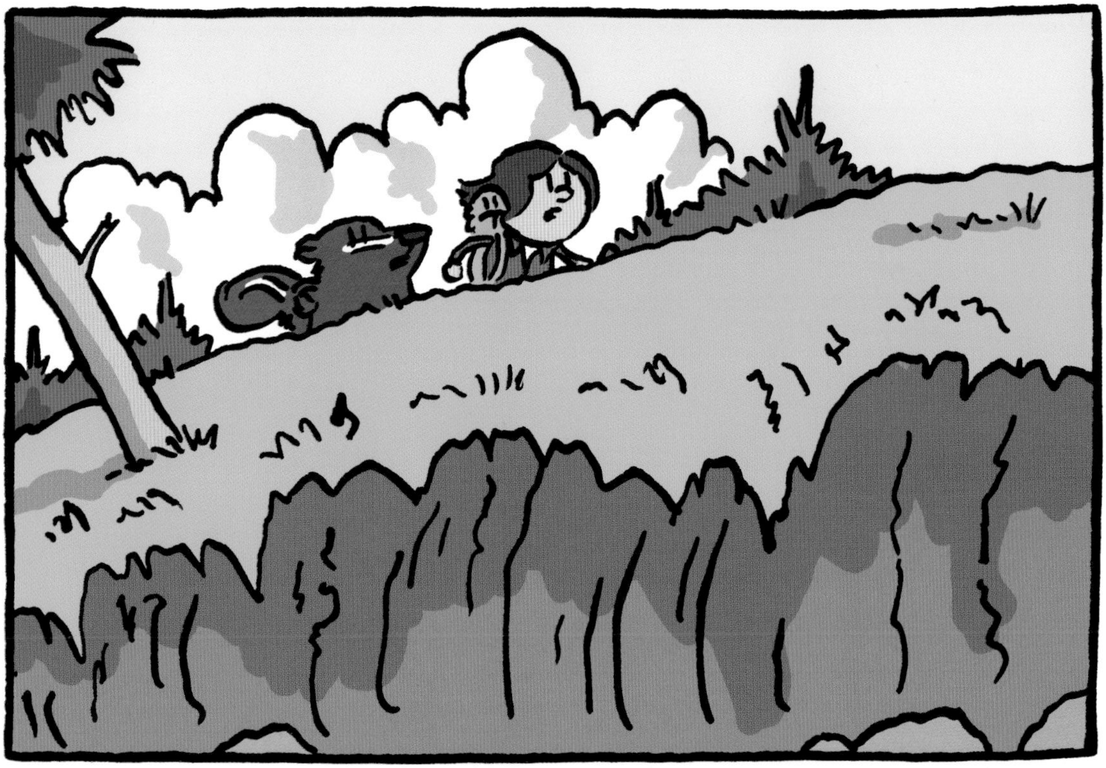

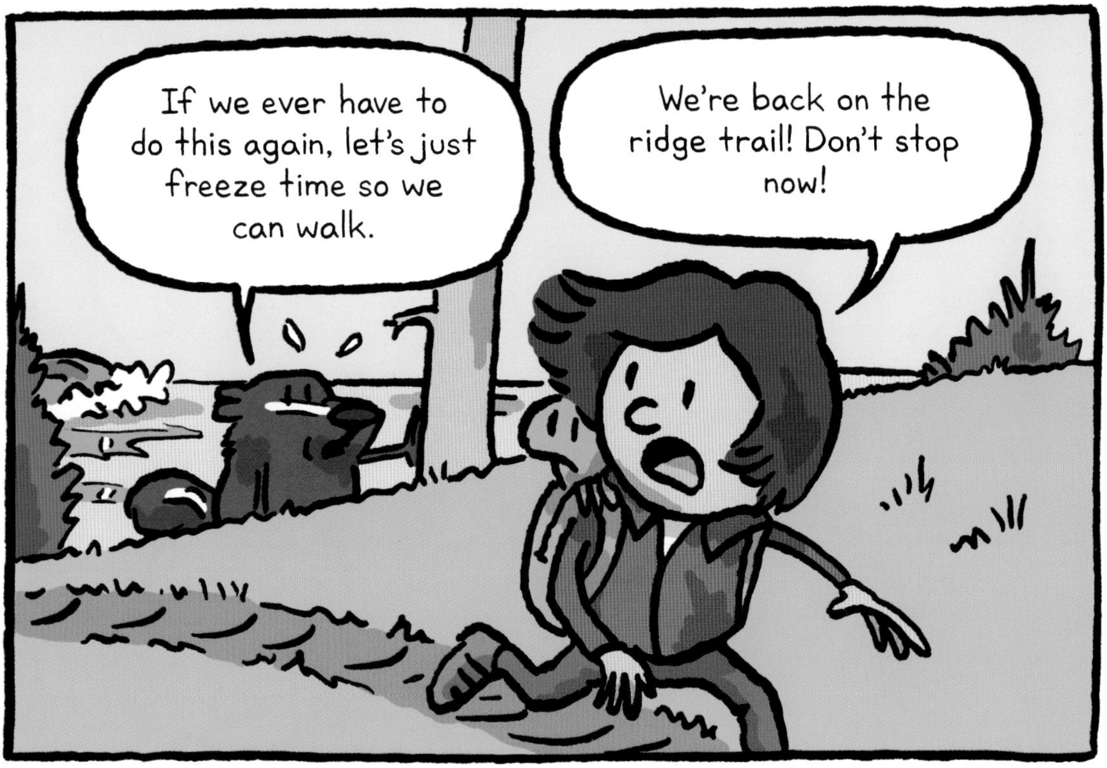

If we ever have to do this again, let's just freeze time so we can walk.
We're back on the ridge trail! Don't stop now!

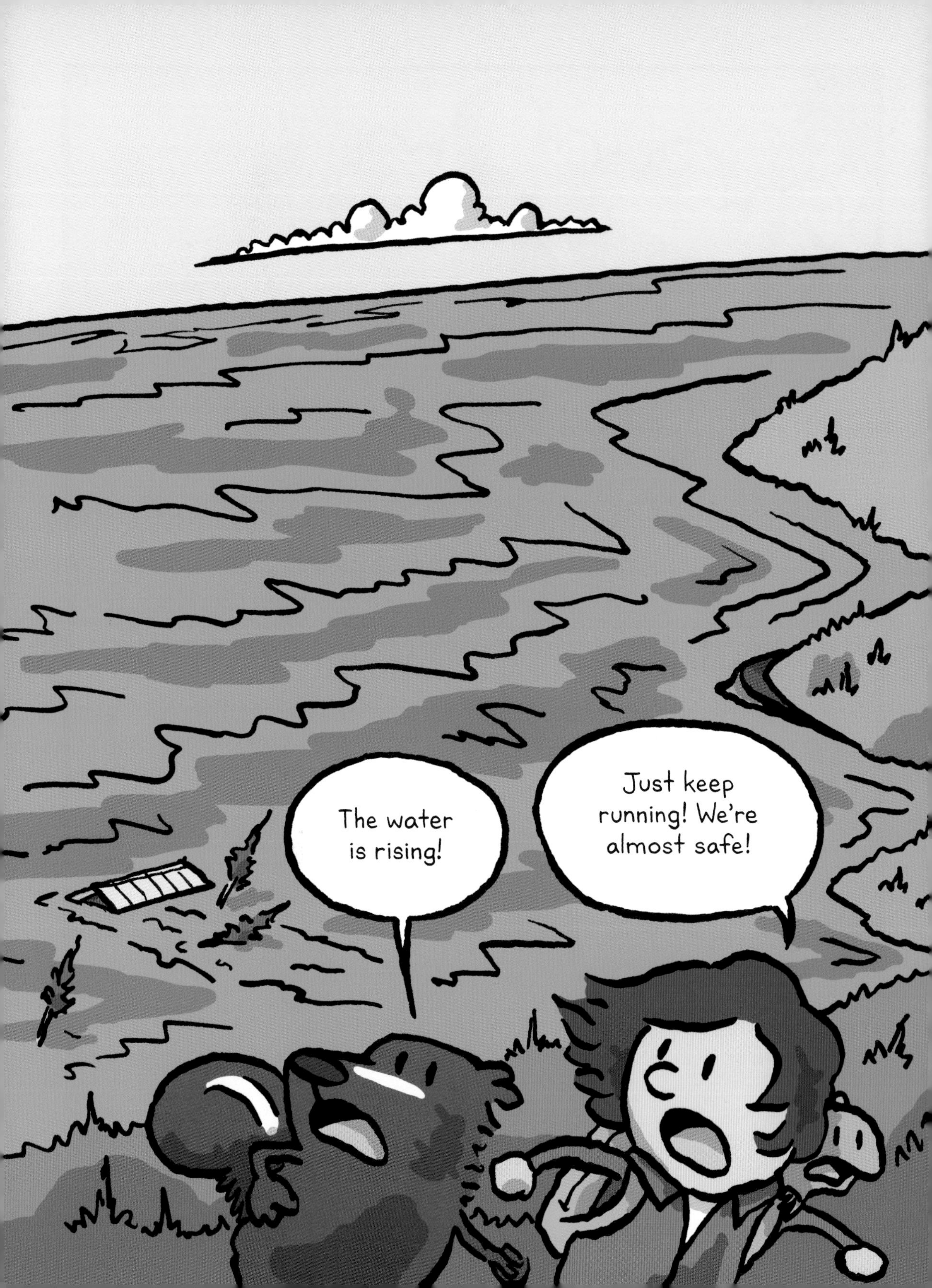
The water is rising!
Just keep running! We're almost safe!

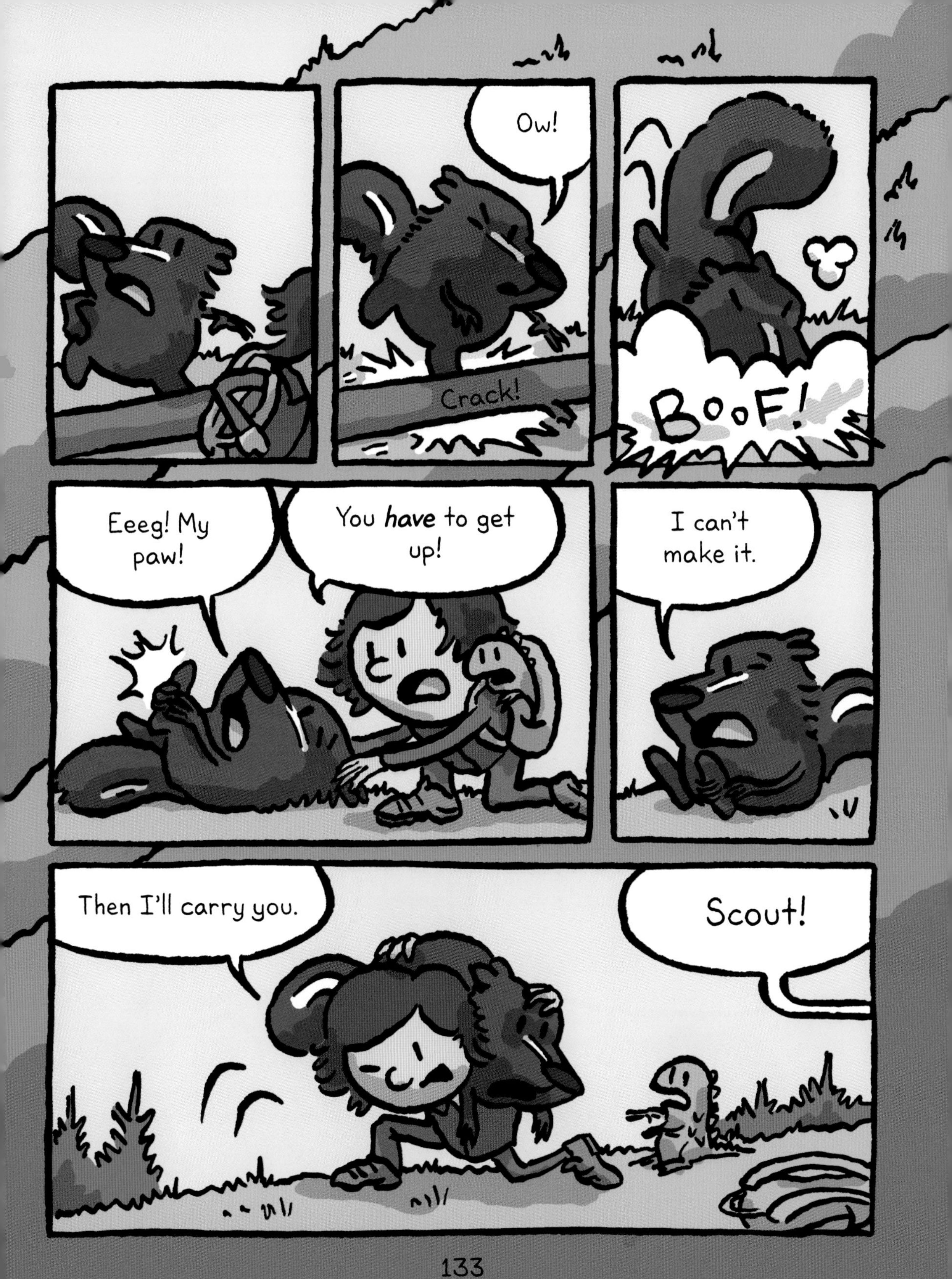

Ow!
Crack!
BOOF!
Eeeg! My paw!
You **have** to get up!
I can't make it.
Then I'll carry you.
Scout!

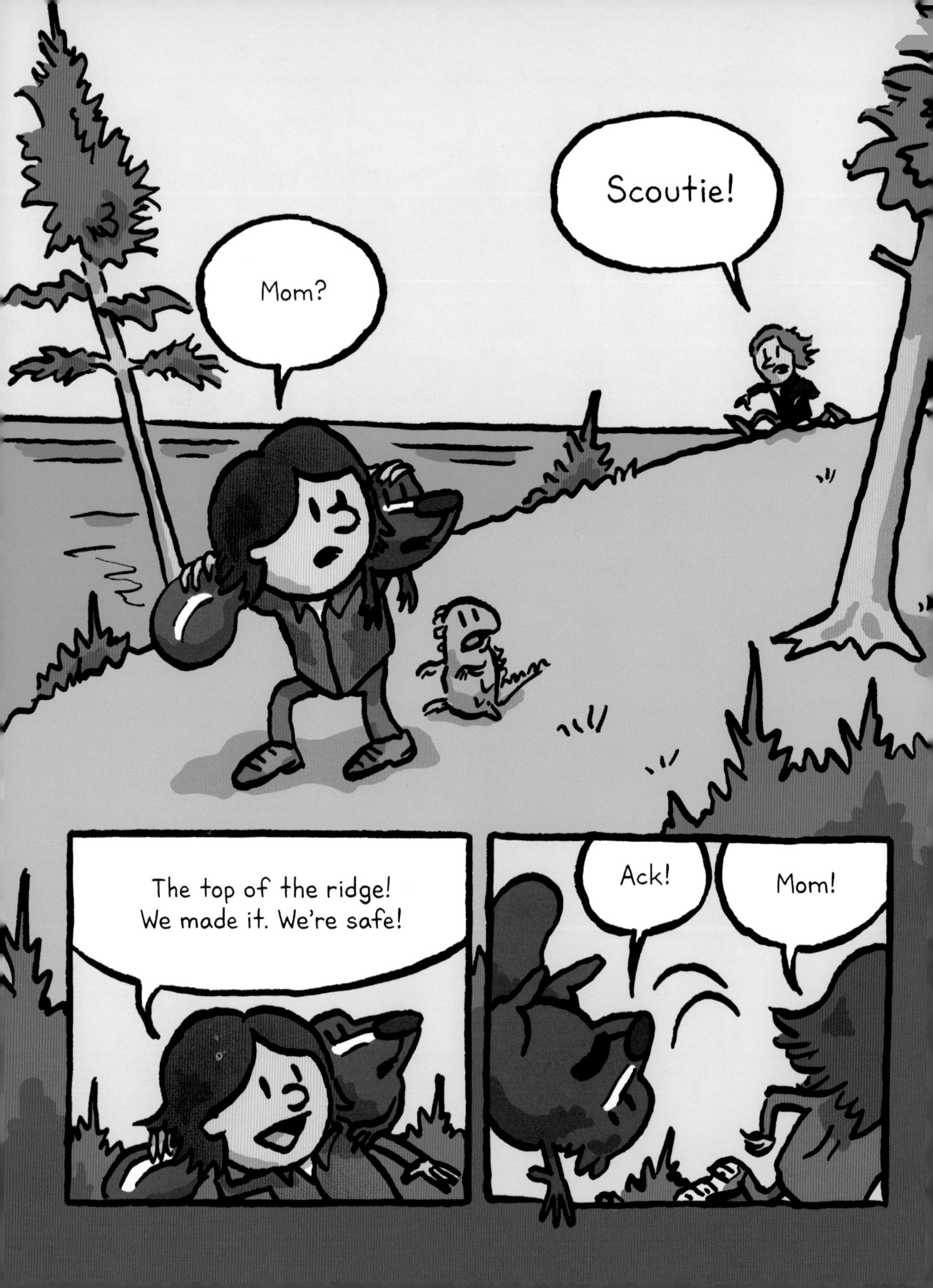
Mom?
Scoutie!
The top of the ridge! We made it. We're safe!
Ack!
Mom!

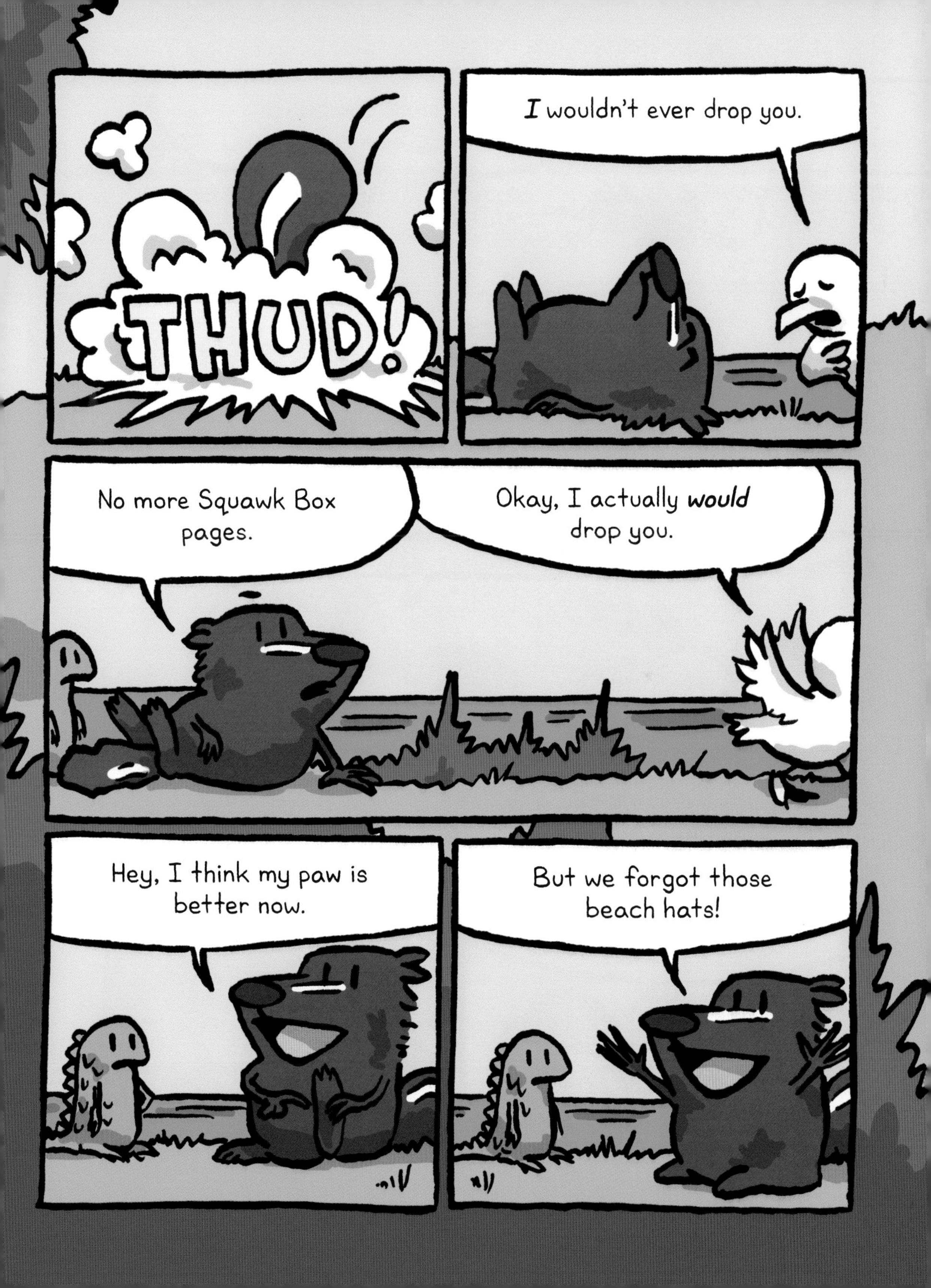
THUD!
I wouldn't ever drop you.
No more Squawk Box pages.
Okay, I actually ***would*** drop you.
Hey, I think my paw is better now.
But we forgot those beach hats!

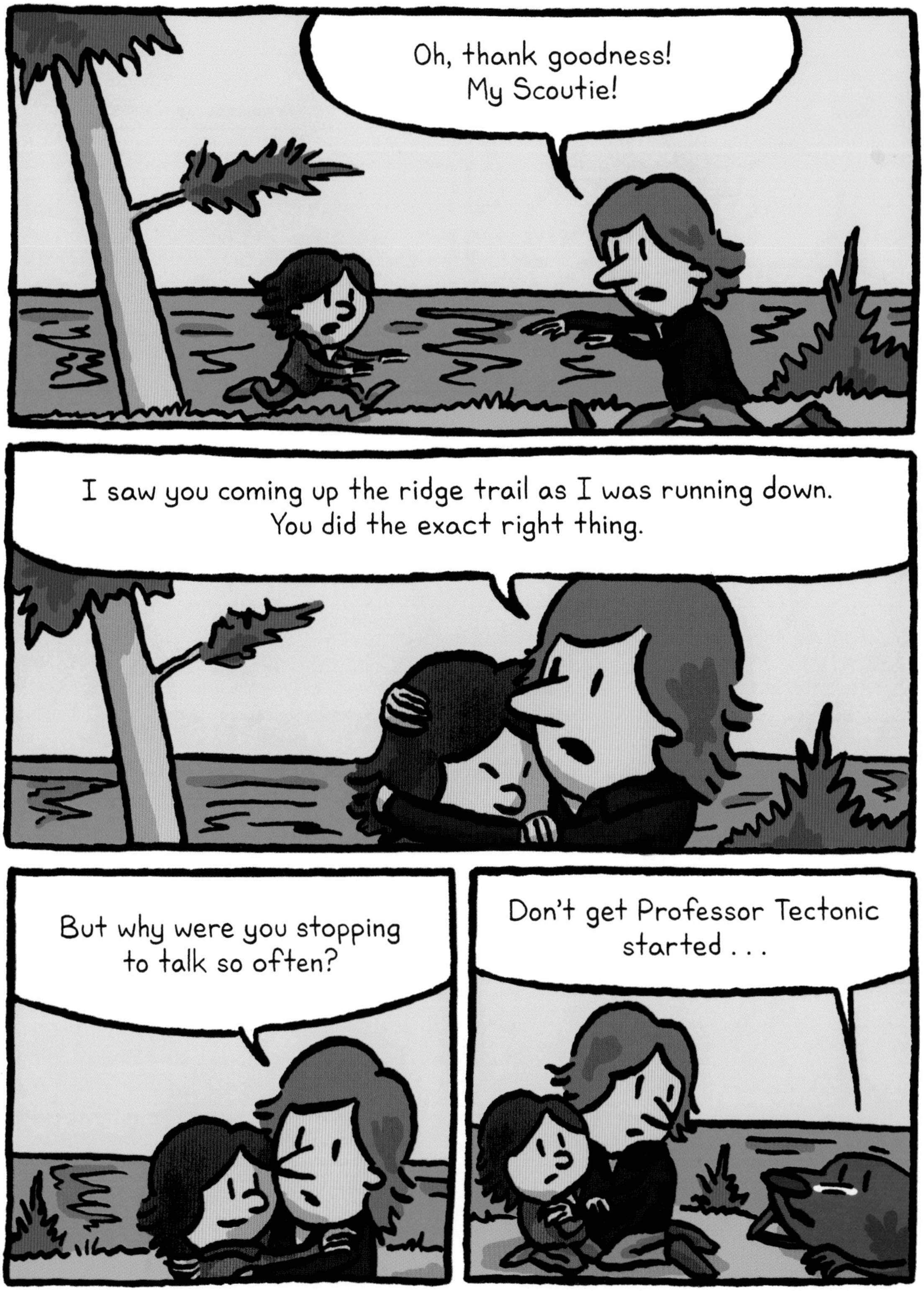
Oh, thank goodness! My Scoutie!
I saw you coming up the ridge trail as I was running down. You did the exact right thing.
But why were you stopping to talk so often?
Don't get Professor Tectonic started . . .

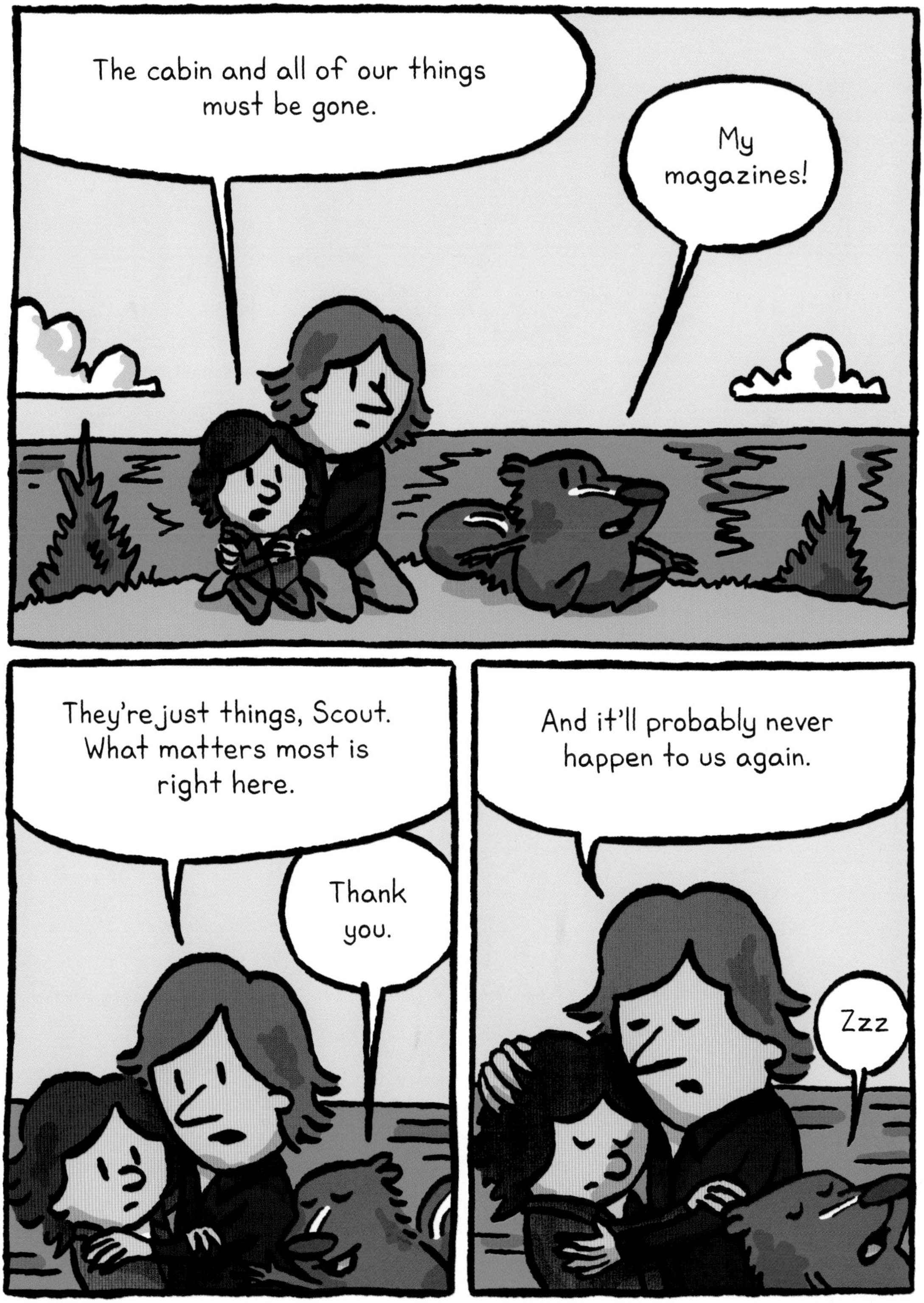
The cabin and all of our things must be gone.
My magazines!
They're just things, Scout. What matters most is right here.
Thank you.
And it'll probably never happen to us again.
Zzz

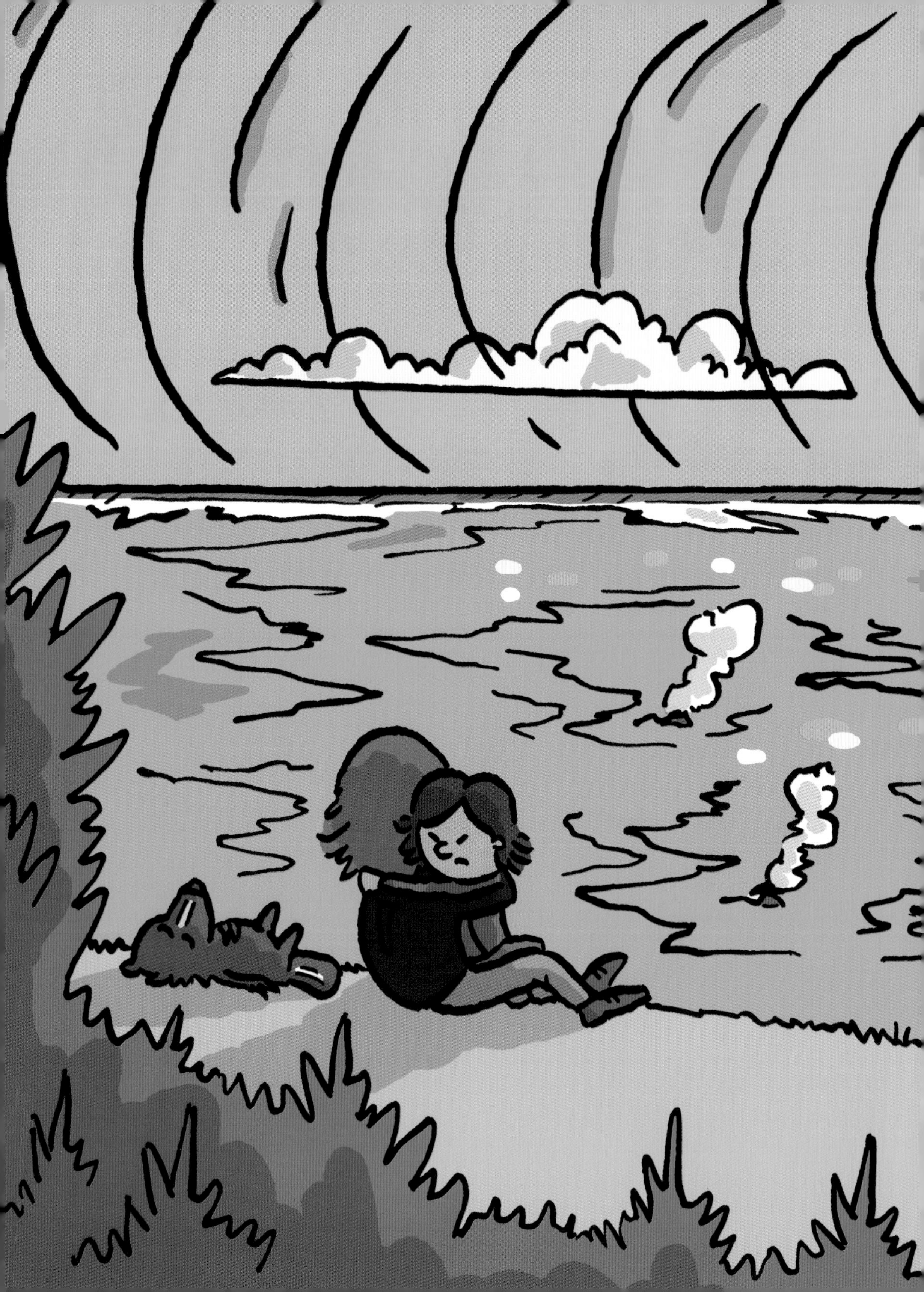

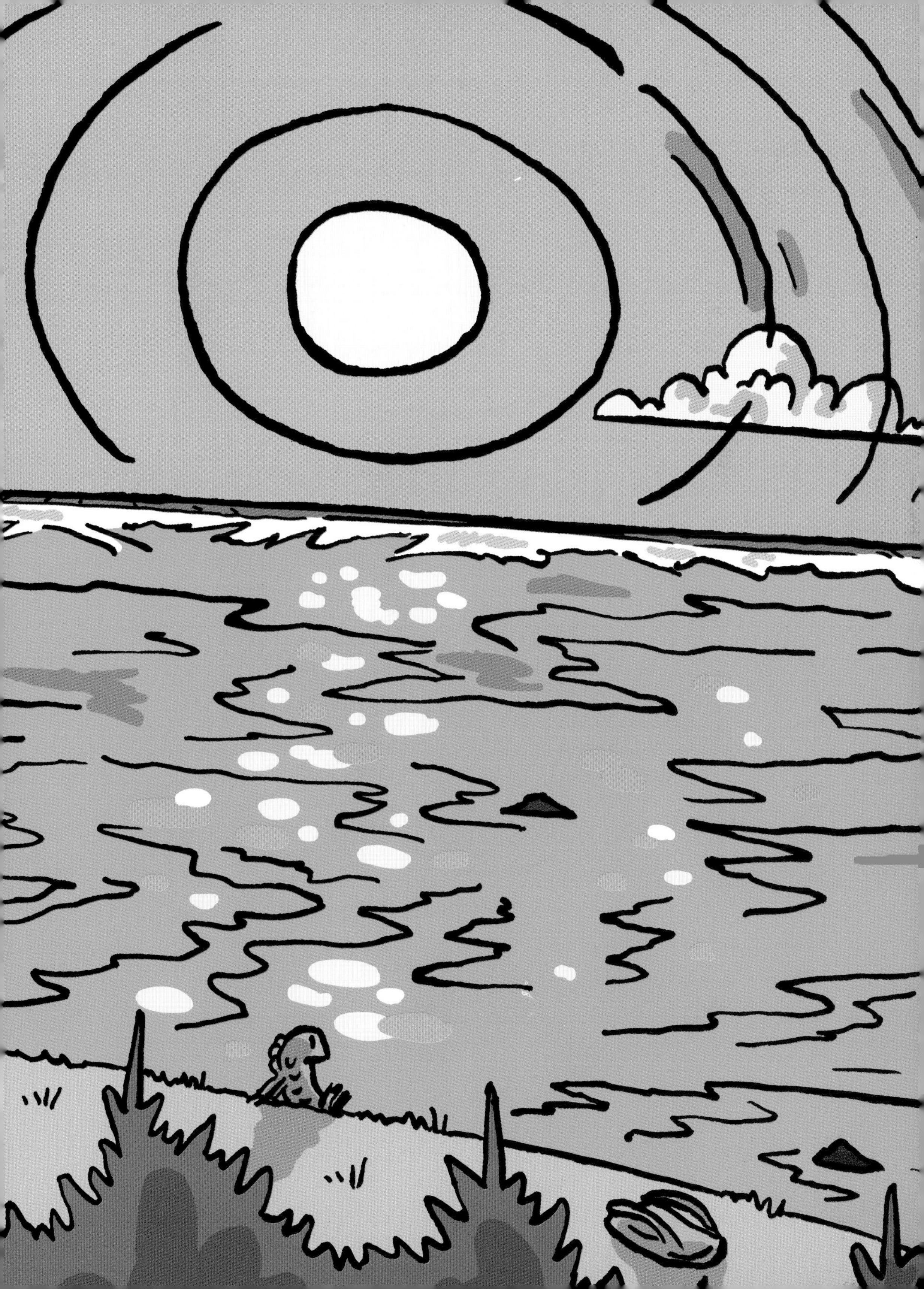

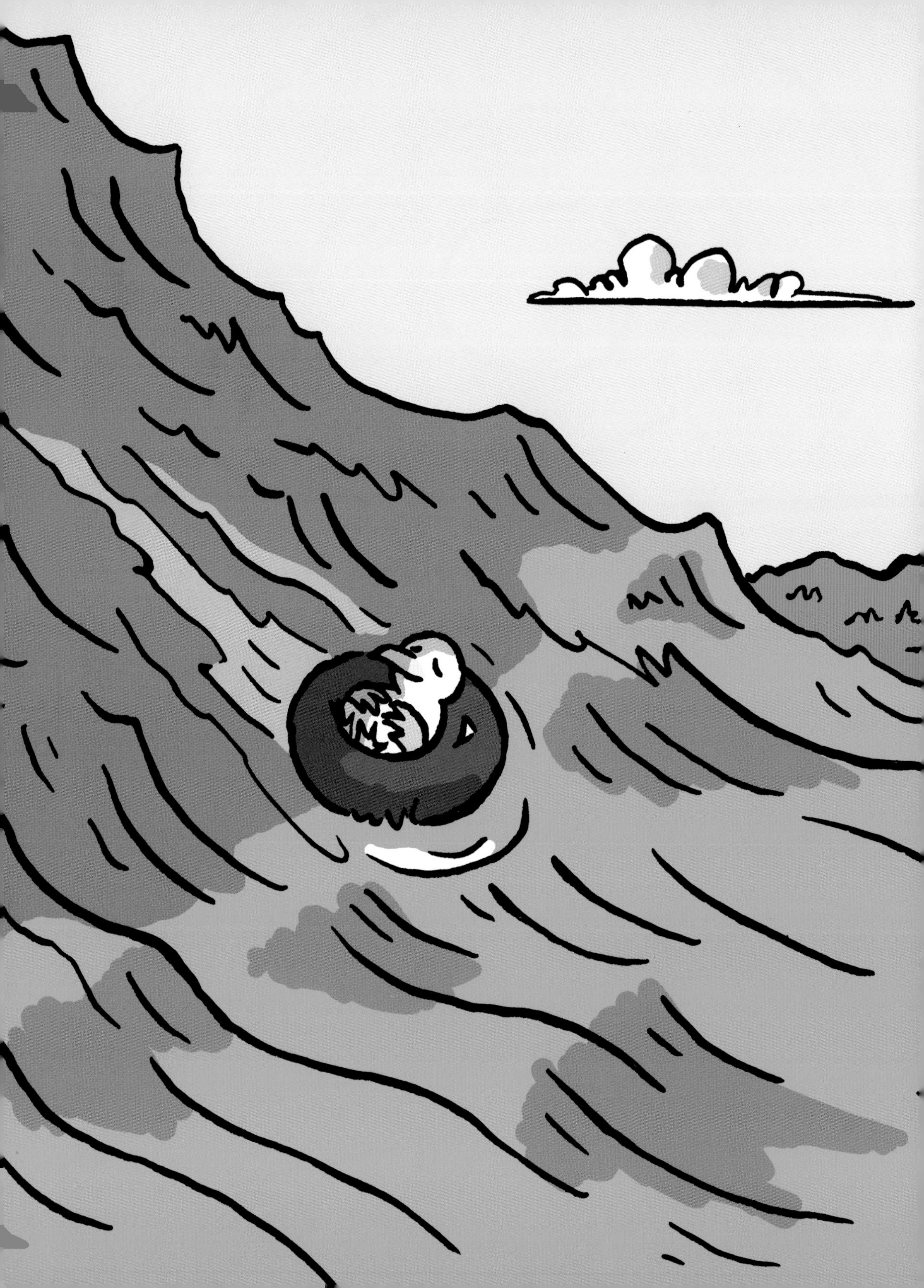

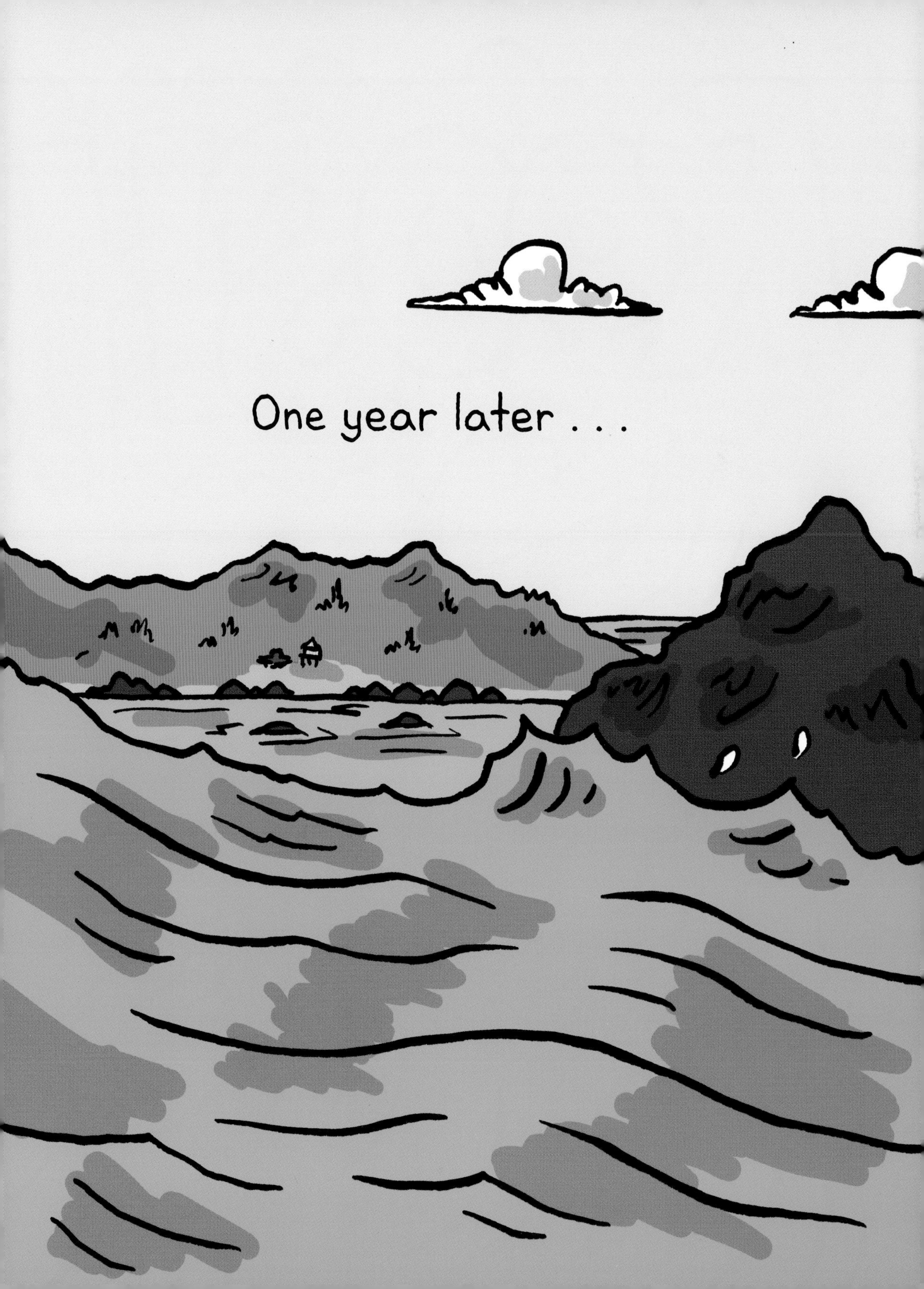
One year later . . .

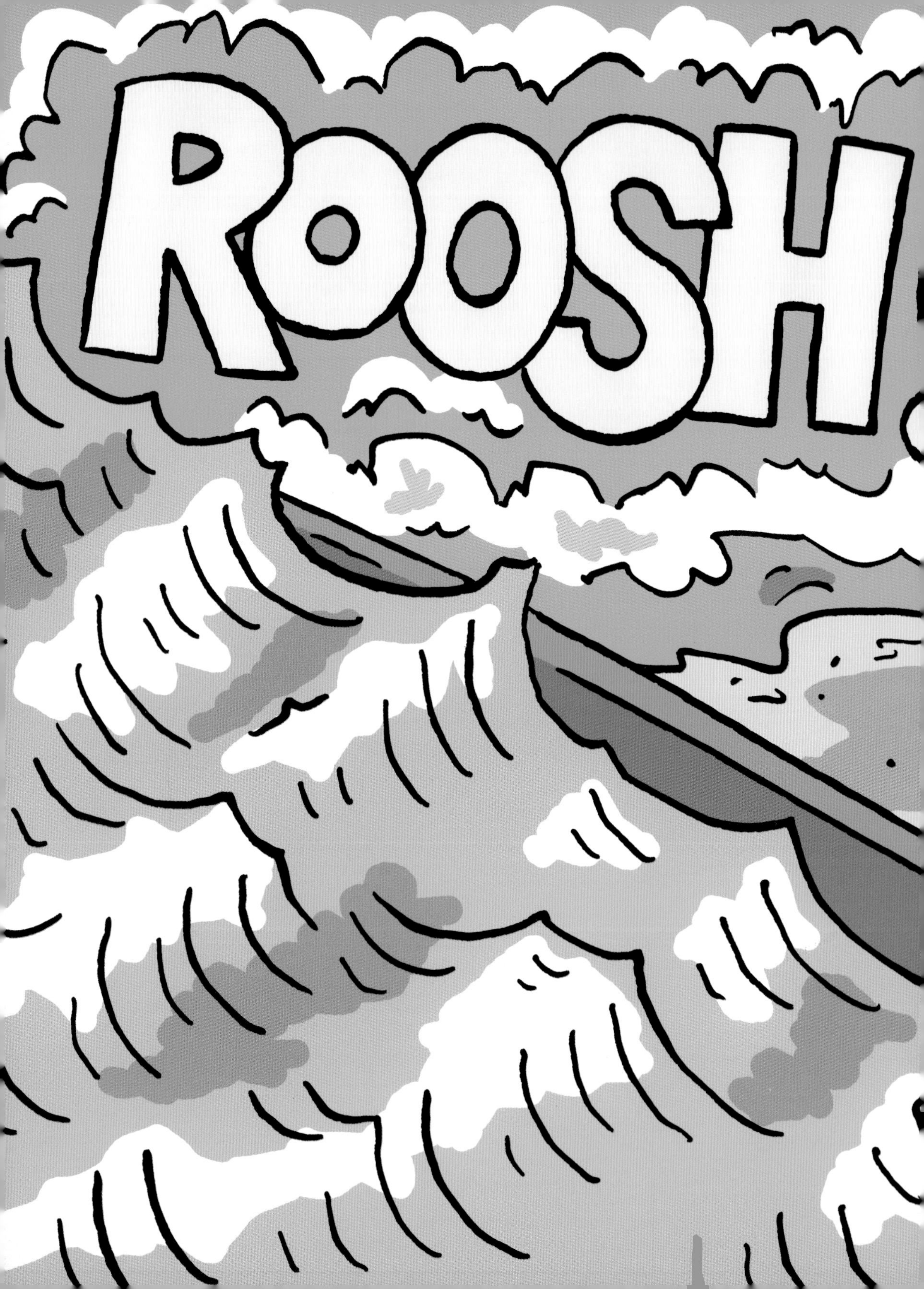
ROOSH!

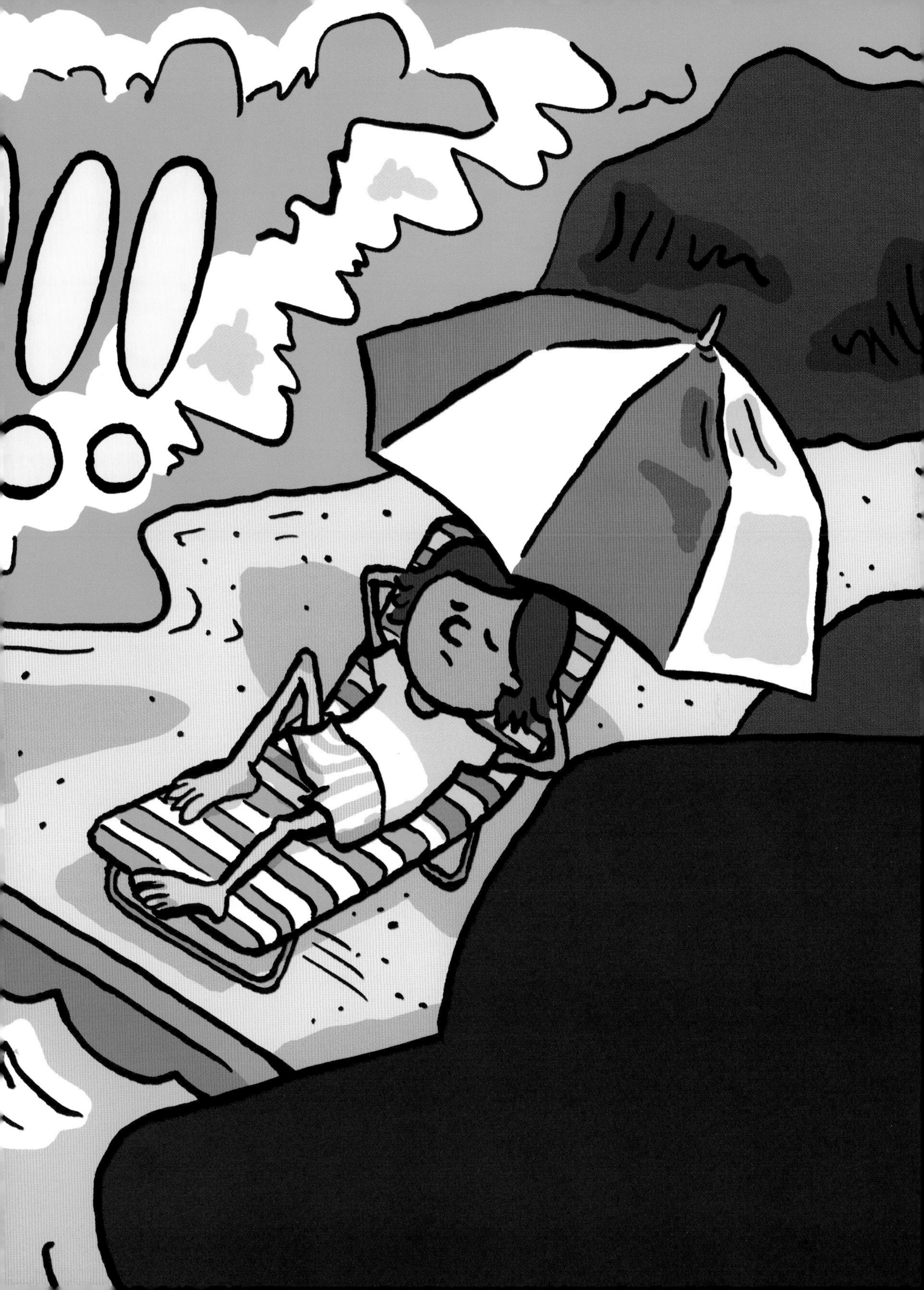
!!

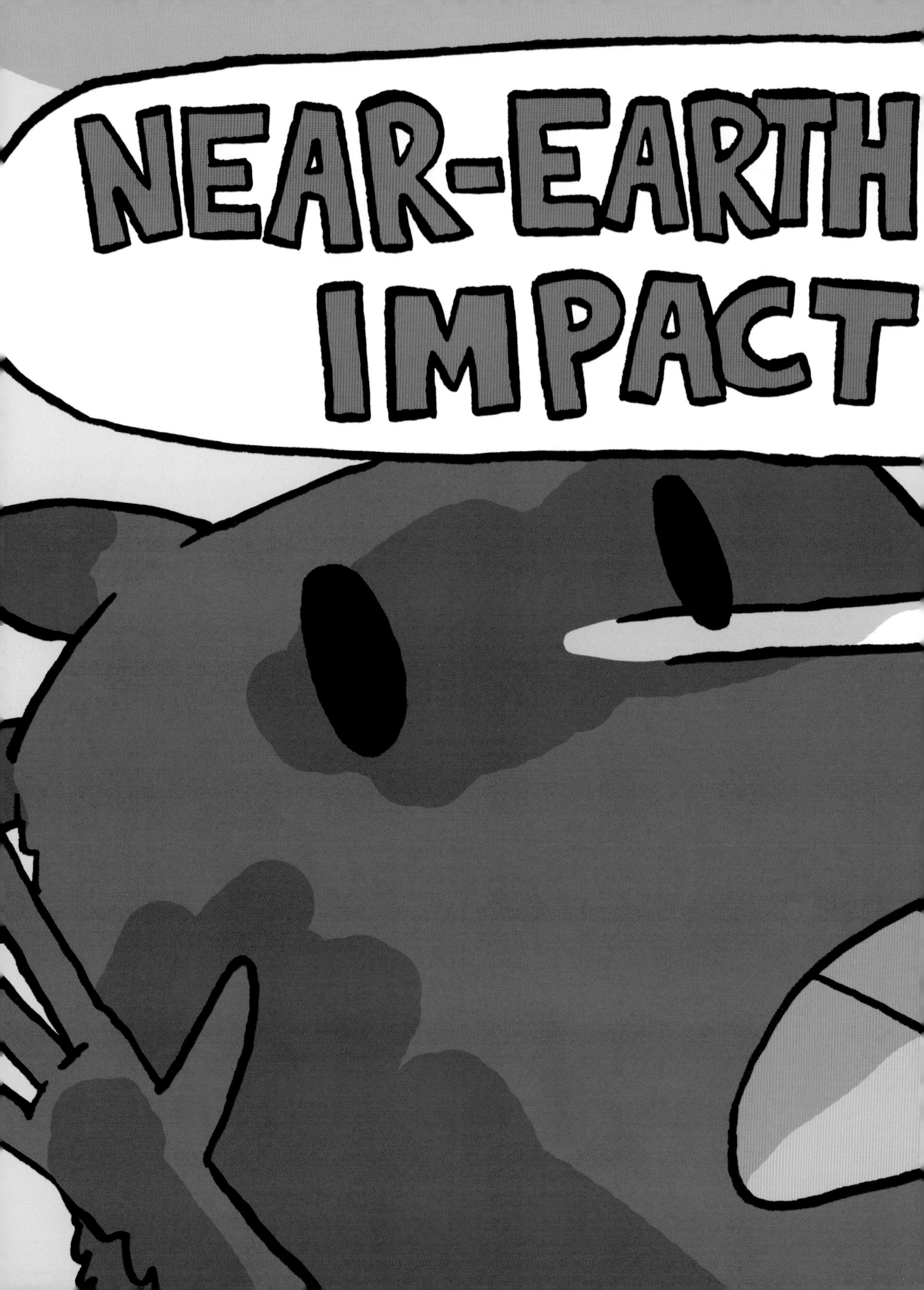
NEAR-EARTH IMPACT

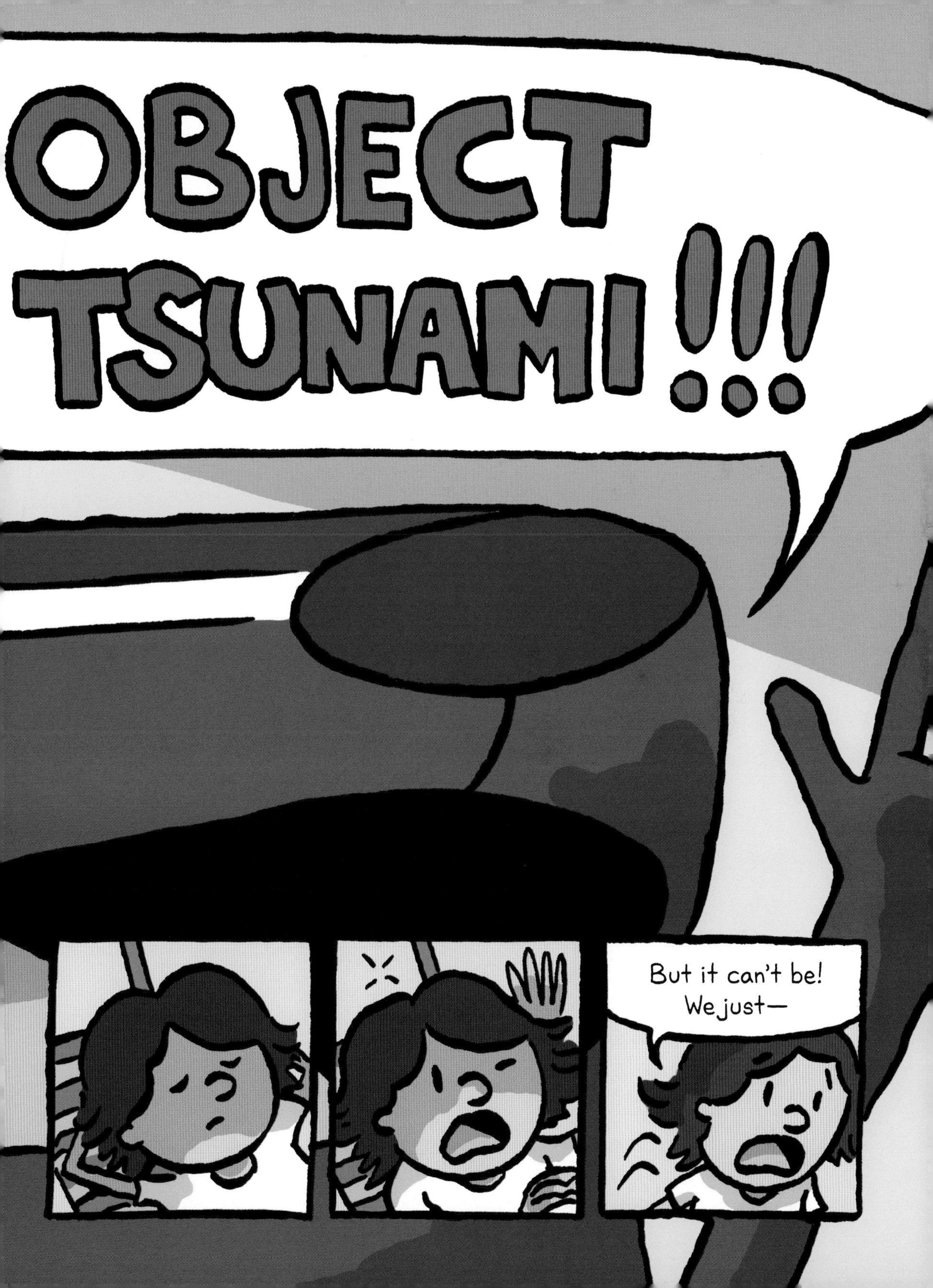
OBJECT TSUNAMI!!!
But it can't be! We just—

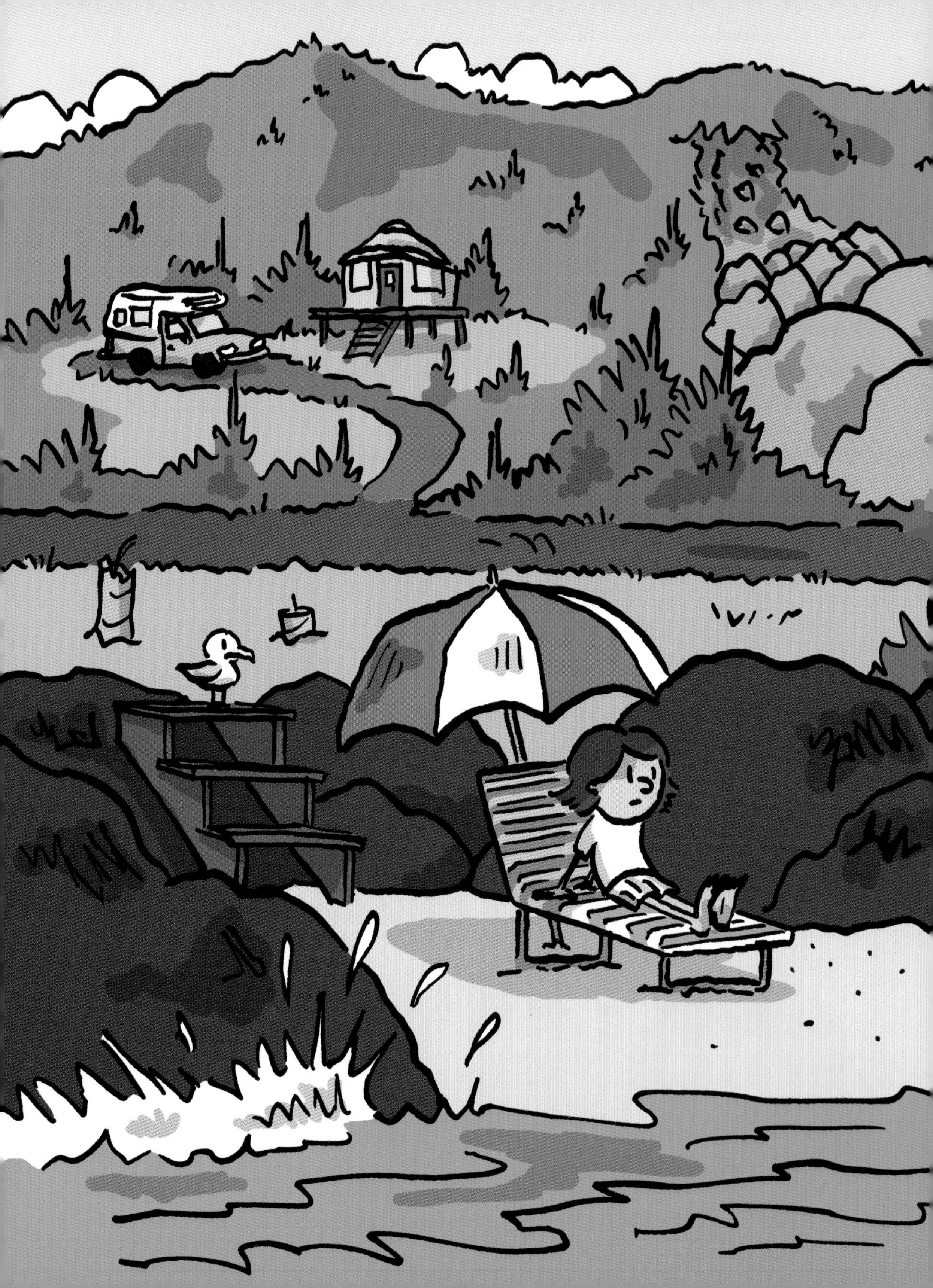

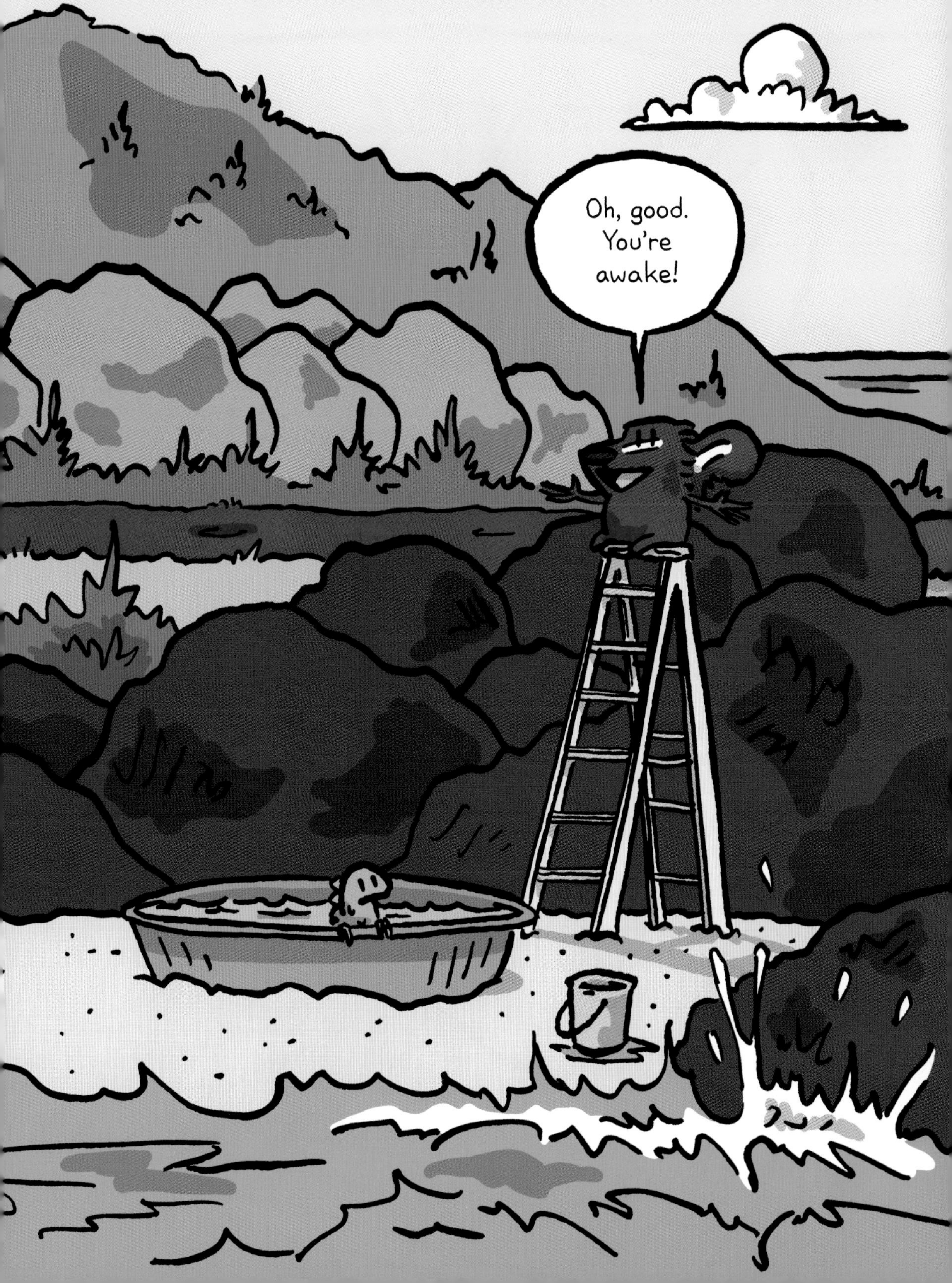
Oh, good. You're awake!

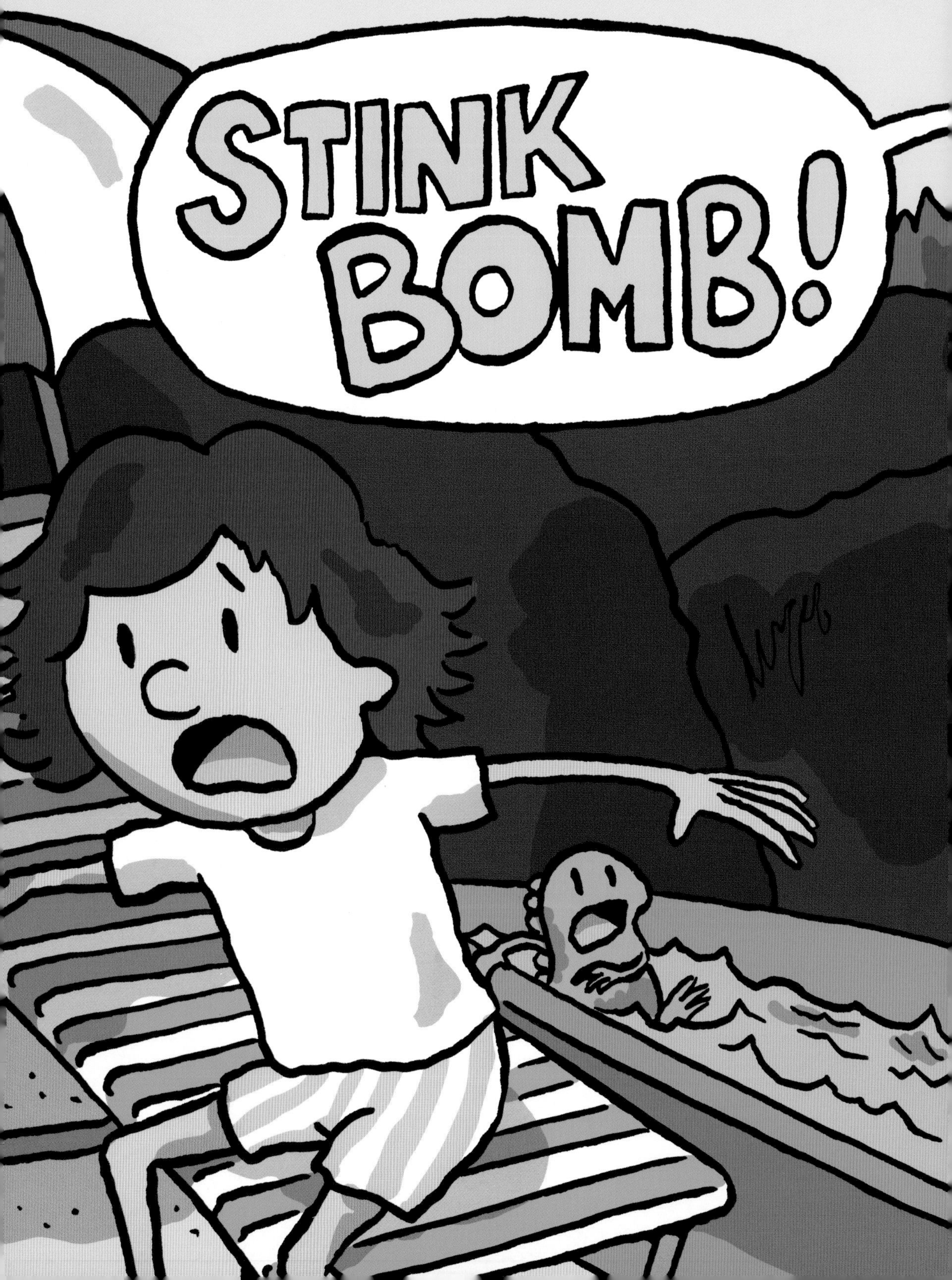
STINK BOMB!

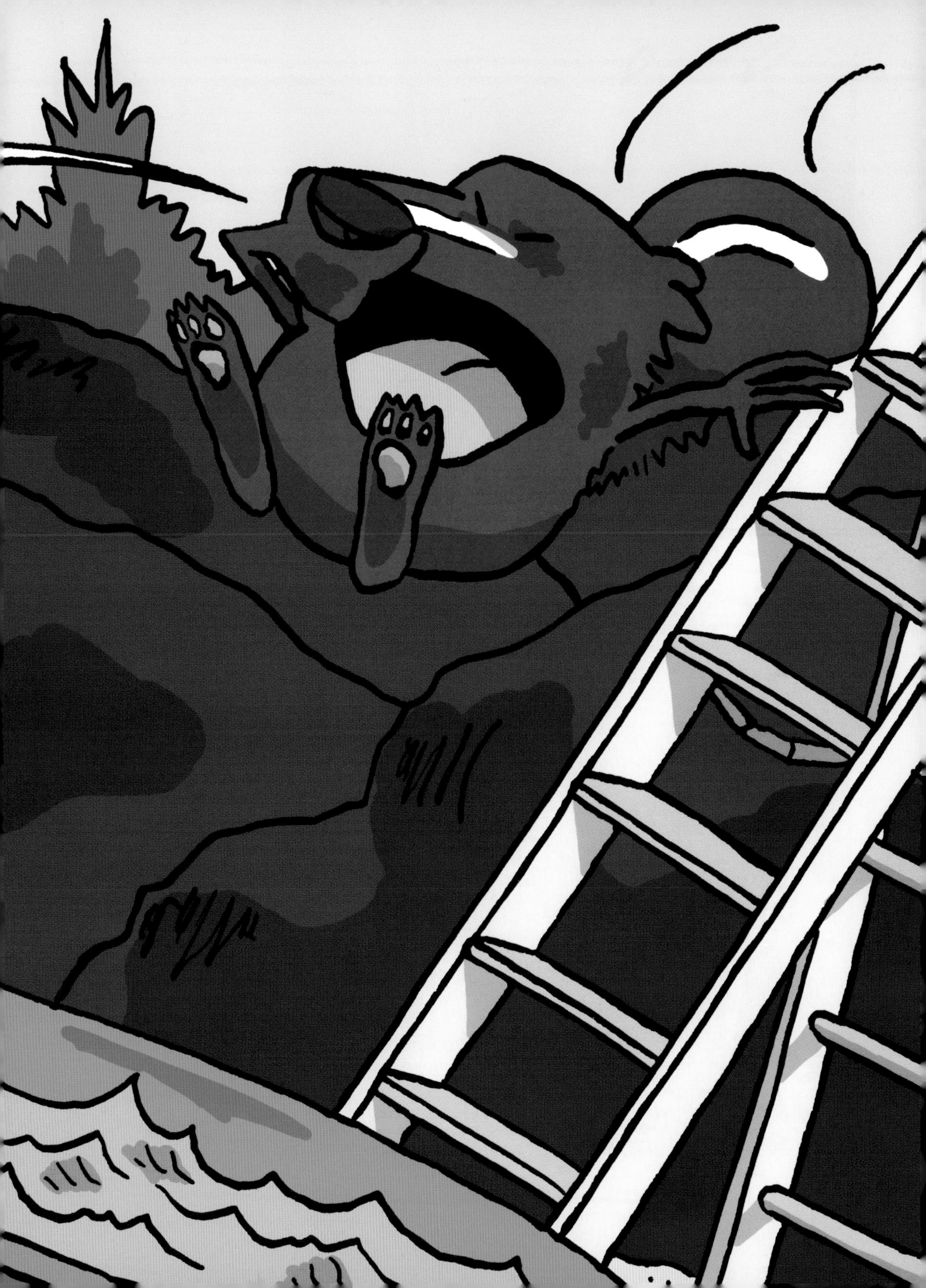

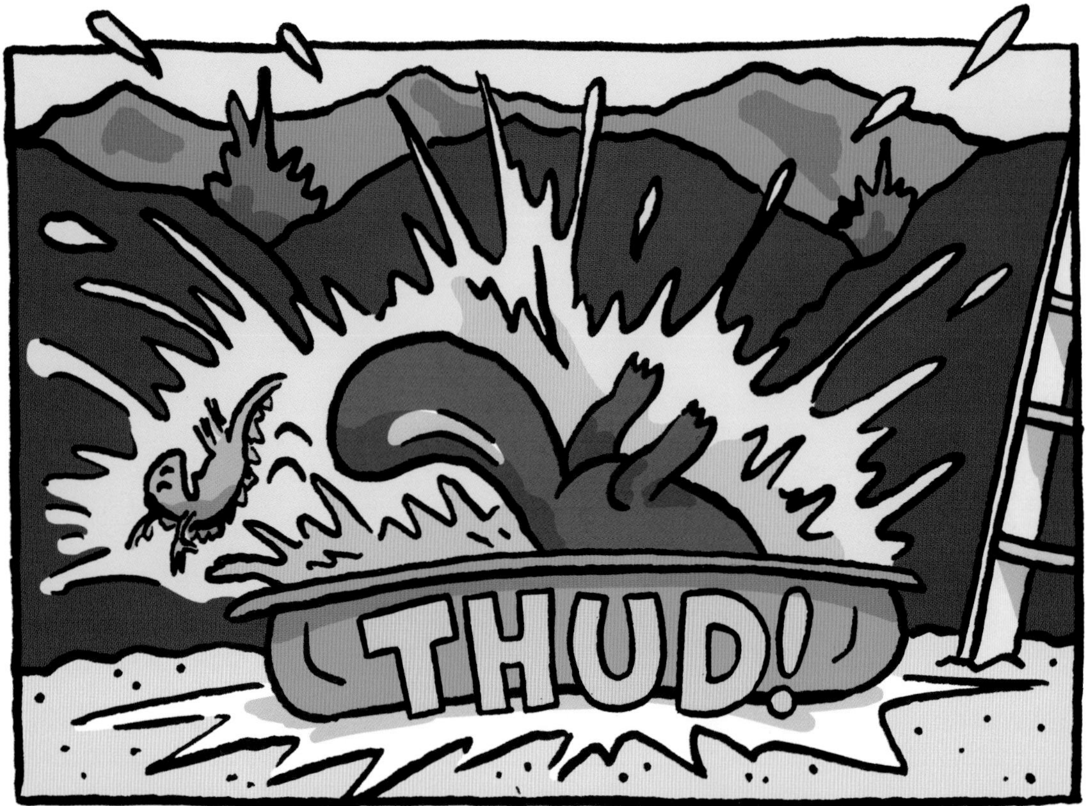
THUD!

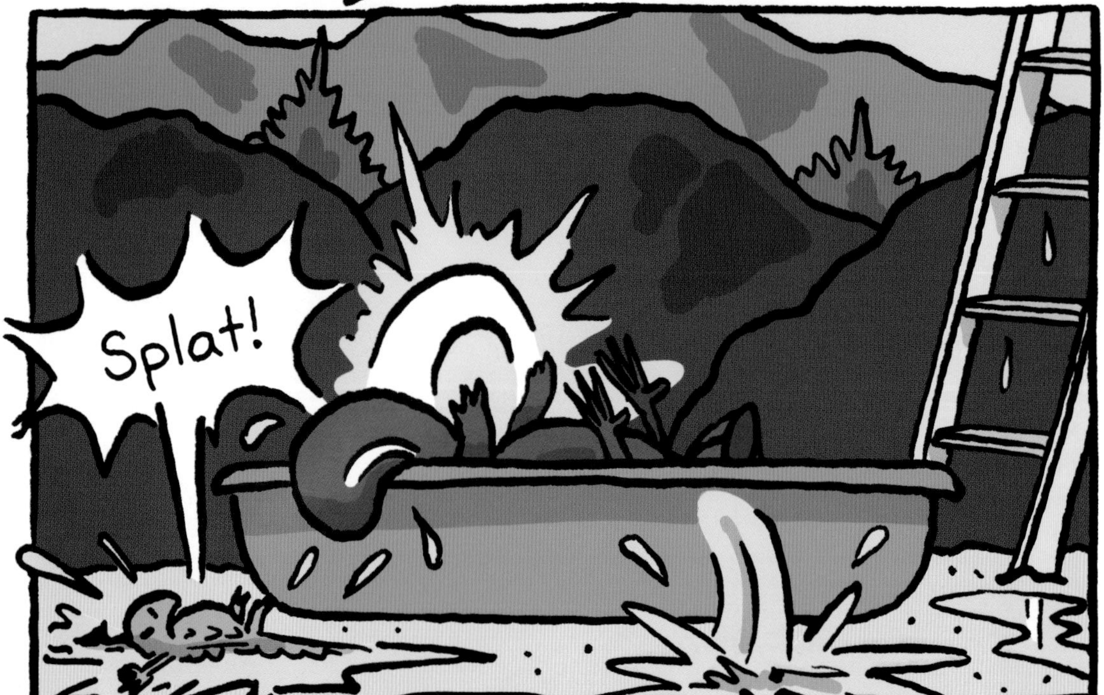
Splat!

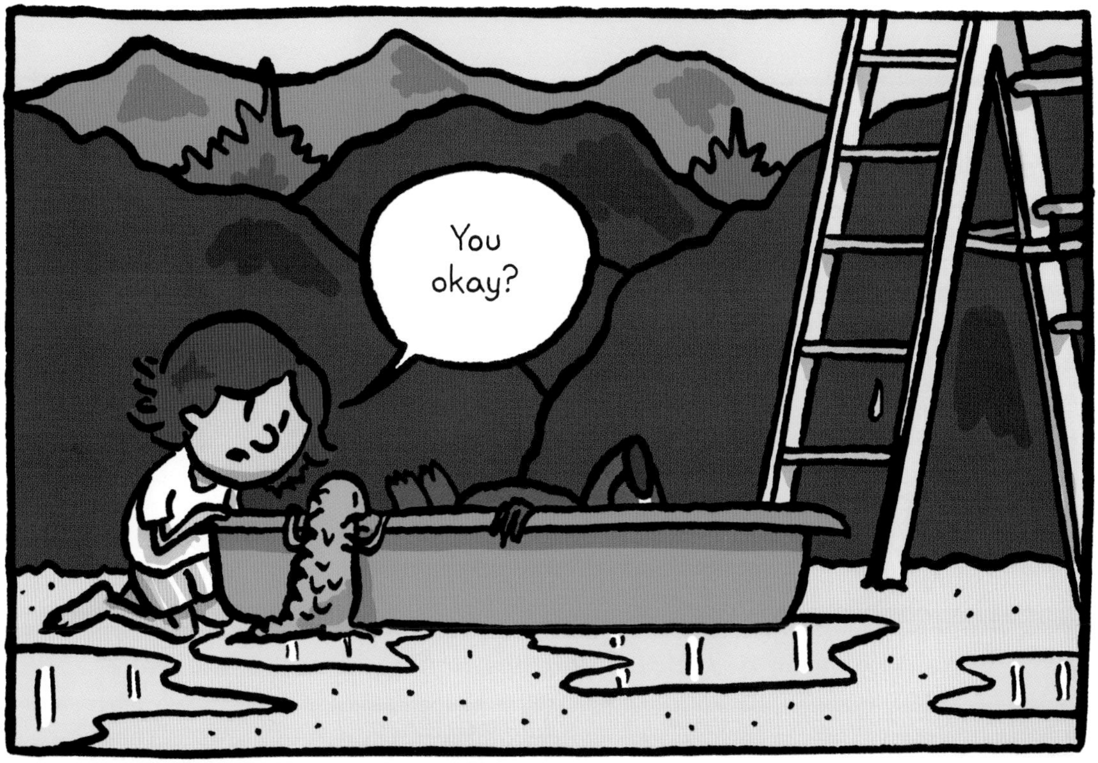
You okay?

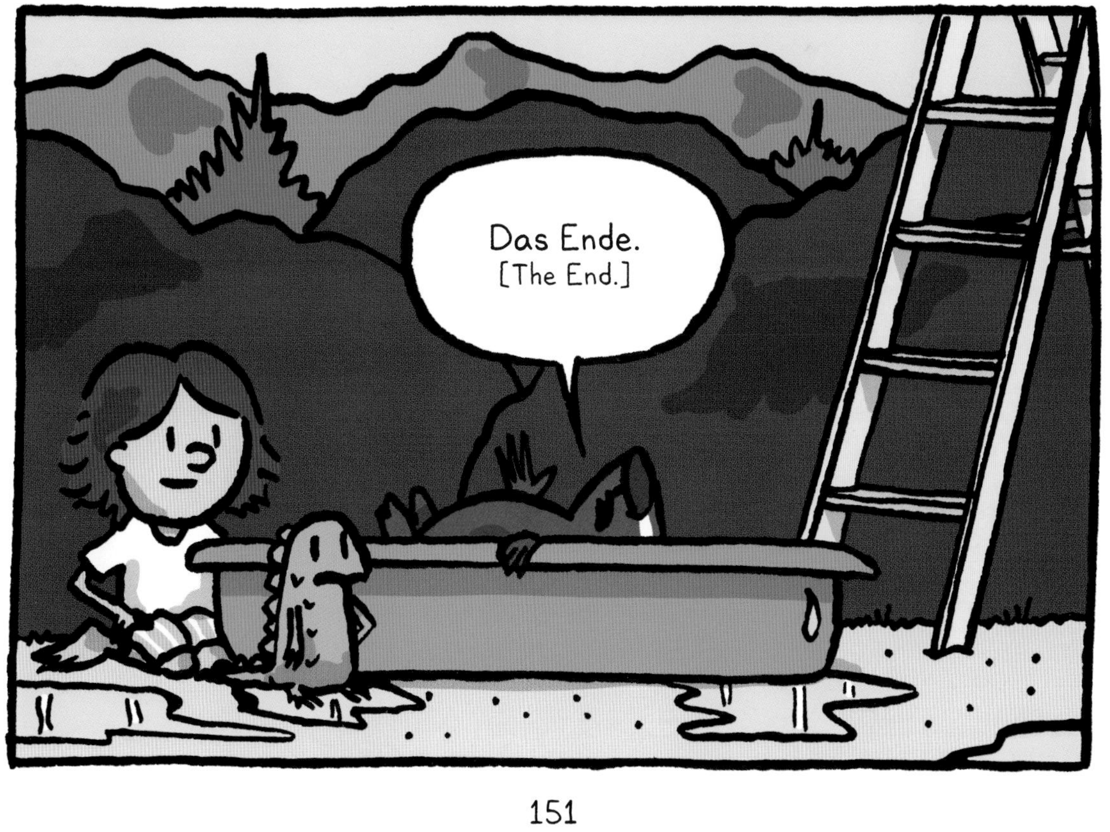
Das Ende.
[The End.]

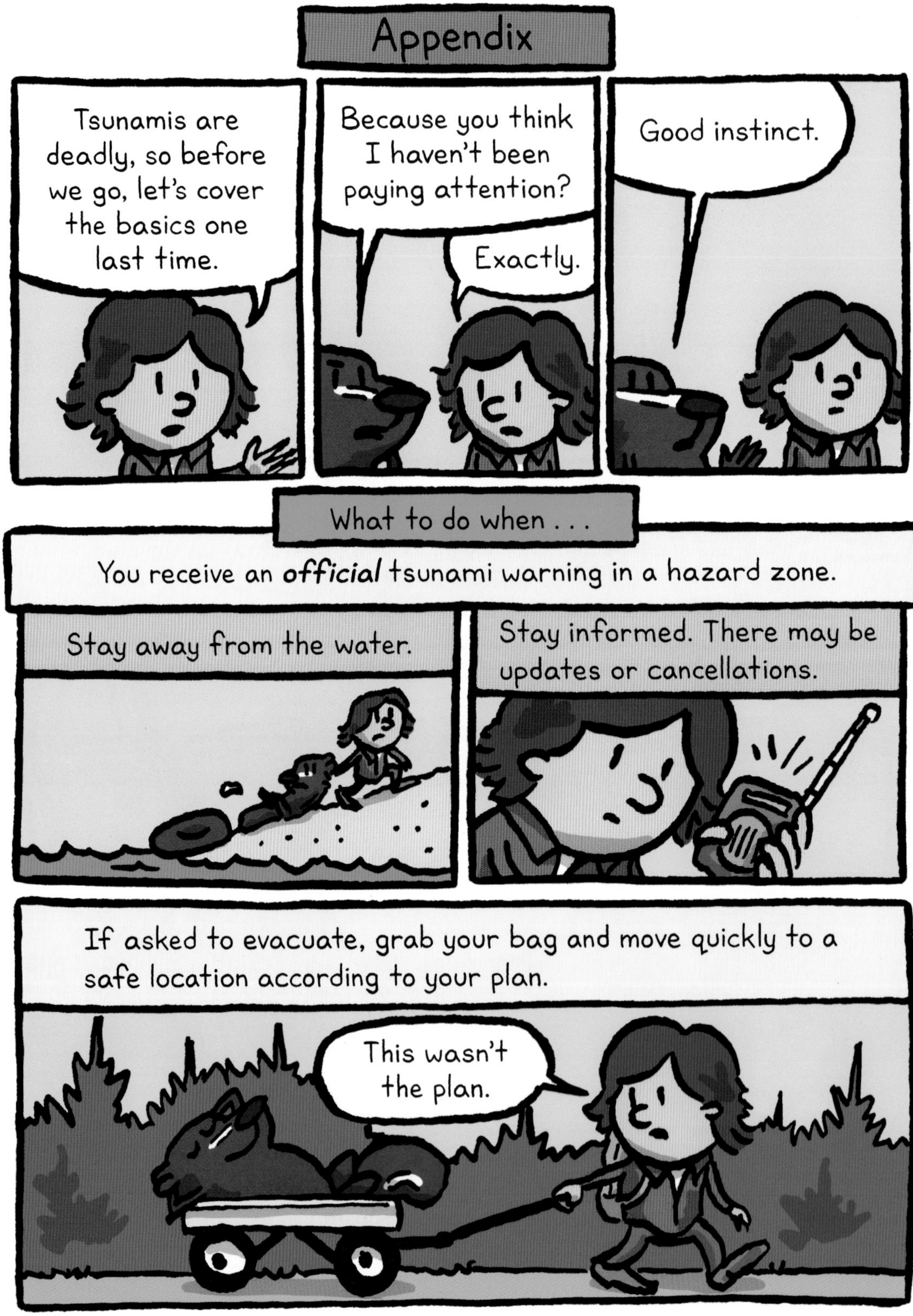
Appendix
Tsunamis are deadly, so before we go, let's cover the basics one last time.
Because you think I haven't been paying attention?
Exactly.
Good instinct.
What to do when . . .
You receive an *official* tsunami warning in a hazard zone.
Stay away from the water.
Stay informed. There may be updates or cancellations.
If asked to evacuate, grab your bag and move quickly to a safe location according to your plan.
This wasn't the plan.

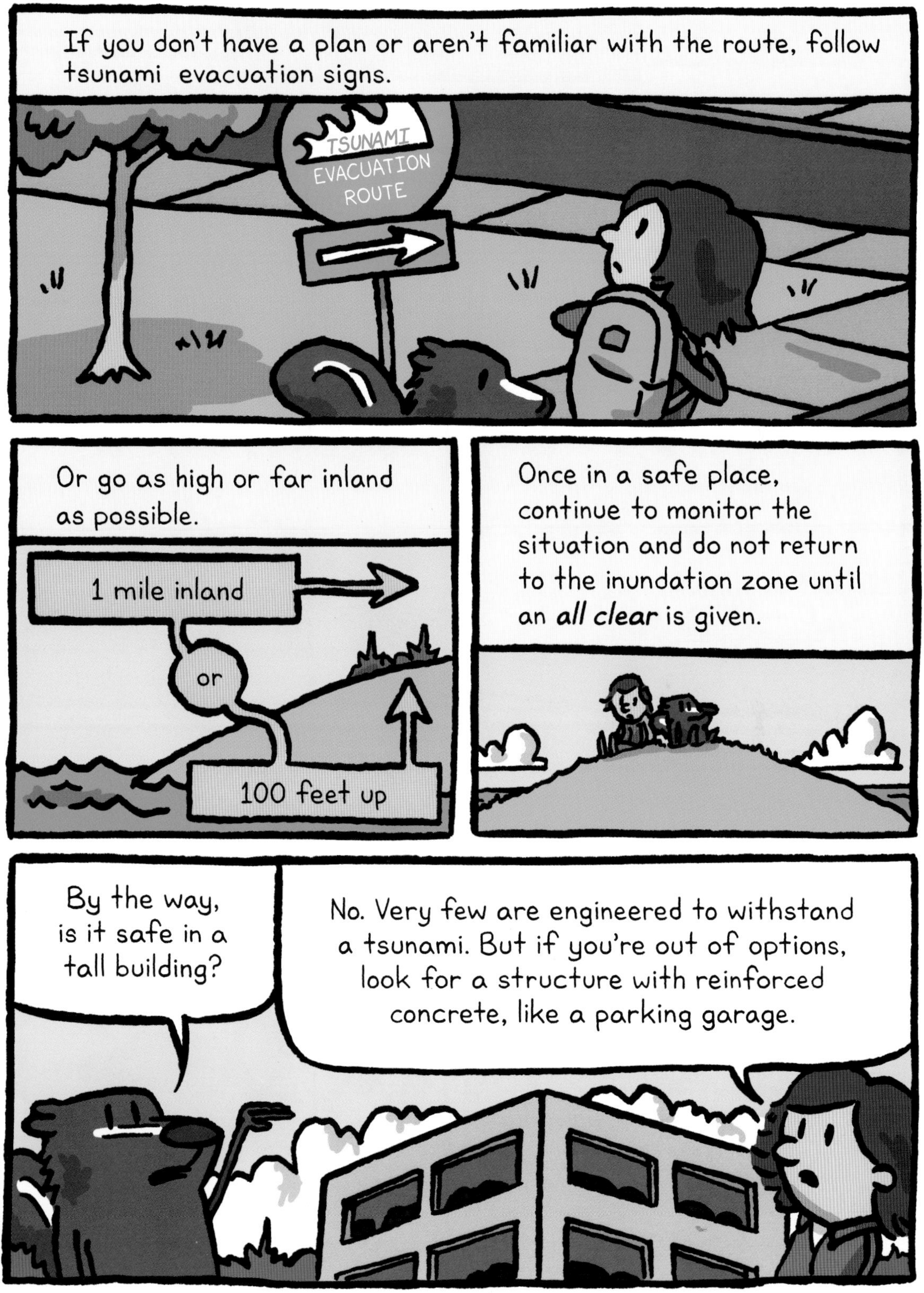
If you don't have a plan or aren't familiar with the route, follow tsunami evacuation signs.
TSUNAMI
EVACUATION ROUTE
Or go as high or far inland as possible.
1 mile inland
or
100 feet up
Once in a safe place, continue to monitor the situation and do not return to the inundation zone until an *all clear* is given.
By the way, is it safe in a tall building?
No. Very few are engineered to withstand a tsunami. But if you're out of options, look for a structure with reinforced concrete, like a parking garage.

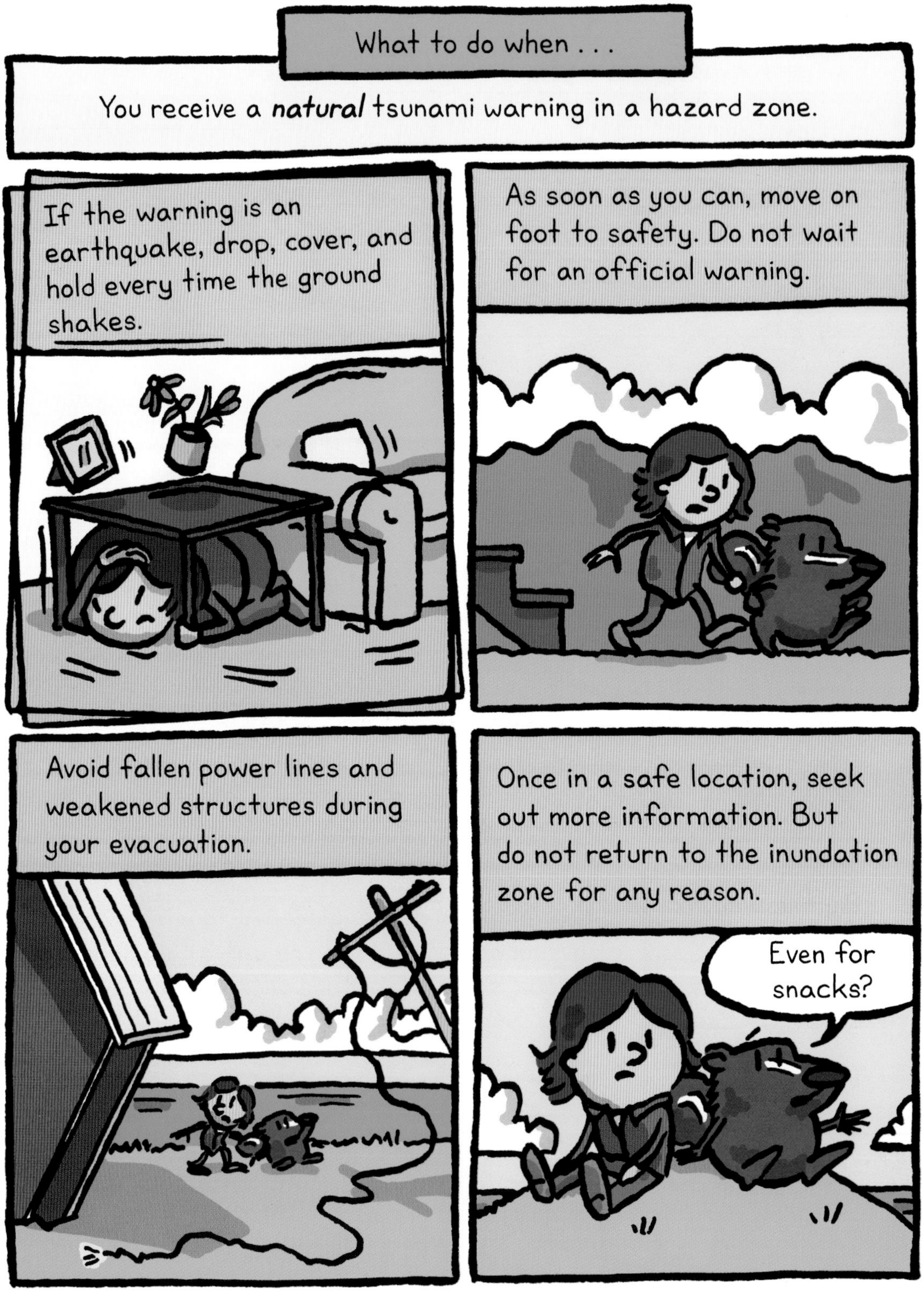
What to do when . . .
You receive a **natural** tsunami warning in a hazard zone.
If the warning is an earthquake, drop, cover, and hold every time the ground shakes.
As soon as you can, move on foot to safety. Do not wait for an official warning.
Avoid fallen power lines and weakened structures during your evacuation.
Once in a safe location, seek out more information. But do not return to the inundation zone for any reason.
Even for snacks?

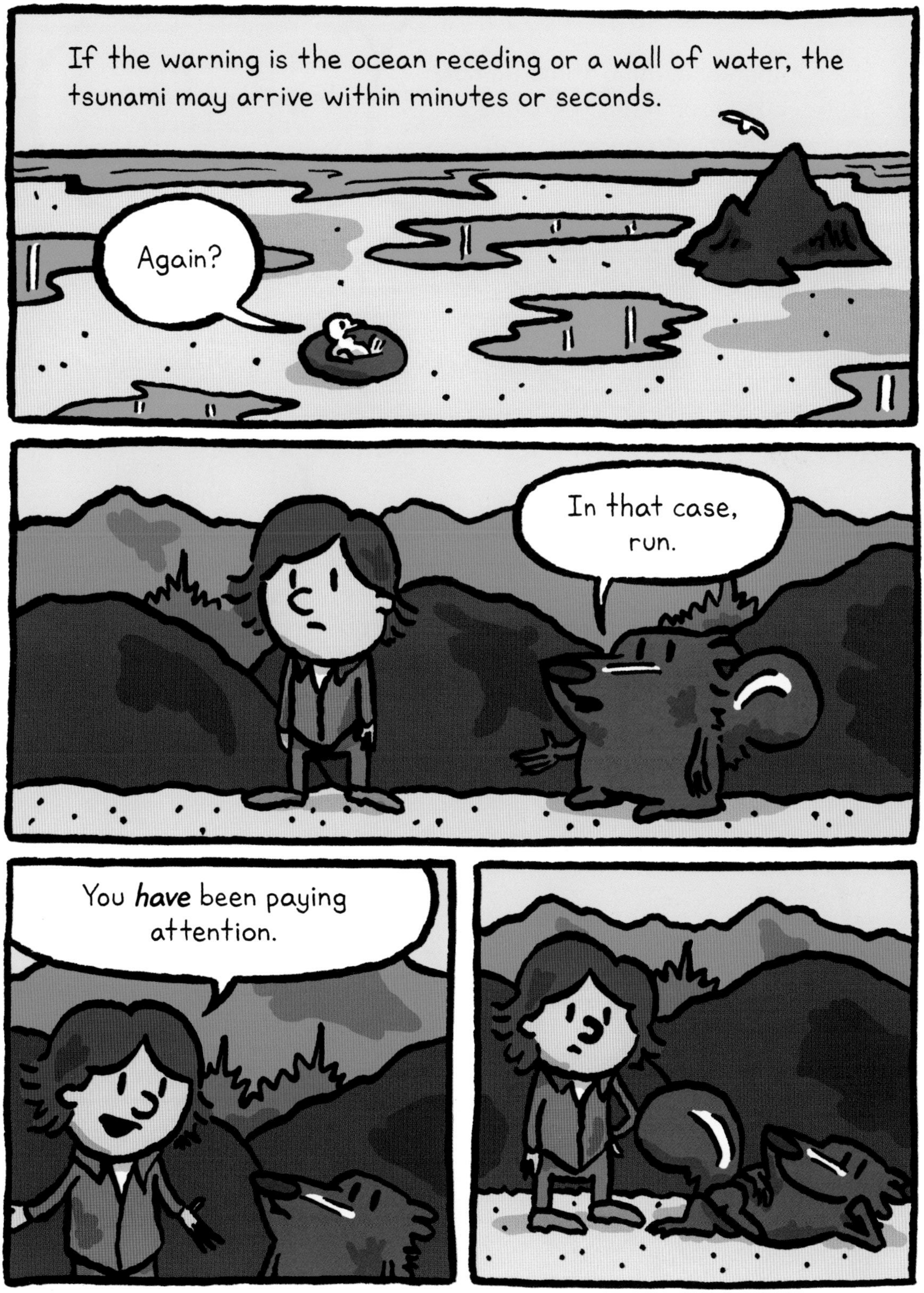
If the warning is the ocean receding or a wall of water, the tsunami may arrive within minutes or seconds.
Again?
In that case, run.
You *have* been paying attention.

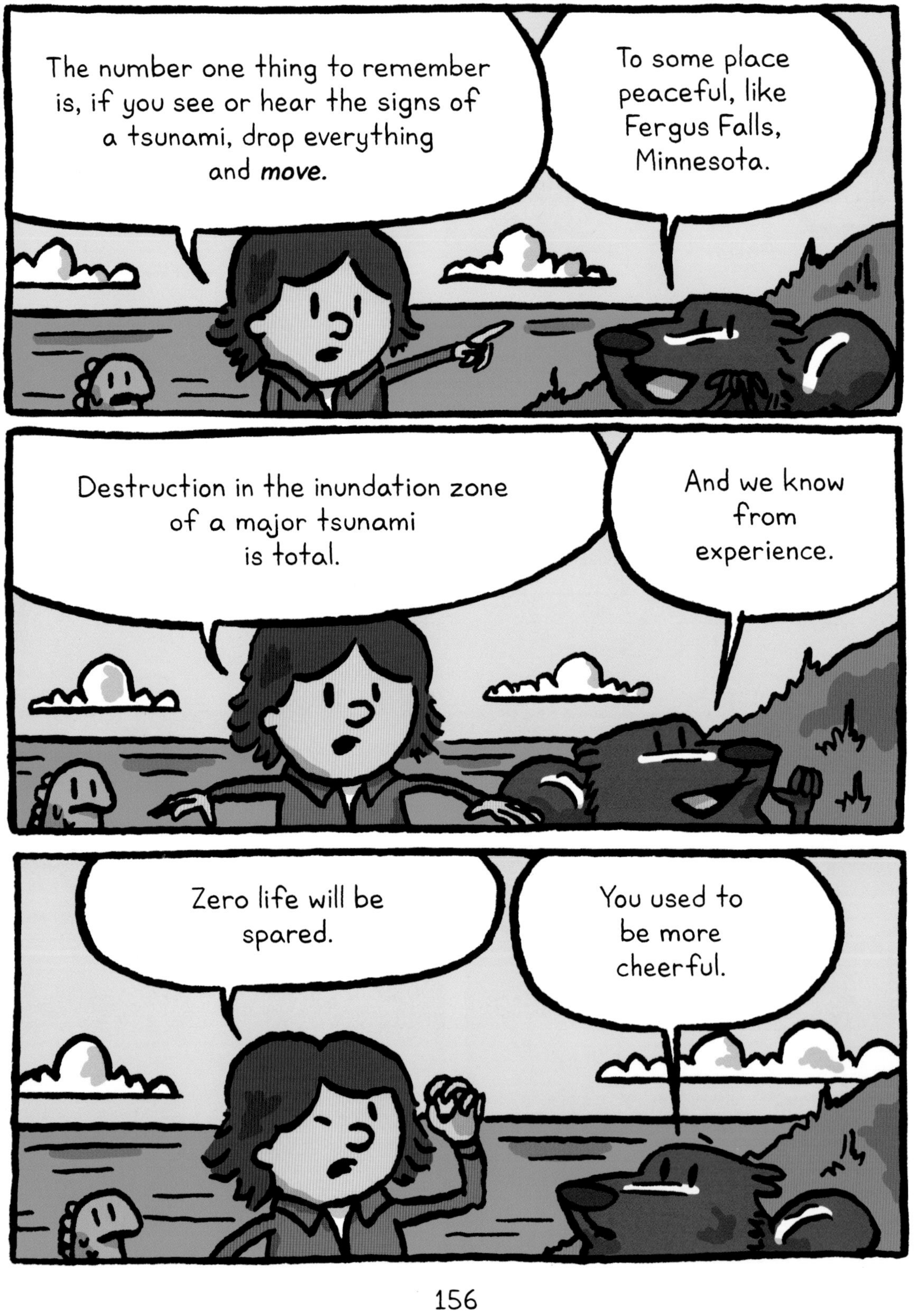
The number one thing to remember is, if you see or hear the signs of a tsunami, drop everything and *move.*
To some place peaceful, like Fergus Falls, Minnesota.
Destruction in the inundation zone of a major tsunami is total.
And we know from experience.
Zero life will be spared.
You used to be more cheerful.

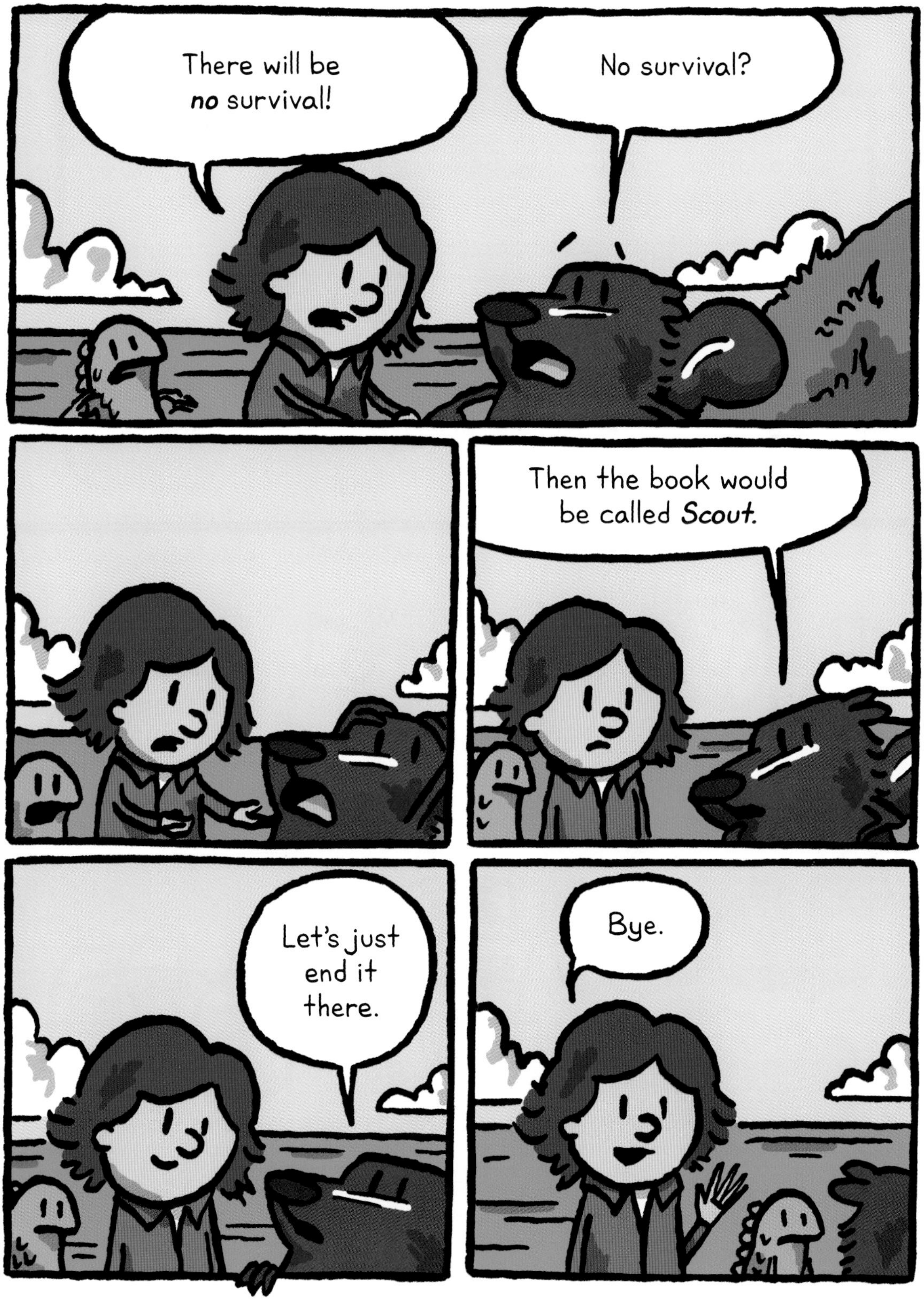
There will be *no* survival!
No survival?
Then the book would be called *Scout*.
Let's just end it there.
Bye.

Emergency Supplies

In addition to a ***Go Bag,*** below are some essential items to keep handy for any emergency, wherever you live.

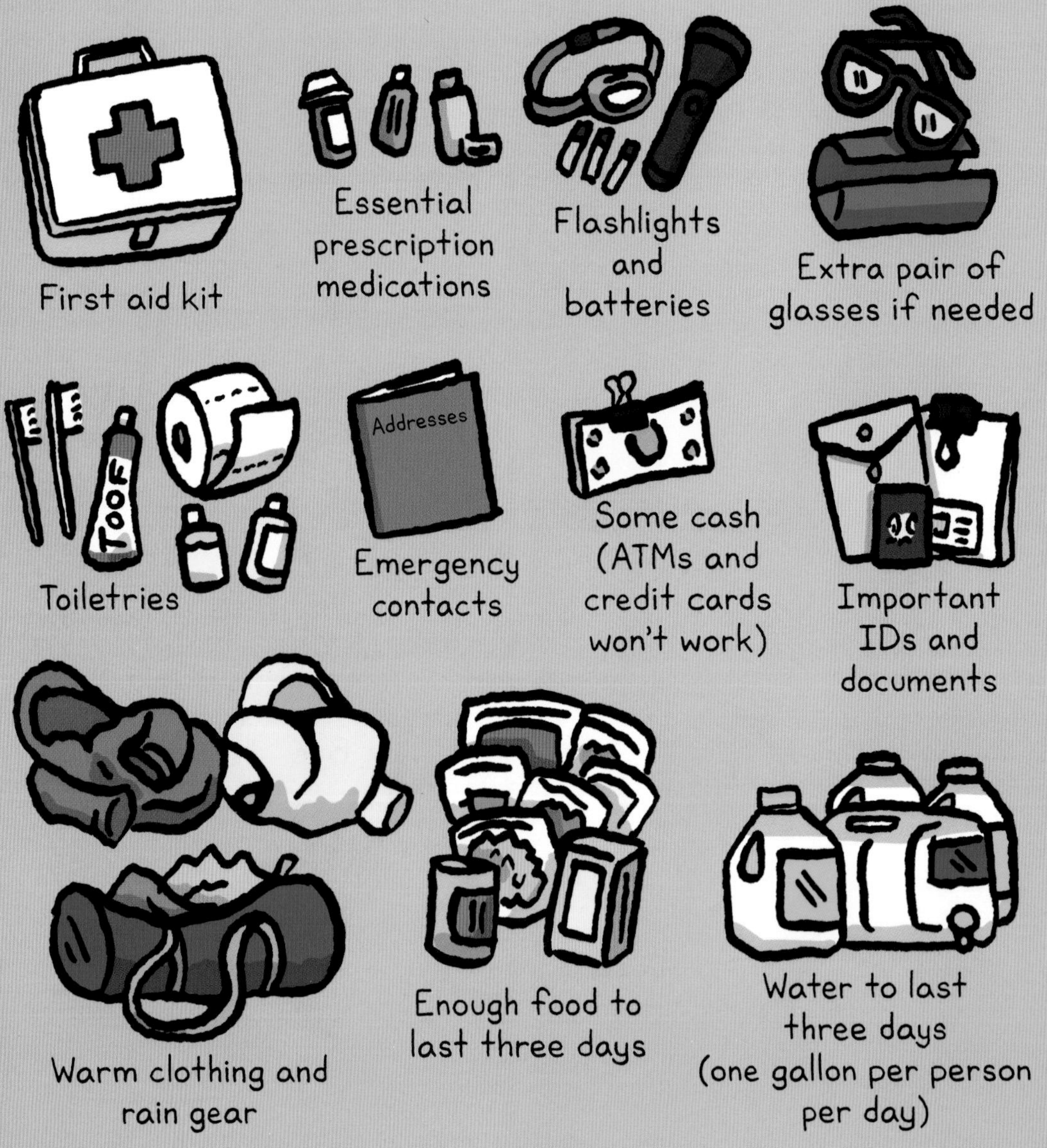
First aid kit
Essential prescription medications
Flashlights and batteries
Extra pair of glasses if needed
TOOF
Toiletries
Addresses
Emergency contacts
Some cash (ATMs and credit cards won't work)
Important IDs and documents
Warm clothing and rain gear
Enough food to last three days
Water to last three days (one gallon per person per day)

A few more earthquake preparations for houses

Find out how to turn off the water and gas.

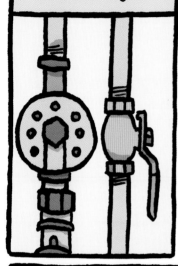

Strap the water heater to the wall so it doesn't tip and break water or gas lines.

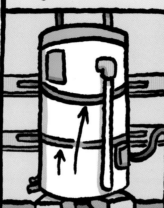

See if the frame is bolted to the foundation.

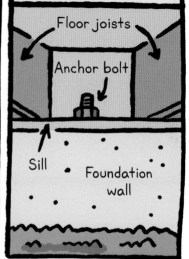

Floor joists

Anchor bolt

Sill

Foundation wall

Useful and interesting tsunami information

National Weather Service Station Broadcast Frequencies, https://www.weather.gov/nwr/station_ listing.

"Oregon's Tsunami Risk: Between the Devil and the Deep Blue Sea," Kathryn Schulz, *The New Yorker*, July 1, 2019.

The Tsunami Zone, http:tsunamizone.org/knowyourzone.

National Tsunami Hazard Mitigation Program, https://nws.weather.gov/nthmp/maps.html

University of Alaska Fairbanks Earthquake Center, https://earthquake.alaska.edu.

U.S. Tsunami Warning System, http://tsunami.gov.

A note from the author

Tsunamis are incredibly dangerous natural events that have caused countless deaths. And while this is a frightening subject, I hope the reader gains both an appreciation and wonder for the scale of the gears at work in the natural world and the knowledge and awareness needed to react when those gears start spinning.

Remember, if you live or travel where tsunamis are a possibility and you witness the warning signs, head to higher ground immediately. Don't wait. Don't pack. Don't chat. Move!

Stay safe out there.

Published by Roaring Brook Press
Roaring Brook Press is a division of Holtzbrinck Publishing Holdings Limited Partnership • 120 Broadway, New York, NY 10271
mackids.com • Copyright © 2023 by Maxwell Eaton III. All rights reserved. • Our books may be purchased in bulk for promotional, educational, or business use. Please contact your local bookseller or the Macmillan Corporate and Premium Sales Department at (800) 221-7945 ext. 5442 or by email at MacmillanSpecialMarkets@macmillan.com.

Library of Congress Control Number: 2023937982

First edition, 2024
Edited by Emily Feinberg
Cover and interior design by Molly Johanson and Casper Manning
Production editing by Nora Milman
The artwork for this book was created with pen and ink on paper and colored digitally.

Printed in China by Toppan Leefung Printing Ltd., Dongguan City, Guangdong Province

ISBN 978-1-250-79045-3 (paperback)
10 9 8 7 6 5 4 3 2 1

ISBN 978-1-250-79044-6 (hardcover)
10 9 8 7 6 5 4 3 2 1

For Scout and Eloise, with a tsunami of love